2017 NAPLEX® Practice Questions

Maryam M. Khazraee, PharmD, RPh

COPYRIGHT

© 2017 NAPLEX® Practice Questions
Copyright© 2017 by Maryam M. Khazraee
Cover by: Maryam M. Khazraee
Published December 2016

All rights reserved. No part of this publication may be reproduced, distributed, or transmitted in any form or by any means, including photocopying, recording, or other electronic or mechanical methods, without the prior written permission of the publisher, except in the case of brief quotations embodied in critical reviews and certain other noncommercial uses permitted by copyright law. For permission requests, write to the publisher, addressed "Attention: Permissions Coordinator," at help@rxpharmacist.com. All trademarks are trademarks of their respective owners and some marked with a registered trademark symbol to notify, with no intention of infringement of the trademark.

DISCLAIMER: The NAPLEX® and NABP® mark are federally registered trademarks owned by the National Association of Boards of Pharmacy (NABP®). RxPharmacist LLC and the author, Maryam M. Khazraee, are not associated with the NABP®, and its products or services have not been reviewed or endorsed by the NABP®.

TERMS OF USE

THE WORK IS PROVIDED "AS IS". RXPHARMACIST AND ITS LICENSORS MAKE NO GUARANTEES OR WARRANTIES AS TO THE ACCURACY, ADEQUACY, OR COMPLETENESS OF OR RESULTS TO BE OBTAINED FROM USING THE WORK, INCLUDING ANY INFORMATION THAT CAN BE ACCESSED THROUGH THE WORK VIA HYPERLINK OR OTHERWISE, AND EXPRESSLY DISCLAIM ANY WARRANTY, EXPRESS OR IMPLIED, INCLUDING BUT NOT LIMITED TO IMPLIED WARRANTIES OF MERCHANTABILITY OR FITNESS FOR A PARTICULARLY PURPOSE.

RxPharmacist, LLC and its licensors do not warrant or guarantee that the functions contained in the work will meet your requirements or that its operation will be uninterrupted or error free. Neither RxPharmacist, LLC nor its licensors shall be liable to you or anyone else for any inaccuracy, error or omission, regardless of cause in the work or for any damages resulting therefrom. RxPharmacist, LLC has no responsibility for the content of any information assessed through the work. Under no circumstances shall RxPharmacist, LLC and/or its licensors be liable for any indirect, incidental, special, punitive, consequential, or similar damages that result from the use of or inability to use the work, even if any of them has been advised of the possibility of such damages. This limitation of liability shall apply to any claim or cause whatsoever whether such claim or cause arises in contact, tort or otherwise

FOREWORD

I understand how it feels being a pharmacy student or professional looking forward to an exciting journey in getting licensed! Let's be honest, this is probably one of the most stressful times in your life studying hard for the NAPLEX® with the fear of not passing. With the exam fees increasing to $575 for the 2017 year just to sit for the exam itself and if you don't pass you have to wait 45 days before another attempt! After recently passing the NAPLEX®, I realized that practicing with more questions would have really boosted my confidence when taking the exam. The goal of this practice question exam book is to help students and fellow pharmacist colleagues in their studies with the most up-to-date material and questions mimicking the actual exam. Hope this guide serves you well! Best of luck!

Copyright © 2016 Maryam M. Khazraee

All rights reserved.

ISBN: 1532924399
ISBN-13: 9781532924392

Table of Contents

Exam Overview 1

Calculation Practice Questions 6
   Section 1: 50 questions, Time: 60 minutes 6
   Section 2: 50 questions, Time: 60 minutes 20
   Section 3: 50 questions, Time: 60 minutes 40

Pharmacotherapy and Case Questions 58
   Section 1: 250 questions, 5.5 hours 58

Practice NAPLEX® Exam 129
   2017 NAPLEX Practice Exam: 250 Questions, 6 hours 129

Section 1 Calculations: Answers and Explanations 196

Section 2 Calculations: Answers and Explanations 210

Section 3 Calculations: Answers and Explanations 222

Section 1 Pharmacotherapy and Case Questions: Answers and Explanations 235

2017 NAPLEX Practice Exam Answers 286

NAPLEX FORMULA SHEET 340

Exam Overview

I would highly recommend to first review the NAPLEX®/MPJE® Registration Bulletin which can be found at: http://www.nabp.net/programs/examination/naplex/registration-bulletin

Be sure to answer EVERY SINGLE QUESTION. You CANNOT return to the previous question to change your answer and you CANNOT skip any questions so try to be cognizant of the amount of time you spend on each question and answer every single question with your first gut instinct.

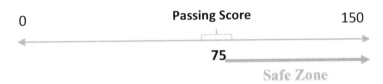

The NAPLEX® does have competency statements but I found them to be a waste of time to read. The main things you need to know is the exam is broken down to two main areas:

- **Area 1**
    - Ensure Safe and Effective Pharmacotherapy and Health Outcomes **(Approximately 67% of Test)**
        - This is basically your pharmacotherapy, so patient cases and working up treatment plans
- **Area 2**
    - Safe and Accurate Preparation, Compounding, Dispensing, and Administration of Medications and Provision of Health Care Products **(Approximately 33% of Test)**
        - This is more of compounding, drug calculations, and identifying medications with proper handling. Hint: Know Sterile Compounding!

Types of Exam Questions

Multiple-Choice Questions (potentially up to a third of the questions)

Which of the following is a known side effect of Lisinopril?

a) Dry Cough
b) Uncontrollable bleeding
c) Dry eyes
d) Yellow discharge from ears

Answer: A

Multiple-Response Questions (potentially up to a third of the questions)

What counselling information should a pharmacist provide to a patient taking fexofenadine? (Select **ALL** that apply)

a) Do not exceed the recommended dose
b) Avoid grapefruit and grapefruit juice
c) Avoid if sensitive to any ingredients of the product
d) Avoid live vaccinations

Answer: A, B, C

You can't use your personal calculator, need to use Pearson Vue's on-screen calculator during

Constructed-Response Questions (Calculation questions, required to use computer calculator)

What is the loading dose, in grams, of a medication for an 82 kg patient if the volume of distribution is 0.43 L/kg and the desired plasma level is 40 mg/L?
(Answer must be numeric; round the answer to the nearest **WHOLE** number.)

| 1.41 | Answer: 1.41 grams

The formula for determining loading dose is: $LD = C_{ss} \times V_d$, C_{ss} is your desired plasma level of 40mg/L and V_d is Volume of distribution so 0.43 L/Kg.

LD= 40 mg/L X 0.43 L/Kg = 17.2 mg/kg   Double Check: 17.2 mg/Kg X (82 Kg) = 1.41 g

Ordered-Response Questions (Very few of these type of questions)

List the compounding garbing in order. (ALL options must be used)
Left-click mouse to highlight, drag, and order the answer options.

Unordered Options	Ordered Response (Answer)
Don Facial Mask	Don shoe covers
Don shoe covers	Don head cover
Don sterile gloves	Don facial mask
Don head cover	Don sterile gloves

Hot Spot Questions (Only got one question like this format but that's just me)

Using the diagram below, identify where in the HIV life-cycle transcription and translation occurs. (Select the **text** response, and left-click the mouse. To change your answer, move the cursor, select alternate **text** response, and click.) **Answer: Step #5 Transcription and Translation**

Picture referenced from: AIDSinfo (NIH): HIV Overview, The HIV Life Cycle http://aidsinfo.nih.gov/education-materials/fact-sheets/19/73/the-hiv-life-cycle

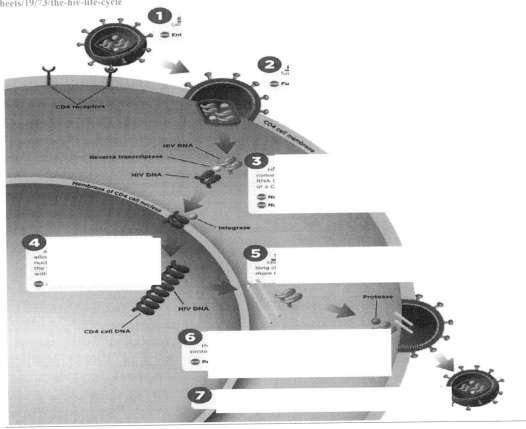

Updates to the exam

On November 1st 2016, the NAPLEX® will increase from 185 to 250 test questions and the test time will increase from 4 hours and 15 minutes to 6 hours. Of the 250 test questions, 200 are used to calculate your score and the other 50 are dispersed throughout the exam so you won't know which ones are not counted toward your score. The NABP online registration for the new test begins October 24 and the new registration fee will increase from $505 to **$575**. You may take the exam up to <u>five attempts</u>, but you must wait 45 days prior to the next attempt at the NAPLEX®.

For 2017 Graduates

If you will graduate in 2017, you will not be eligible to take the current (or now old) NAPLEX®. You may register for the new NAPLEX® starting November 1, 2016.

If you are a 2017 graduate who registers **prior** to November 1, 2016:

- Your record will be closed, and you will receive a partial refund of $360 and be required to re-register for the NAPLEX® at the $575 fee.

For 2018 Graduates

The NAPLEX® will include a communication skills assessment that NABP® will develop to be used by its member boards as an additional component for licensure beginning in 2018. This was created to ensure people speak English so I wouldn't worry too much ☺

How to Test? How to sign up? How does this process look like?

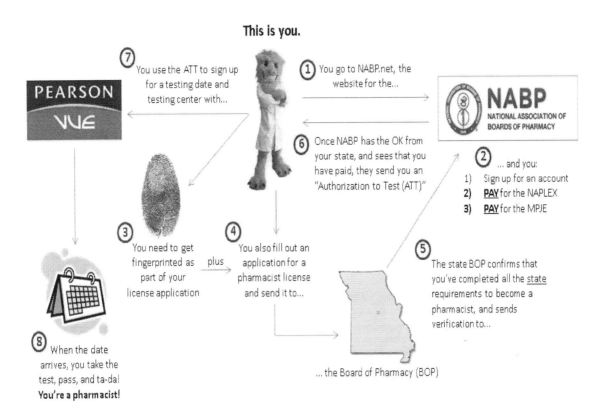

Special thanks to Ruth and her stlcopruth blog for the above diagram. You can visit her website for extra tips on the registration process but the information is outdated so make sure you ask your College of Pharmacy and you may even have to call your state board of pharmacy to ensure you meet all your requirements.

Ruth's blog: https://stlcopruth.wordpress.com

So now that we had a quick overview of the NAPLEX® exam we'll get straight to the practice questions! Ready? Set? Go!

Calculation Practice Questions

There are 150 calculation questions listed in this section. It is important to be well-versed in these questions as you can easily get most if not all of them correct by simply practicing. To make it easier, we have split these into three sets.

Section 1: 50 questions, Time: 60 minutes

1. What is the final concentration (expressed as a ratio strength) of a solution if 8 capsules (54 mg each) are dissolved in 1 pint of simple syrup?

2. You receive the following hyperalimentation solution:

Amino Acids 8.5%	500 ml	Amino Acids 8.5%
Dextrose 70%	500 ml	Dextrose 70%
Sodium Chloride	25 mEq	NaCl 4 mEq/ml
Potassium Chloride	18 mEq	KCl 2 mEq/ml
Magnesium Sulfate	10 mEq	Magnesium Sulfate 4.08 mEq/ml
Calcium Gluconate	15 mEq	Calcium Gluconate 0.465 mEq/ml
Potassium Phosphate	17 mmol	Potassium Phosphate 3 mmol/ml
Multi-Vitamins 12	10 ml	MVI-12 10 ml vial
Trace Elements	3 ml	Trace Elements 3 ml vial

   What is the total volume of the final hyperalimentation solution?

3. How many kilograms of calcium gluconate ($CaC_6H_{11}O_7$) are in 12 moles? (MW Ca=40, C=12, H=1, O=16)

   a) 0.24
   b) 2.34
   c) 2.82
   d) 2820
   e) 2400

4. How many mL of a drug solution should be measured to obtain 36 grams of the solution if the specific gravity is 0.92?

   a) 0.03
   b) 39
   c) 33
   d) 36
   e) 29

5. A mother of a 6-month-old infant requests assistance with an over the counter fever product - acetaminophen 80mg/0.8mL. Her child weighs 15 pounds and the recommended dose of acetaminophen for fever in infants is 10-15mg/kg every 6 to 8 hours. Which of the following would be appropriate instructions for her to follow?

   a) Give 3.3 mL by mouth every 6 to 8 hours
   b) Give 1.5 mL by mouth every 6 to 8 hours
   c) Give 0.5 mL by mouth every 6 to 8 hours
   d) Give 2 mL by mouth every 6 to 8 hours
   e) Give 0.8 mL by mouth every 6 to 8 hours

6. A postmenopausal woman consumes 600 mg of calcium carbonate with breakfast and dinner. How many mEq is she receiving daily? (Molecular weight: Ca 40, C 12, O 16)

7. How much sodium chloride (in mg) is needed to make the solution below isotonic?

		E value
Drug X	0.004% w/v	0.92
Drug Y	1.2%	0.36
Purified water qs 30 mL		☐

8. An order is received for a new patient admitted to the hospital. The loading dose is 5 mg/kg ideal body weight. The maintenance dose is 2 mg/kg ideal body weight per hour. The patient is a 56-year-old female weighing 157 lbs. She is 5'7" tall. Calculate the maintenance dose for this patient. How much drug (in grams) will this patient receive over a 48-hour period?

   a) 6851 grams
   b) 5.91 grams
   c) 6.9 grams
   d) 122 grams
   e) 5866 grams

9. How much, in liters, of a 12% w/v solution can be made if you have 500 mL of a 25% solution and 2 liters of a 3% solution?

   a) 0.2 L
   b) 1.2 L
   c) 3.3 L
   d) 205 mL
   e) 1222 mL

10. A medication order is received for prednisolone 60 mg/m2/day in 3 divided doses for 2 weeks followed by 45 mg/m2/day in 2 divided doses for 2 weeks followed by 30 mg/m2 once daily for 2 weeks followed by 20 mg/m2 every other day for 2 weeks. Prednisolone is available as a 125 mg/5 mL solution. The patient is a 63-year-old man weighing 246 lbs and standing 5'11 tall. What is the morning dose, in mg, of prednisolone during the second phase of the taper? ☐

11. A pharmacist compounding 8 ounces of ointment needs to add 56 grams of a solution (density = 0.62), which contains the active ingredient. What volume, in L, of solution is needed?

   a) 0.01
   b) 0.09
   c) 0.72
   d) 90
   e) 720

12. How many grams of a 4.6% w/w ointment can you prepare with 1 kg of a 10.7% w/w ointment and 500 g of a 2.9% w/w ointment?

   a) 391
   b) 639
   c) 1794
   d) 2294
   e) 4588

13. A 57-year-old, 142 lb woman presented to the Emergency Department with a fever of 102.7 degrees F for 3 days. She has an open ulceration on her left leg determined to be cellulitis. She is admitted to the hospital to receive IV antibiotics. A culture determines sensitivity to cephalosporins. Cefazolin at a dose of 1.5 g IV every 8 hours for 3 days is started. The physician orders the Cefazolin (1g/50ml) to be infused at 2g/hr. On the 4th day, The patient is released from the hospital and is prescribed cephalexin 500mg, 4 times daily for 7 days.

   How many bags of IV antibiotics are needed over the 3 days?

14. A medication order is received for gentamicin 1.7 mg/kg IV every 8 hours in 50 mL NS. The patient is a 56-year-old female weighing 145 lb and standing 5'4 tall. Gentamicin is available in a 2 mL single use vial (40 mg/mL). How many mg of gentamicin will the patient receive daily?

   a) 43
   b) 94
   c) 128
   d) 280
   e) 337

15. A pharmacist compounding 6 ounces of ointment needs 26 grams of coal tar solution (specific gravity 0.84). What volume, in mL, of solution is needed?
   a) 0.03
   b) 22
   c) 31
   d) 131
   e) 53

16. If 250 mL of a 20% (v/v) solution is diluted to 2000 mL, what will be the final percent strength (v/v)?

17. How many milligrams of sodium citrate ($Na_3C_6H_5O_7$) are in 3 moles? (MW Na=23, C=12, H=1, O=16)

18. A male patient is 6'4 tall and weighs 258 pounds. He presents to the outpatient infusion center today to receive "Drug x" in a dose of 17.5 mcg/kg. Calculate, in milligrams, the dose of "Drug x" he will receive.

   a) 0.002
   b) 2.05
   c) 4.5
   d) 2053
   e) 4115

19. A 31-year-old, 5'3", 156 lb woman presented to the emergency department with severe dysphagia and has been receiving hemodialysis twice a week. She is admitted to the hospital for dehydration. She is to receive fluid replacement for dehydration 4 times daily and total parenteral nutrition every 3 days for caloric needs. She is released from the hospital on day 6 and will be re-evaluated on an outpatient basis for nutritional needs.

How many mls of a 50% dextrose solution is needed for this patient? Assume amino acids = 0.75g/kg body weight and provides 4 kcal/g; lipids = 30% of total daily calories and provide 9 kcal/g; and dextrose = 3.4 kcal/g. Assume a stress factor adjustment of 1.2 due to hemodialysis.

Male = 66 + (13.7xW) + (5xH) - (6.8xA)   Female = 655 + (9.6xW) + (1.8xH) - (4.7xA)

A = age in years, W = weight in kg, H = height in cm

20. A 49-year-old, 220 lb man, presented to the emergency department with a pulse ox reading of 89, blood pressure of 180/92, and a pulse of 126. He is administered O2 via nasal cannula and 1 liter of normal saline over 3 hours. He has a history of diabetes and hypertension. He is admitted to the hospital on observational status to monitor his vital signs. Once admitted, he is given Cipro, 400 mg/200ml, every 12 hours, infused at 500 mg/hr.

What is the flow rate (ml/hr) of the normal saline?
a) 450
b) 250
c) 336
d) 332
e) 333

21. How many milliliters of methyl salicylate should be used in compounding the following prescription?

Methyl salicylate 8% (v/v); Liniment base ad 300 mL
Sig: For external use

a) 23 mL
b) 24 mL
c) 200 mL
d) 19 mL
e) 240 mL

22. If a prescription is written for an elixir that contains 50 mcg of a specific active ingredient in 1 ml, what would be the equivalent amount of active ingredient if the total amount to be dispensed is 3 ml?

a) 151 mg
b) 15 mg
c) 1.5 mg
d) 0.15 mg
e) 1510 mg

23. A pharmacist receives a prescription for lactulose 4 tablespoonsful 3 times daily. How much lactulose, in liters, would be dispensed for a 30-day supply?

a) 5.2
b) 5.3
c) 5.4
d) 5400
e) 540

24. A 34-year-old, 178-lb male hiker presents with a rash covering his legs and feet. He is given 0.75 mg/kg dose of IM Depo-Medrol (40mg/ml) for immediate relief of urticaria and rash. He is also prescribed a topical calamine compound and a prednisone taper to be taken over 5 days.

Calamine	100 mg
Phenol	600 mg
Zinc Oxide	300 mg

How many grams of phenol is needed to make 2 oz of the calamine mixture?

a) 33
b) 350
c) 38
d) 34
e) 340

25. A nutritional supplement contains:

Protein	6.9 g/100 ml
Fat	3.2 g/100 ml
Carbohydrate	15 g/100 ml

What is the total number of calories received from 8 ounces of the supplement?

☐

26. A medication order is received for gentamicin 1.7 mg/kg IV every 8 hours in 50 mL NS. The patient is a 56-year-old female weighing 165 lb and standing 5'4 tall. Gentamicin is available in a 2 mL single use vial (40 mg/mL). If the infusion is administered over 30 minutes and the administration set delivers 20 drops per mL, how many drops per minute will the patient receive?

☐

27. A 34-year-old, 178 lbs. male hiker presents with a rash covering his legs and feet. He is given 0.75 mg/kg dose of IM Depo-Medrol (40mg/ml) for immediate relief of urticaria and rash. He is also prescribed a topical calamine compound and a prednisone taper to be taken over 5 days.

   Calamine   100 mg
   Phenol   600 mg
   Zinc Oxide   300 mg

   What is the Depo-Medrol concentration expressed as a ratio strength?

   a) 1:26 (w/v)
   b) 25:1 (w/v)
   c) 1:41 (w/v)
   d) 1:25 (w/v)
   e) 40:1 (w/v)

28. An asthmatic patient had been stabilized on IV aminophylline 40 mg/hr with therapeutic theophylline level. The patient is now to be discharged from the hospital. What daily oral dose of Theo-24 (a sustained theophylline product with assumed bioavailability of 100%) should he receive?

   a) 800 mg/day
   b) 850 mg/day
   c) 900 mg/day
   d) 750 mg/day
   e) 700 mg/day

29. Drug X (380 mg) is dissolved in 120 mL of purified water. What is the resulting concentration, expressed as a ratio?

   a) 1:333
   b) 1:33
   c) 1:316
   d) 1:335
   e) 1:361

30. A 70 kg patient is to receive dopamine infused intravenously at 10 micrograms/kg/minute. The hospital currently has premixed 250ml bags containing 400mg of Dopamine in each bag. The nurse asks you to confirm the patient's IV infusion rate.

   What infusion rate is correct in this case?
   a) 24.25 ml/hr
   b) 25.25 ml/hr
   c) 26.25 ml/hr
   d) 27.25 ml/hr
   e) 25 ml/hr

31. What is the final concentration if 37.5 grams of a 12.2% w/w ointment are mixed with 62.5 grams of a 17.6% w/w ointment?

32. How many mEq of potassium are in a 100 mL solution containing 0.5 g of KCl (molecular weights: K = 39; Cl = 35.5)?

33. What is the concentration, in mOsm/L if 500 mg of potassium chloride is dissolved in 250 mL of normal saline? (Molecular weight: K 39, Cl 35.5, Na 23)

34. How many millimoles of dietary potassium does a person consume if he ingests ¼ of a pear (680 mg potassium/½ melon)? (MW K=39, Cl=35.5)

35. If 25 liters of drug z weighs 55020 g, what is its density?

   a) 2.2 g/mL
   b) 2.5 g/mL
   c) 2.8 g/mL
   d) 3.0 g/nL
   e) 2.0 g/mL

36. You received a prescription order of an elixir containing 100 ppm of an active ingredient. Which of the following would represent an equivalent amount of the active ingredient?

   a) 1 gm in 1,000 mL
   b) 1 gm in 10,000 mL
   c) 1 gm in 100 mL
   d) 1 gm in 1 mL
   e) 1 gm in 10 mL

37. How many calories would be provided to a patient who receives 1 liter of D5W?

   a) 180 kcal
   b) 190 kcal
   c) 170 kcal
   d) 200 kcal
   e) 150 kcal

38. A 59-year-old, 156 lb. female presents to her physician with hot flashes. Her provider prescribes Estrogen/Progesterone sublingual drops. The directions are "Place 1 drop under the tongue daily."

Estrogen	0.5 g
Progesterone	0.8 g
Saccharin	100 mg
Silica gel	200 mg
Cherry flavor	10 gtts
Almond Oil	10 ml

   How many milligrams/day of progesterone is the patient receiving per dose if the dropper delivers 15 gtts/ml?

39. A 24-year-old male comes into the pharmacy with the following prescription for his upper respiratory infection:

    Ciprofloxacin suspension 500 mg/5 mL Q12H #100 mL
    Sig: 1 tsp BID tat

    How many days will this patient's therapy last?

    a) 5 days
    b) 10 days
    c) 15 days
    d) 3 days
    e) 7 days

40. A man is brought to the ED unresponsive and has a strong smell of alcohol on his breath. He begins to become slightly responsive and the staff is notified by the patient he is an alcoholic. The ED physician orders a "banana bag," aka rally pack, to be administered over 6 hours.

    "Banana Bag" (aka rally pack)
    liter normal saline
    -thiamine (100mg/ml, 2ml) 100 mg
    -folic acid (5mg/ml, 10ml) 1 mg
    -MVI (1 ml vial) 1 vial
    -magnesium sulfate (0.5g/ml, 2ml) 3 g

    How much magnesium sulfate (ml) is needed to make the patient's bag plus an additional 4 bags?

    a) 33 mL
    b) 30 mL
    c) 35 mL
    d) 40 mL
    e) 29 mL

41. A patient is using a drug solution containing 10 mg of clindamycin per ml in a 30 ml package. What is the strength of clindamycin in the solution used by the patient?

42. A patient needs to change his regular human insulin product from the U-100 formulation to the U-500 formulation. If he has been taking 0.4 ml of the initial formulation with good control, how much (ml) of the new formulation would you advise him to take?

43. A pharmacist compounding 2 ounces of ointment needs 5 grams of drug X solution (specific gravity 0.43). What volume, in mL, of solution is needed?

44. How many millimoles of dietary potassium does a patient consume if she ingests 3 servings of soup (240 mg potassium/serving)? (MW K=39, Cl=35.5)

   a) 11.5
   b) 15.5
   c) 18
   d) 18.5
   e) 19

45. A 47-year-old, 6'1", 198 lb man presented to the Emergency Department with COPD exacerbation. He is admitted to the hospital for pneumonia as confirmed on a chest x-ray. He receives temporary nutritional replenishment via TPN due to esophageal cancer. He is to receive fluid replacement for dehydration 4 times daily and total parenteral nutrition every 3 days for caloric needs. The patient is released from the hospital on day 8 and will be re-evaluated on an outpatient basis for nutritional needs.

   Calculate the resting metabolic energy according to the Harris-Benedict equation. Assume amino acids = 0.75g/kg body weight and provides 4 kcal/g; lipids = 30% of total daily calories and provide 9 kcal/g; and dextrose = 3.4 kcal/g.
   Male = 66 + (13.7xW) + (5xH) - (6.8xA)   Female = 655 + (9.6xW) + (1.8xH) - (4.7xA)
   A = age in years, W = weight in kg, H = height in cm

a) 1907 kcal
b) 2107 kcal
c) 2000 kcal
d) 2300 kcal
e) 1800 kcal

46. How many kilograms of potassium chloride are in 5 moles? (MW K=39, Cl = 35.5)

a) 0.30
b) 0.37
c) 0.20
d) 0.25
e) 0.40

47. A 57-year-old, 142 lb woman presented to the Emergency Department with a fever of 102.7 degrees F for 3 days. She has an open ulceration on her left leg determined to be cellulitis. She is admitted to the hospital to receive IV antibiotics. A culture determines sensitivity to cephalosporins. Cefazolin at a dose of 1.5 g IV every 8 hours for 3 days is started. The physician orders the Cefazolin (1g/50ml) be infused at 2g/hr. On the 4th day, the patient is released from the hospital and is prescribed cephalexin 500mg 4 times daily for 7 days.

At what flow rate (gtt/min) is the antibiotic to be infused if the drop factor is 18 gtt/ml?

48. How many kilograms of ferrous gluconate ($C_{12}H_{22}FeO_{14}$) are in 3 moles? (MW Fe=56, C=12, H=1, O=16)

a) 1.3
b) 1338
c) 1200
d) 1.2
e) 446

49. What is the total volume, in ml, of a 2.7% solution that can be made by diluting one ounce of a 10.7% solution?

a) 119
b) 150

c) 100
d) 89
e) 41

50. How many milligrams is 154 nanograms? ☐

Section 2: 50 questions, Time: 60 minutes

This second section will provide you more case scenario type practice calculation questions to help you better practice your calculations. It's recommended to time yourself giving 60 minutes to complete each 50 question set.

1.

Patient Profile

Patient Name: Charlie Tolino Address: 21 Rivershore, Daytona Beach, FL
Age: 55   Sex: M   Race: W Height: 5' 9"   Weight: 300 lbs
Allergies: NKDA   Diagnoses: Chronic Kidney Disease

Medications						
Date	Rx#	Prescriber	Drug	Quantity	Sig	Refills
12/01/17	4308	Dr. Strange, MD	Ferric Citrate 1 g tab	30	1 tab PO TID x 2 weeks	1
Additional Info						
Date	Urine Protein	Creatinine Clearance (CrCl)	Serum Phosphate	BP	HR	Temp
12/01/17	2+	35 ml/min	4.6	130/80	67	99 F

How many milligrams of ferric ion (Fe^{3+}, 55.85 g/mol) are provided by each 1 gram ferric citrate (MWave = 265.93 g/mol)?

a) 200 mg
b) 230 mg
c) 210 mg
d) 250 mg
e) 266 mg

2. In the metric system, "mega" is how many times bigger than "kilo"?

3. You receive the following hyperalimentation solution:

Amino Acids 8.5%	500 ml	Amino Acids 8.5%
Dextrose 70%	500 ml	Dextrose 70%
Sodium Chloride	25 mEq	NaCl 4 mEq/ml
Potassium Chloride	18 mEq	KCl 2 mEq/ml
Magnesium Sulfate	10 mEq	Magnesium Sulfate 4.08 mEq/ml
Calcium Gluconate	15 mEq	Calcium Gluconate 0.465 mEq/ml
Potassium Phosphate	17 mmol	Potassium Phosphate 3 mmol/ml
Multi-Vitamins 12	10 ml	MVI-12 10 ml vial
Trace Elements	3 ml	Trace Elements 3 ml vial

What is the volume of Calcium Gluconate needed in the final solution?

a) 32.36 mL
b) 33 mL
c) 32.26 mL
d) 34 mL
e) 31 mL

4. How much sodium chloride (in g) is needed to make the solution below isotonic?

		E value
Drug Z	0.05% w/v	0.82
Drug X	2.7%	0.07
Purified water qs 60 mL		

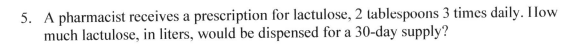

5. A pharmacist receives a prescription for lactulose, 2 tablespoons 3 times daily. How much lactulose, in liters, would be dispensed for a 30-day supply?

a) 2
b) 2700
c) 27
d) 2.7
e) 270

6. A pharmacist receives the following order for a hyperalimentation solution:

Amino Acids 8.5%	500 ml	Amino Acids 8.5%
Dextrose 70%	500 ml	Dextrose 70%
Sodium Chloride	25 mEq	NaCl 4 mEq/ml
Potassium Chloride	18 mEq	KCl 2 mEq/ml
Magnesium Sulfate	10 mEq	Magnesium Sulfate 4.08 mEq/ml
Calcium Gluconate	15 mEq	Calcium Gluconate 0.465 mEq/ml
Potassium Phosphate	17 mmol	Potassium Phosphate 3 mmol/ml
Multi-Vitamins 12	10 ml	MVI-12 10 ml vial
Trace Elements	3 ml	Trace Elements 3 ml vial

What is the volume of potassium chloride needed in the final solution?
a) 6.7 mL
b) 7 mL
c) 5.6 mL
d) 8 mL
e) 9 mL

7. A pharmacist compounding 4 ounces of ointment needs 15 grams of coal tar solution (specific gravity 0.84). What volume, in mL, of solution is needed?

8. A 49-year-old, 186 lb male housepainter is admitted to the hospital for severe dehydration. He is given a 500 ml bolus of normal saline, followed by 1000 ml of normal saline with 30 mg propranolol for tachycardia in a 50 ml piggyback. The piggyback runs over 1 hour and the additional 1000 ml normal saline runs for an additional 7.5 hours.

What is the ratio strength and corresponding percentage strength of the propranolol solution?

a) 1:333 (w/v), 0.3%
b) 1:1,666 (w/v), 0.06%
c) 1:3,333 (w/v), 0.03%
d) 1:6,666 (w/v), 0.06%
e) 1:3,333 (w/v), 0.3%

9. How much sodium chloride (in mg) is needed to make the solution below isotonic?

		E value
Drug A	0.5% w/v	0.54
Drug B	2%	0.26
Purified water qs 180 mL		

10. The pharmacy received a TPN order for 1.5 mEq of magnesium in 100 mL of IV fluid. The valence of Mg is +2 and molecular weight is 24. What would be the corresponding strength of magnesium?

    a) 460 mg/L
    b) 560 mg/L
    c) 180 mg/L
    d) 360 mg/L
    e) 300 mg/L

11. What is the volume of magnesium sulfate needed in the final solution?

Amino Acids 8.5%	500 ml	Amino Acids 8.5%
Dextrose 70%	500 ml	Dextrose 70%
Sodium Chloride	25 mEq	NaCl 4 mEq/ml
Potassium Chloride	18 mEq	KCl 2 mEq/ml
Magnesium Sulfate	10 mEq	Magnesium Sulfate 4.08 mEq/ml
Calcium Gluconate	15 mEq	Calcium Gluconate 0.465 mEq/ml
Potassium Phosphate	17 mmol	Potassium Phosphate 3 mmol/ml
Multi-Vitamins 12	10 ml	MVI-12 10 ml vial
Trace Elements	3 ml	Trace Elements 3 ml vial

   a) 3 mL
   b) 2.45 mL
   c) 4 mL
   d) 6 mL
   e) 5 mL

12. How many milligrams of sodium bicarbonate (NaHCO3) are in 7 moles? (MW Na=23, C=12, H=1, O=16)

   a) 588 mg
   b) 600 mg
   c) 600,000 mg
   d) 588,000 mg
   e) 84 mg

13. How much of a 7% w/v solution can be made if you have 360 mL of a 12.5% solution and 2 liters of a 3% solution?

14.
Patient Profile

Patient Name: Mika Rose   Address: 3659 Longfellow Road, Perry, FL

Age: 35   Sex: M   Race: W   Height: 4' 9"   Weight: 158.4 lb

Allergies: NKDA   Diagnoses: Uveitis

Medications						
Date	Rx#	Prescriber	Drug	Quantity	Sig	Refills
1/01/18	4668-01	Dr. Strange, MD	Homatropine 5% Opth. Drops	5 mL	1 gtt o.d. TID	0
1/10/18	4668-02	Dr. Strange, MD	Prednisolone Acetate 1% Opth. Drops	5 mL	2 gtt o.d. QID	1

The homatropine ophthalmic solution must be compounded as a preservative-free product using homatropine hydrobromide, USP (E = 0.17). According to the USP XXI, solubilization of homatropine requires Sorensen's Modified Phosphate Buffer. If it is recommended that a buffer comprises at least 1/3 of the solution volume, what is the minimum volume of Sorensen's Modified Phosphate Buffer (pH 7.4) that is required to prepare this product?

15. A hospital pharmacist received an order for piperacillin/tazobactam sodium 3.375 g IV every 6 hours in 100 mL normal saline infused over 30 minutes. If the administration set delivers 15 drops of solution per mL, how many drops per minute must be regulated to deliver the medication as prescribed?

    a) 50 drops/minute
    b) 60 drops/minute
    c) 55 drops/minute
    d) 49 drops/minute
    e) 58 drops/minute

16.

Patient Profile

Patient Name: Donald Trimp   Address: 56 Carol Road, Jacksonville, FL

Age: 69   Sex: M   Race: AA   Height: 5'8"   Weight: 185 lb

Allergies: Penicillin   Diagnoses: HTN, Type 2 DM, COPD

Medications						
Date	Rx#	Prescriber	Drug	Quantity	Sig	Refills
2/01/17	77-1	Dr. Strange, MD	Metformin 500 mg	30	1 tablet PO daily	4
2/10/17	77-2	Dr. Strange, MD	Lisinopril 5 mg	30	1 tablet PO BID	5

What is the patient's BMI?

a) 26
b) 27
c) 28
d) 29
e) 30

17. A patient gives you a prescription for a prednisone taper: prednisone 30 mg daily x 5 days, then decrease by 5 mg every 3 days until taper ends. How many prednisone 5 mg tablets will be dispensed to fill this prescription?

18. A female patient is 5'5 tall and weighs 140 pounds. She presents to the outpatient infusion center today to receive herceptin 6 mg/kg. Calculate, in grams, the dose of herceptin she will receive?

a) 0.38 g
b) 0.40 g
c) 360 g
d) 381.6 g
e) 63.6 g

19. What would be the equivalent ratio strength of a 10% w/v solution?

a) 1:10
b) 1:100
c) 1: 1,000
d) 1:11
e) 1:1

20. You receive the following order:

Amino Acids 8.5%	500 ml	Amino Acids 8.5%
Dextrose 70%	500 ml	Dextrose 70%
Sodium Chloride	20 mEq	NaCl 4 mEq/ml
Potassium Chloride	15 mEq	KCl 2 mEq/ml
Magnesium Sulfate	8 mEq	Magnesium Sulfate 4.08 mEq/ml
Calcium Gluconate	12 mEq	Calcium Gluconate 0.465 mEq/ml
Potassium Phosphate	23 mmol	Potassium Phosphate 3 mmol/ml
Multi-Vitamins 12	10 ml	MVI-12 10 ml vial

How many kcal/day would this patient receive if the flow rate of the TPN is 150ml/hr? Assume 4 kcal/g provided by amino acids, 3.4 kcal/g provided by parenteral dextrose, and 9 kcal/g provided by lipids.

21. You received the following order for a 120 lb patient:

Amino Acids 8.5%	1.5 g/kg	Amino Acids 8.5%, 1000 mL bottle
Dextrose 70%	5 g/kg	Dextrose 70%, 500 mL bottle
Sodium Chloride	10 mEq	NaCl 4 mEq/ml
Potassium Chloride	20 mEq	KCl 2 mEq/ml
Magnesium Sulfate	8 mEq	Magnesium Sulfate 4.08 mEq/ml
Calcium Gluconate	10 mEq	Calcium Gluconate 0.465 mEq/ml
Potassium Phosphate	20 mmol	Potassium Phosphate 3 mmol/ml
Multi-Vitamins 12	10 ml	MVI-12 10 ml vial

What volume of 70% dextrose solution is needed to prepare this hyperalimentation solution?

22. A pharmacist compounding 46 ounces of ointment needs 24 grams of drug N solution (specific gravity 0.62). What volume, in L, of solution is needed?

a) 0.03 L
b) 0.3 L
c) 0.4 L
d) 0.44 L
e) 0.04 L

23.

Patient Profile

Patient Name: Hilleary Clifton   Address: 227 George Bush Road, Sig, Ohio

Age: 67   Sex: F   Race: W   Height: 5'4"   Weight: 185 lb

Allergies: Quinolones   Diagnoses: Psoriasis, dermatitis

Date	Rx#	Prescriber	Drug	Quantity	Sig	Refills
11/16	778	Dr. Strange, MD	Triamcinolone acetonide 0.025%	60 g	Apply to AA QID PRN	4
11/16	779	Dr. Strange, MD	Crude Coal tar gel	33 g	Apple to AA at hs	5

How many mL of triamcinolone acetonide suspension 40 mg/mL would be needed to compound the prescription of 11/16?

24.

Patient Profile

Patient Name: Bernie Sands   Address: 34 Kennedy Way, Jesuit, Montana

Age: 10   Sex: M   Race: W   Height: 4'4"   Weight: 33.3 kg

Allergies: Lipitor   Diagnoses: Moderate Asthma

Medications					
Date	Rx#	Prescriber	Drug	Quantity	Sig
12/16	888	Dr. Bled, MD	Advair 250/50 mcg	1 Diskus	Inhale 1 puff PO BID
12/16	889	Dr. Bled, MD	Singulair 10 mg	30	Take 1 tablet PO HS

12/25 Patient goes to see Dr. Santheimer c/o sore throat, cough, and rhinorrhea. Patient has a fever of 101.3 degrees F. Dr. Santheimer diagnoses him with an URI and states he will call in a prescription for Amoxicillin to the local pharmacy. While you are on duty at the pharmacy, Dr. Santheimer calls in Amoxicillin and wants you to calculate the dose. He wants the patient to receive 30mg/kg/day PO divided q 12 hours for 10 days. What do you dispense?

   a) Amoxicllin 250 mg/5 mL sig 5 teaspoonfuls PO Q12hr x 10 days
   b) Amoxicillin 250 mg/5 mL sig 3 teasoonfuls PO Q12hr x 10 days
   c) Amoxicillin 250 mg/5 mL sig 2 teasoonfuls PO Q12hr x 10 days
   d) Amoxicillin 250 mg/5 mL sig 4 teasoonfuls PO Q12hr x 10 days
   e) Amoxicillin 250 mg/5 mL sig 1 teasoonfuls PO Q12hr x 10 days

25. If 785 mL of alcohol weighs 775 g, what is its density?

26. What is the osmolarity of a solution, in mOsm/L, if 750 mg of potassium chloride injection is added to 500 mL of normal saline? (Molecular weight: K+ 39, Cl- 35.5, Na+ 23)

   a) 348
   b) 337
   c) 300
   d) 174
   e) 340

27.

Patient Profile

Patient Name:	Bugs Bunny		Address: 6 Looney Tunes Way, Hollywood, CA		
Age: 31	Sex: M	Race: W	Height: 5'3"		Weight: 180 lbs
Allergies: Sulfa drugs			Diagnoses:		Bipolar disorder, allergies

Medications					
Date	Rx#	Prescriber	Drug	Quantity	Sig
10/16	888	Dr. Acme, MD	ProAir HFA	1 inhaler (200 puffs)	Inhale 2 puffs PO QID PRN
10/16	889	Dr. Acme, MD	Abilify 15 mg	30	Take 1 tablet PO daily

During allergy season, if the patient uses Rx #889 as prescribed to the max, for how many days will each prescription last?

28. Which of the following dextrose solutions is isotonic?

   a) 2.5% dextrose in water
   b) 50% dextrose in water
   c) 5% dextrose in water
   d) 10% dextrose in water
   e) 20% dextrose in water

29.

Patient Profile

Patient Name:	Criggy Lust		Address: 5 bashful way, Cleveland, OH	
Age: 41	Sex: F	Race: AA	Height: 5'6"	Weight: 132 lbs
Allergies: lisinopril			Diagnoses: ESRD, HTN	

Medications					
Date	Rx#	Prescriber	Drug	Quantity	Sig
12/24	999	Dr. Codex, MD	Valcyte 450 mg	60	Take 1 tablet PO BID
12/24	997	Dr. Codex, MD	Propranolol 25 mg	30	Take 1 tablet PO daily

This patient's serum creatinine at 6 months post-transplant was measured at 1.9 mg/dL. Using the Cockcroft-Gault equation, what is the best estimate of this patient's creatinine clearance?

30.

Patient Profile

Patient Name:	Salem Witch		Address: 17 N Washington Square, Salem, MA	
Age: 21	Sex: F	Race: W	Height: 5'3"	Weight: 109 lbs
Allergies: Lopressor			Diagnoses: Allergies	

Medications

Date	Rx#	Prescriber	Drug	Quantity	Sig
12/28	967	Dr. Blodd, MD	Zantac Injection in NSS	50 mg 100 mL	IV infusion over 20 minutes q8h
12/28	968	Dr. Blodd, MD	Quetiapine 10 mg	30	Take 1 tablet PO daily

Zantac (ranitidine HCl) Injection, USP is available as a 25 mg/mL solution (see label). What is an appropriate infusion rate for the drug product if an IV administration set calibrated to 20 drops/mL is used?

a) 100 drops/minute
b) 150 drops/minute
c) 200 drops/minute
d) 10 drops/minute
e) 20 drops/minute

31.

Patient Profile

Name: Lucy Ball   Address: 67 Famous Way, Hollywood, CA

Age: 7   Sex: F   Race: W   Height: 3'3"   Weight: 39 lbs

Allergies: Sulfa drugs   Diagnoses: Depression, ADHD

Medications

Date	Rx#	Prescriber	Drug	Quantity	Sig
12/29	567	Dr. Kim, MD	Vyvanse 30 mg	30	1 tablet PO QAM

Dr. Harrison calls and wants you to dispense Omnicef 250 mg/5 ml and wants you to calculate the dose giving 14 mg/kg q 24 hours for 10 days. Calculate an appropriate dosing volume of Omnicef suspension for this patient.

a) 7.5 mL PO daily for 10 days
b) 6 mL PO daily for 10 days

c) 4 mL PO daily for 10 days
d) 5 mL PO daily for 10 days
e) 8 mL PO daily for 10 days

32. How much sodium chloride (in g) is needed to make the solution below isotonic?
Purified water qs 480 mL
Drug A 0.75% w/v   E value 0.52
Drug B 3% w/v   E value 0.13

33. A 59-year-old, 136 lb. female nurse presents to her family physician with hot flashes and fatigue. Her provider prescribes a compound for Estrogen/Progesterone sublingual drops. The directions for this compound are "Place 1 drop under the tongue once daily."

Estrogen 0.5 g
Progesterone 0.8 g
Saccharin 100 mg
Silica Gel 200 mg
Cherry Flavor 10 gtts
Almond Oil 10 mL

How many milliliters of cherry flavor is needed to prepare 45 ml of the Estrogen/Progesterone compound with a drop factor of 15 gtt/ml?

34. A 49-year-old, 186 lb male housepainter is admitted to the hospital for severe dehydration. He is given a 500 ml bolus of normal saline, followed by 1000 ml of normal saline with 30 mg propranolol for tachycardia in a 50 ml piggyback. The piggyback runs over 1 hour and the additional 1000 ml normal saline runs for an additional 7.5 hours.

What is the flow rate (ml/min) of the second normal saline bag over its 8.5 hour administration period if the drop factor is 15 gtt/ml?

35. You receive the following order:
    Amino Acids 8.5%   1.5 g/kg   Amino Acids 8.5%, 1000 mL bottle
    Dextrose 70%   5 g/kg   Dextrose 70%, 500 mL bottle

Sodium Chloride	10 mEq	NaCl 4 mEq/ml
Potassium Chloride	20 mEq	KCl 2 mEq/ml
Magnesium Sulfate	8 mEq	Magnesium Sulfate 4.08 mEq/ml
Calcium Gluconate	12 mEq	Calcium Gluconate 0.465 mEq/ml
Potassium Phosphate	20 mmol	Potassium Phosphate 3 mmol/ml
Multi-Vitamins 12	10 ml	MVI-12 10 ml vial

What is the volume of calcium gluconate needed in the final solution?

a) 27 mL
b) 28 mL
c) 26 mL
d) 25 mL
e) 24 mL

36. A nutritional supplement contains:
    Protein 8.3g/100 mL
    Fat   3.6g/100 mL
    Carb   15g/100 mK

    What number of calories are received from fat in 4 ounces of the supplement?

    a) 35 Kcal
    b) 38 Kcal
    c) 34 Kcal
    d) 30 Kcal
    e) 39 Kcal

37. A 35-year-old, 5'5", 136 lb woman presented to the emergency department with severe dysphagia and has been receiving hemodialysis twice a week. She is admitted to the hospital for dehydration. She is to receive fluid replacement for dehydration 4 times daily and total parenertal nutrition every 3 days for caloric needs. She is released from the hospital on day 6 and will be re-evaluated on an outpatient basis for nutritional needs.

Calculate the total daily calories needed for this patient. Assume amino acids = 0.75g/kg body weight and provides 4 kcal/g; lipids = 30% of total daily calories and provide 9 kcal/g; and dextrose = 3.4 kcal/g. Assume a stress factor adjustment of 1.2 due to hemodialysis.

Male = 66 + (13.7xW) + (5xH) - (6.8xA)
Female = 655 + (9.6xW) + (1.8xH) - (4.7xA), A = age in years
W = weight in kg, H = height in cm

38. A pharmacist receives a prescription for drug y in a dose of 3 teaspoons every 8 hours for 14 days. How much drug y, in milliliters, will be dispensed?

   a) 600 mL
   b) 45 mL
   c) 630 mL
   d) 6.3 mL
   e) 15 mL

39.

Patient Profile

Name: Caymen Atio   Address: 56 Longfellow, Sanctuary, PR

Age: 37   Sex: M   Race: AA   Height: 5'7"   Weight: 153 lbs

Allergies: Sulfa drugs   Diagnoses: 3rd degree burns left arm, left leg

Medications				
Date	Rx#	Prescriber	Drug	Sig
01/29	555	Dr. Hosseni, MD	Gentamicin sulfate injection, 10 mg/mL	1.5 mg/kg IBW IM Q8-12hrs x 14 days

Test	Normal Value	Results
SCr	0.5- 1.1 mg/dL	0.8 mg/dL
01/29	Gentamicin dosing interval based on CrCl. Q8h for CrCl > 60 ml/min; Q12h for CrCl 40-60 mL/min; Q24h for CrCl 20-40	

	mL/min; <20 ml/min give loading dose and monitor levels
01/28	Gentamicin sulfate comes in 10mg/mL and 40 mg/mL sterile solution for injection

What is an appropriate gentamicin dose and dosing interval for this patient?

a) 92 mg TID
b) 99 mg BID
c) 95 mg BID
d) 90 mg BID
e) 100 mg TID

40. How much water, in mL, must be added to a 0.12% solution to obtain 1 pint of a 0.07% solution?

a) 197
b) 192
c) 100
d) 97
e) 79

41. You receive the following order:

Amino Acids 8.5%	500 ml	Amino Acids 8.5%
Dextrose 70%	500 ml	Dextrose 70%
Sodium Chloride	20 mEq	NaCl 4 mEq/ml
Potassium Chloride	15 mEq	KCl 2 mEq/ml
Magnesium Sulfate	8 mEq	Magnesium Sulfate 4.08 mEq/ml
Calcium Gluconate	12 mEq	Calcium Gluconate 0.465 mEq/ml
Potassium Phosphate	23 mmol	Potassium Phosphate 3 mmol/ml
Multi-Vitamins 12	10 ml	MVI-12 10 ml vial

What is the total volume of the final hyperalimentation solution?

a) 1058 mL
b) 1061 mL

c) 1050 mL
d) 1060 mL
e) 1100 mL

42. You receive a compound for Estrogen/Progesterone sublingual drops.

   Estrogen 0.8 g
   Progesterone 0.8 g
   Cherry Flavor 10 gtts

   How many milliliters of cherry flavor is needed to prepare 45 ml of the Estrogen/Progesterone compound with a drop factor of 15 gtt/ml?

43.

Patient Profile

Name: Rose Blood   Address: 32 Resident Evil Way, Gambro, NC

Age: 87   Sex: F   Race: W   Height: 6'9"   Weight: 183 lbs

Allergies: Penicillins   Diagnoses: CKD, Asthma, COPD

Medications				
Date	Rx#	Prescriber	Drug	Sig
08/29	655	Dr. Mo, MD	Proventil Inhaler	1 puff q4-6 hrs PRN SOB

What is Mr. Roy's estimated Ideal Body Weight (IBW)?

a) 95 kg
b) 94 kg
c) 96 kg
d) 92 kg
e) 93 kg

44. A 35-year-old, 5'3", 166 lb man presented to the emergency department with severe dysphagia and has been receiving hemodialysis twice a week. He is admitted to the hospital for dehydration. He is to receive fluid replacement for dehydration 4 times daily and total parenteral nutrition every 3 days for caloric needs. He is released from the hospital on day 6 and will be re-evaluated on an outpatient basis for nutritional needs.

How many mls of a 7% amino acid solution are needed? Assume amino acids = 0.75g/kg body weight and provides 4 kcal/g; lipids = 30% of total daily calories and provide 9 kcal/g; and dextrose = 3.4 kcal/g. Assume a stress factor adjustment of 1.2g/kg/day due to hemodialysis.

Male = 66 + (13.7xW) + (5xH) - (6.8xA)   Female = 655 + (9.6xW) + (1.8xH) - (4.7xA)
A = age in years, W = weight in kg, H = height in cm

45.

Patient Profile

Name: Jin Lao   Address: 23 Forest View Way, Fresco, SC

Age: 1   Sex: M   Race: W   Height: N/A   Weight: 13 lbs

Allergies: Penicillins   Diagnoses: Asthma

Medications				
Date	Rx#	Prescriber	Drug	Sig
08/29	655	Dr. ke, MD	Ranitidine 15 mg/mL	1 ml BID; 11 refills

What is Jin's dose of ranitidine in milligrams/kg/dose?

a) 5.91 mg/kg/dose
b) 2.54 mg/kg/dose
c) 5.1 mg/kg/dose
d) 7 mg/kg/dose
e) 4 mg/kg/dose

46. The pediatric dose of a drug is 375 mg/m2. Determine the dose for an 8-year-old girl who is 3'8" tall and weighs 70 lbs

47. You receive the following order:

Amino Acids 8.5%	500 ml	Amino Acids 8.5%
Dextrose 70%	500 ml	Dextrose 70%
Sodium Chloride	20 mEq	NaCl 4 mEq/ml
Potassium Chloride	15 mEq	KCl 2 mEq/ml
Magnesium Sulfate	8 mEq	Magnesium Sulfate 4.08 mEq/ml
Calcium Gluconate	12 mEq	Calcium Gluconate 0.465 mEq/ml
Potassium Phosphate	25 mmol	Potassium Phosphate 3 mmol/ml

What is the volume of potassium phosphate in the final solution?

48. How many moles of dietary sodium does a patient consume if he ingests 2 eggs (171 mg sodium/egg), 3 slices of bacon (192 mg sodium/slice), and 2 slices of toast (148 mg sodium/slice) with 4 tsp. butter (27 mg sodium/tsp) for breakfast? (MW Na=23, Cl=35.5)

a) 0.02
b) 23
c) 0.5
d) 0.06
e) 0.6

49. A pharmacist receives a prescription for lactulose 4 tablespoons every 8 hours for 48 hours. How much lactulose, in milliliters, will be dispensed?

a) 150 mL
b) 200 mL
c) 180 mL
d) 320 mL
e) 360 mL

50. A 59-year-old, 227 lb man, presented to the emergency department with a pulse ox reading of 89, blood pressure of 190/96, and a pulse of 136. He is administered O_2 via nasal cannula and 1 liter of normal saline over 4 hours. He has a history of diabetes and hypertension. He is admitted to the hospital on observational status to monitor. Once admitted, he is given Cipro, 400 mg/200ml, every 12 hours, infused at 500 mg/hr.

What is the flow rate (ml/hr) of the antibiotic?

a) 280 ml/hr
b) 230 ml/hr
c) 250 ml/hr
d) 300 ml/hr
e) 200 ml/hr

Section 3: 50 questions, Time: 60 minutes

This third, final section will provide some calculation type questions not covered in the previous two sections to help you better practice your calculations. It's recommended to time yourself giving 1 hour to complete each 50 question set.

1.

Patient Profile

Name: Melanie Pierce Address: 64 Front Drive, Silver Springs, MD

Age: 38 Sex: F Race: AA Height: 5'3" Weight: 130 lbs

Allergies: Sulfa drugs Diagnoses: Eye Infection

Medications					
Date	Rx#	Prescriber	Drug	Quantity	Sig
12/19	765	Dr. Mo, MD	Cefazolin Sodium	0.35%	2 gtt OU BID
			Thimerosal	0.002%	
			0.09% NaCl for Injection, USP	qs 15 mL	

The directions on a 500 mg vial of cefazolin for injection, USP indicates the addition of 2.0 mL of sterile water for injection, USP to the vial, 2.2 mL of cefazolin sodium solution is obtained. What volume of sterile cefazolin for injection, USP is required to provide the required amount of cefazolin in the prescription order?

2. How many mL of a 25% w/v solution of calcium chloride must be mixed with a 10% solution to prepare 240 mL of a 15% solution?

   a) 80
   b) 60
   c) 40
   d) 20
   e) 100

3. A 34-year-old, 178 lb male hiker presents to Urgent Care with a rash covering his legs and feet. He is given 0.75 mg/kg dose of IM Depo-Medrol (40mg/ml) for immediate relief of urticaria and rash. He is also prescribed a topical calamine compound and a prednisone taper to be taken over 5 days.

   Calamine   100 mg
   Phenol   600 mg
   Zinc Oxide 300 mg
   Almond Oil 50 mg

   How much calamine is needed to make 30 grams of the topical calamine mixture?

   a) 2 g
   b) 4 g
   c) 3 g
   d) 5 g
   e) 1 g

4. How many mOsm are present when 950 mg of calcium chloride injection is dissolved in 1 liter of water? (Molecular weight: Ca^{2+} =40, Cl^{1-} =35.5)

5. 480 mL of a 15% w/v solution is mixed with 1 liter of water. What is the new strength, in % w/v, of this solution?

   a) 5.1%
   b) 4.0%
   c) 4.5%
   d) 4.9%
   e) 6%

6. A medication order is received for prednisolone 60 mg/m2/day in 3 divided doses for 2 weeks followed by 45 mg/m2/day in 2 divided doses for 2 weeks followed by 30 mg/m2 once daily for 2 weeks followed by 20 mg/m2 every other day for 2 weeks. Prednisolone is available as a 125 mg/5 mL solution. The patient is a 63-year-old man weighing 346 lbs and standing 6'11 tall. What is this patient's body surface area?

7.

Patient Profile

Name: Michael Jackson   Address: 46 TradePost Way, Wellpinit, WA

Age: 38   Sex: M   Race: NA   Height: 5'6"   Weight: 150 lbs

Allergies: Sulfa drugs   Diagnoses: Metabolic acidosis

Medications					
Date	Rx#	Prescriber	Drug	Quantity (mmol/L)	Sig
01/19	7885	Dr. Qi, MD	Sodium Bicarbonate Potassium Bicarbonate Sodium Chloride In Sterile water for infusion, USP	180 150 90 2.5 L	Infuse IV, 0 refils

The molecular weights for the ingredients are as follows:
Sodium bicarbonate, 84 g/mole   Potassium chloride, 74.5 g/mole
Sodium chloride, 58.5 g/mole

The following sterile drug products are available:
Sodium Bicarbonate for Injection, USP, 8.4%
Potassium Chloride for Injections Concentrate, USP, 500 mEq/250 mL
Sodium Chloride for Injection Concentrate, USP, 14.6%

What volume of 8.4% Sodium Bicarbonate for Injection, USP should be added to the Sterile Water for Infusion, USP IV bag?

a) 400 mL
b) 450 mL
c) 500 mL
d) 600 mL
e) 300 mL

8. A pharmacist receives a prescription for lactulose 2 tablespoons every 8 hours for 48 hours. How much lactulose, in milliliters, will be dispensed?

9. A man is brought to the ED unresponsive and has a strong smell of alcohol on his breath. He begins to become slightly responsive and the staff is notified by the patient he is an alcoholic. The ED physician orders a "banana bag," to be administered over 6 hours.

"Banana Bag"
1 liter normal saline
-thiamine (100mg/ml, 2ml) 100 mg
-folic acid (5mg/ml, 10ml) 1 mg
-MVI (1 ml vial) 1 vial
-magnesium sulfate (0.5g/ml, 2ml) 3 g

The physician ordered 3g of magnesium sulfate in the banana bag and it is to be infused at 0.5 g/hr. What is the flow rate of the banana bag if the drop factor is 18 gtt/ml?

a) 42 gtt/min
b) 45 gtt/min
c) 48 gtt/min
d) 50 gtt/min
e) 40 gtt/min

10. How many mL of a 17.5% w/v solution of calcium chloride must be mixed with a 5% solution to prepare 480 mL of a 15% solution?

a) 384 mL
b) 288 mL
c) 480 mL
d) 350 mL
e) 380 mL

11. How many mOsm are present when 550 mg of calcium chloride ($CaCl_2$) are dissolved in 1 liter of water? (molecular weight: Ca^{2+} 40, Cl^{-1} 35.5)

a) 14 mOsm
b) 15 mOsm
c) 16 mOsm
d) 31 mOsm
e) 10 mOsm

12. An order is received for a new patient admitted to the hospital. The loading dose is 5 mg/kg ideal body weight. The maintenance dose is 2 mg/kg ideal body weight per hour. The patient is a 36-year-old female weighing 167 lbs. She is 5'5" tall. What is the loading dose for this patient, in mg?

   a) 280 mg
   b) 300 mg
   c) 285 mg
   d) 330 mg
   e) 250 mg

13. A 48-year-old, 142 lb man presented to the Emergency Department with a fever of 103.7 degrees F for 3 days. He has an open ulceration on his right leg determined to be cellulitis. He is admitted to the hospital to receive IV antibiotics. A culture determines sensitivity to cephalosporins. Cefazolin at a dose of 1.5 g IV every 8 hours for 3 days is started. The physician orders the Cefazolin (1g/50ml) be infused at 2g/hr. On the 4th day, the patient is released from the hospital and is prescribed cephalexin 500mg 4 times daily for 7 days.

If Cephalexin suspension contains 250 mg of Cephalexin in each 5 ml dose, how many grams of Cephalexin are contained in a 200 ml bottle of suspension?

14. You receive the following order:

Amino Acids 8.5%	500 ml	Amino Acids 8.5%	
Dextrose 70%	500 ml	Dextrose 70%	
Sodium Chloride	20 mEq	NaCl 4 mEq/ml	
Potassium Chloride	15 mEq	KCl 2 mEq/ml	
Magnesium Sulfate	8 mEq	Magnesium Sulfate 4.08 mEq/ml	
Calcium Gluconate	12 mEq	Calcium Gluconate 0.465 mEq/ml	
Potassium Phosphate	25 mmol	Potassium Phosphate 3 mmol/ml	

The physician orders this solution be infused at 200 ml/hr. At what flow rate (gtt/min) should it be infused if the drop factor is 15 gtts/ml?

15.

Patient Profile

Name: Frazier Stevenson   Address: The Trading Post, Wellpinit, WA

Age: 33   Sex: M   Race: NA   Height: 5'8"   Weight: 160 lbs

Allergies: NKDA   Diagnoses: Burkitt's Lymphoma

Medications				
Date	Rx#	Prescriber	Drug	Quantity	Sig
03/19	8590	Dr. Sig, MD	Vincristine Sulfate	1.4 mg/m^2	IV in 50 mL NS over 15 minutes

What volume of a 2 mg/2 mL vincristine sulfate solution for injection should be injected into the 50 mL NS infusion bag?

16. A 31-year-old, 5'3", 156 lb woman presented to the emergency department with severe dysphagia and has been receiving hemodialysis twice a week. She is admitted to the hospital for dehydration. She is to receive fluid replacement for dehydration 4 times daily and total parenteral nutrition every 3 days for caloric needs. She is released from the hospital on day 6 and will be re-evaluated on an outpatient basis for nutritional needs.

How many kcal are provided from a 7% amino acid solution? Assume amino acids = 0.75g/kg body weight and provides 4 kcal/g; lipids = 30% of total daily calories and provide 9 kcal/g; and dextrose = 3.4 kcal/g. Assume a stress factor adjustment of 1.2g/kg/day due to hemodialysis.

Male = 66+(13.7xW)+(5xH)-(6.8xA)
Female = 655 + (9.6xW) + (1.8xH) - (4.7xA), A = age in years
W = weight in kg, H = height in cm

a) 210
b) 211
c) 200
d) 213
e) 221

17. A 59-year-old, 136 lb. female nurse presents to her family physician with hot flashes and fatigue. Her provider prescribes a compound for Estrogen/Progesterone sublingual drops. The directions for this compound are "Place 2 drops under the tongue once daily."

Estrogen 0.5 g
Progesterone 0.8 g
Saccharin 100 mg
Silica Gel 200 mg
Fruity Tutti Flavor 8 gtts
Sesame Seed Oil QS to 5 mL

How many grams of Progesterone are needed to prepare 45 ml of the Estrogen/Progesterone compound?

a) 3.6 g
b) 4.5 g
c) 5.1 g
d) 3.0 g
e) 2.6 g

18. A medication order is received for prednisolone 60 mg/m²/day in 3 divided doses for 2 weeks followed by 45 mg/m²/day in 2 divided doses for 2 weeks followed by 30 mg/m² once daily for 2 weeks followed by 20 mg/m² every other day for 2 weeks. Prednisolone is available as a 125 mg/5 mL solution. The patient is a 49-year-old woman weighing 246 lbs and standing 5'11 tall. What is the total volume of prednisolone solution, in mL, needed to complete the course of therapy?

19. Drug X (826 mg) is dissolved in 500 mL of purified water. What is the resulting concentration, expressed as a ratio strength?

a) 1:666

b) 1:600
c) 1:605
d) 1:604
e) 1:603

20. A 38-year-old, 5'3", 156 lb woman presented to the emergency department with severe dysphagia and has been receiving hemodialysis twice a week. She is admitted to the hospital for dehydration. She is to receive fluid replacement for dehydration 4 times daily and total parenertal nutrition every 3 days for caloric needs. She is released from the hospital on day 6 and will be re-evaluated on an outpatient basis for nutritional needs.

Calculate the resting metabolic energy according to the Harris-Benedict equation. Assume amino acids = 0.75g/kg body weight and provides 4 kcal/g; lipids = 30% of total daily calories and provide 9 kcal/g; and dextrose = 3.4 kcal/g. Assume a stress factor adjustment of 1.2g/kg/day due to hemodialysis.
Male = 66 + (13.7xW) + (5xH) - (6.8xA)
Female = 655 + (9.6xW) + (1.8xH) - (4.7xA), A = age in years
W = weight in kg, H = height in cm

21.
Patient Profile

Name: Freddy Flintstone   Address: 4 Lane, Tacoma, Wyoming

Age: 43   Sex: M   Race: W   Height: 6'1"   Weight: 190 lbs

Allergies: NKDA   Diagnoses: Knee replacement

Medications					
Date	Rx#	Prescriber	Drug	Quantity	Sig
04/19	8790	Dr. Kit, MD	Fentanyl Citrate	100 mcg	Slow IV pre-op

Fentanyl citrate (MW = 528.6 g/mole) is available as a sterile solution for injection containing fentanyl citrate, which the label indicates as equivalent to 50 mcg/mL fentanyl base (MW = 336.5 g/mole). What volume of the injectable solution should be administered to the patient to provide the indicated dose of fentanyl citrate?

a) 1.20 mL
b) 1.30 mL
c) 63.7 mL
d) 1.50 mL
e) 1.27 mL

22. 300 mL of a 15% w/v solution is mixed with 200 mL of water. What is the new strength, in % w/v, of this solution?

a) 8%
b) 9%
c) 10%
d) 11%
e) 5%

23. A pharmacist receives a prescription for "Drug x" in a dose of 4 tablespoons every 6 hours. How much "Drug x", in liters, would be dispensed for a 30-day supply?

24. A hospital pharmacist receives an order for piperacillin/tazobactam sodium 3.375 g IV every 6 hours in 150 mL normal saline infused over 1 hour. If the administration set delivers 30 drops of solution per mL, how many drops per minute must be regulated to deliver the medication as prescribed?

25.

Patient Profile

Name: Captain Jacks   Address: 4 Pirate View Way, Smithson, Maine

Age: 46   Sex: M   Race: W   Height: 5'8"   Weight: 190 lbs

Allergies: Lisinopril   Diagnoses: Asthma, Allergies

		Medications			
Date	Rx#	Prescriber	Drug	Quantity	Sig
06/19	8788	Dr. Bin, MD	Prednisone 60 mg daily x 3 days, then taper by 5 mg q3d to 10 mg daily	Qs 30 days	UD

Prednisone 5 mg tablets are available to fill this patient's prescription. How many tablets should be dispensed to this patient to fill the order for the first 30 days

26.

Patient Profile

Name: Berry Blast   Address: 21 Berry Lane, Frutti Tutti, Kansas

Age: 6   Sex: M   Race: W   Height: 2'8"   Weight: 30 lbs

Allergies: Penicillin   Diagnoses: Allergies

		Medications			
Date	Rx#	Prescriber	Drug	Quantity	Sig
02/19	8778	Dr. Fun, MD	Desloratidine 0.5 mg/mL	250 mL	5 mg PO QD PRN

If taken maximally every day as prescribed, how many days will rx#8778 last this patient?

a) 20 days
b) 25 days
c) 30 days
d) 15 days
e) 10 days

27. What is the final concentration (as a ratio strength) of a solution if four 100 mg tablets are dissolved in 250 mL of water?

   a) 1:625
   b) 1:325
   c) 1:525
   d) 1:425
   e) 1:250

28. A female patient is 5'9 tall and weighs 190 pounds. She presents to the outpatient infusion center today to receive herceptin 6 mg/kg. Calculate, in grams, the dose of herceptin she will receive

   a) 0.518 g
   b) 518 g
   c) 514 g
   d) 0.514 g
   e) 0.6 g

29.

Patient Profile

Name: Clark Kent Address: 24 Metropolis Lane, NY, NY

Age: 29 Sex: M Race: W Height: 5'9" Weight: 210 lbs

Allergies: NKDA Diagnoses: Metabolic acidosis

Medications					
Date	Rx#	Prescriber	Drug	Quantity (mmol/L)	Sig
05/19	8889	Dr. Doom, MD	Sodium Bicarbonate Potassium Chloride Sodium Chloride In Sterile Water for infusion, USP	180 150 90 2.5 L	Infuse IV

The molecular weight of NaCl is 58.5 g/mole. What volume of 14.6% Sodium Chloride for Injection Concentrate, USP should be added to the Sterile Water for Infusion, USP IV bag?

30.

Patient Profile

Name: Marcus Kent   Address: 453 Middle of Nowhere, Kansas

Age: 49   Sex: M   Race: W   Height: 5'6"   Weight: 250 lbs

Allergies: NKDA   Diagnoses: Type 2 DM, HTN

Medications					
Date	Rx#	Prescriber	Drug	Quantity	Sig
06/19	889	Dr. Day, MD	Metformin 1000 mg	30	Take 1 tablet PO BID

What is the patient's BMI? ☐

31. A 48-year-old, 193 lb. male retired teacher has under gone several rounds of chemotherapy for lung cancer. He was given this prescription for "Miracle Mouthwash" to help with mouth ulcerations he developed from chemotherapy. The directions for this compound are "Swish, gargle, and spit 1 teaspoonful every 6 hours as needed for sore throat."

1 part	Viscous Lidocaine 2%
2 parts	Maalox
1 part	Diphenhydramine (12.5 mg/5 mL)
1.8 parts	Nystatin 100,000 Units Suspension

How many milliliters of Nystatin should be used to prepare 240 ml?

a) 65.5 mL
b) 74.5 mL
c) 70 mL
d) 80 mL
e) 66 mL

32. A medication order is received for gentamicin 1.7 mg/kg IV every 8 hours in 50 mL NS. The patient is a 56-year-old woman with an ideal body weight of 75 kg. Gentamicin is available in a 2 mL single use vial (40 mg/mL).

How many vials of gentamicin solution are needed to prepare a 5-day course of therapy (assume all doses are prepared in the morning and the expiration is 24 hours)?

a) 28
b) 23
c) 25
d) 40
e) 20

33. Which of the following factors is the most appropriate for calculating the dose of a drug to achieve a specific plasma concentration?

a) Half-Life
b) Volume of Distribution
c) Bioavailability
d) Protein Binding
e) Clearance

34.

Patient Profile

Name: Thomas Smith   Address: 34 Road, Blountstown, FL

Age: 9   Sex: M   Race: AA   Height: 2'9"   Weight: 56 lbs

Allergies: NKDA   Diagnoses: Allergies, Hay Fever

Date	Rx#	Prescriber	Drug	Quantity	Sig
01/27	889	Dr. Slow, MD	Cefdinir 125 mg/5 mL	Qs	7 mg/kg q12hrs x 7 days

What dose of Cefdinir should the patient receive?

a) 6 mL every 12 hours for 7 days
b) 5 mL every 12 hours for 7 days
c) 3 mL every 12 hours for 7 days
d) 8 mL every 12 hours for 7 days
e) 7 mL every 12 hours for 7 days

35.

Patient Profile

Name: Medlinda Wood   Address: 47 hunt way, Perry, FL

Age: 76   Sex: F   Race: AA   Height: 162 cm   Weight: 79 kg

Allergies: Penicillin   Diagnoses: Hyperlipidemia

Medications					
Date	Rx#	Prescriber	Drug	Quantity	Sig
06/26	8764	Dr. Gel, MD	Crestor 10 mg	30	1 tablet PO daily HS

Using the Cockcroft Gault equation, what is the best estimate of this patient's creatinine clearance?

36. You receive the following order for a 150 lb patient:

Amino Acids 8.5%	1.5 g/kg	Amino Acids 8.5%, 500 mL bottle
Dextrose 70%	5 g/kg	Dextrose 70%, 500 mL bottle
Sodium Chloride	20 mEq	NaCl 4 mEq/ml
Potassium Chloride	15 mEq	KCl 2 mEq/ml
Magnesium Sulfate	8 mEq	Magnesium Sulfate 4.08 mEq/ml
Calcium Gluconate	12 mEq	Calcium Gluconate 0.465 mEq/ml
Potassium Phosphate	25 mmol	Potassium Phosphate 3 mmol/ml

What volume of 8.5% Amino Acid solution is needed to prepare this hyperalimentation solution?

a) 1,200 mL
b) 1,250 mL
c) 1,203 mL
d) 1,205 mL
e) 1,202 mL

37. A 50-year-old, 153 lb. female retired CIA agent has under gone several rounds of chemotherapy for breast cancer. She was given this prescription for "Miracle Mouthwash" to help with mouth ulcerations she developed from chemotherapy. The directions for this compound are "Swish, gargle, and spit 1 teaspoonful every 6 hours as needed for sore throat."
1 part   Viscous Lidocaine 2%
2 parts Maalox
1 part   Diphenhydramine (12.5 mg/5 mL)
1.8 parts   Nystatin 100,000 Units Suspension

How many milliliters of viscous lidocaine should be used to prepare 240 ml?

38. Using the same case as #37, how many milliliters of Maalox should be used to prepare 240 ml?

39. You receive the following order:

Amino Acids 8.5%	1.5 g/kg	Amino Acids 8.5%, 500 mL bottle
Dextrose 70%	5 g/kg	Dextrose 70%, 500 mL bottle
Sodium Chloride	45 mEq	NaCl 4 mEq/ml
Potassium Chloride	15 mEq	KCl 2 mEq/ml
Magnesium Sulfate	8 mEq	Magnesium Sulfate 4.08 mEq/ml
Calcium Gluconate	12 mEq	Calcium Gluconate 0.465 mEq/ml
Potassium Phosphate	25 mmol	Potassium Phosphate 3 mmol/ml

What is the volume of sodium chloride needed in the final solution?

40. A 57-year-old, 156 lb. female nurse presents to her family physician with hot flashes and fatigue. Her provider prescribes a compound for Estrogen/Progesterone sublingual drops. The directions for this compound are "Place 1 drop under the tongue once daily."

Estrogen 0.5 g
Progesterone 0.8 g   Saccharin 100 mg
Silica Gel 200 mg   Fruity Tutti Flavor 8 gtts
Sesame Seed Oil QS to 5 mL

How many milligrams/day of Estrogen is the patient receiving if the dropper delivers 15 gtts/ml?

41. A 46 year old male has been receiving vancomycin for 1 week for a MRSA pneumonia. He is 5'9" and weighs 160 lbs. His admission SCr was 1 mg/dL. The pharmacist was called by a nurse, because his SCr is now 1.6 mg/dL. Several vancomycin levels have been drawn. The following information is available:

Vancomycin regimen: 750 mg IV Q24H at 2100 (stable regimen since 1/1/17)
Last vancomycin dose: 1/7/17 @ 2100
Vancomycin random level: 1/8/17 @ 1000 = 28 mg/L
Vancomycin random level: 1/8/17 @ 1300 = 24.7 mg/L

Calculate MK's vancomycin half-life.

42. Drug P03E6 has a volume of distribution of 80 L and a clearance of 9.37 L/hr. What is the half-life of this drug?

   a) 4
   b) 6
   c) 3
   d) 2
   e) 5

43. A new antibiotic has the following properties listed in it's monograph:
   Dosing (IV): 675 mg IV Q8H
   Dosing (PO): 675 mg PO TID
   Protein binding: 18%
   Metabolism: partially hepatic
   Half-life (elimination): 1.6 - 2.1 hours

What is the bioavailability of this new drug?

a) 0%
b) 10%
c) 100%
d) 50%
e) 25%

44. A dose of 750 mg of naproxen is administered to a patient. A blood sample is drawn one hour after the dose is administered. The concentration of naproxen is measured as 8 mcg/mL (which is 8 mg/L). Naproxen has a volume of distribution of 51 L. Determine the total amount of drug remaining in the body 1 hour after dose administration.

45. An oral drug is administered as a 225 mg dose. The resulting AUC is 52 mg x hr/mL. Bioavailability of the oral formulation is 50%. What is the clearance of this drug?

46. Following a 400 mg dose of cefdinir, the terminal elimination rate constant was determined to be 0.38 hr^{-1}. Calculate the half-life of cefdinir.

47. Amoxicillin has a clearance of 4.5 L/hr and a volume of distribution of 65 L. Calculate the half-life of amoxicillin.

48. Following a 400 mg dose of voriconazole IV the area under the curve is measured at 38.0 mcg x hr/mL. Calculate the apparent clearance.

49. Following an oral dose of 400 mg of cefdinir, the terminal elimination rate constant was determined to be 0.38 hr^{-1}, and the AUC was determined to be 25.18 mg x hr/L. Calculate the volume of distribution of cefdinir.

50. What is the pH of a solution prepared to be 0.5 M sodium bicarbonate and 0.05 M ascorbic acid (pKa for ascorbic acid = 3.13)?

   a) 4.0
   b) 4.5
   c) 4.2
   d) 4.13
   e) 4.10

Pharmacotherapy and Case Questions

Now that you have practiced your calculations, we will provide a section of 250 general pharmacotherapy and case scenario questions to help you master your knowledge.

This section will be composed of compounding Sterile and Nonsterile Products and Reviewing, Dispensing, and Administering Drugs and Drug Products along with pharmacotherapy questions.

Section 1: 250 questions, 5.5 hours

1. Another name for Enbrel is:

    a) Efavirenz
    b) Etanercept
    c) Eptifibatide
    d) Enfurvirtide
    e) Entidronate

2. A patient asks the pharmacist about a severe hangover from drinking vodka last night. He awakened with heartburn, nausea, tremor, dizziness, fatigue, body aches, headache, and depression. What is the worst combination of ingredients for him?

    a) Caffeine (i.e. Coffee), calcium carbonate
    b) Ibuprofen, calcium carbonate
    c) Naproxen, calcium carbonate
    d) Tums
    e) Advil, Maalox

3. After you ask for her allergies, an elderly woman mentions that she is allergic to capsules. She says that capsules never seem to get into her throat correctly and she hates swallowing them. She says that even after a full glass of water she still feels the capsule right in her mouth. After looking at her profile, you find out that 4 out of 7 of her medications are capsules.

Which of the following is likely to help her swallow?

   a) Do not use water
   b) Empty capsule contents into apple juice, then drink
   c) Extend head upward, when feeling capsule in back of throat swallow
   d) Take a sip of water with capsule, flex the head forward, and swallow
   e) Swallow with some food

4. Another name for Macrobid is:

   a) Nitrofurantoin
   b) Gentamicin
   c) Bactrim DS
   d) Metronidazole
   e) Clarithromycin

5. Combivent is also known as:

   a) Albutcrol/Formoterol
   b) Albuterol/Fluticasone
   c) Albuterol/Salmeterol
   d) Albuterol/Budesonide
   e) Albuterol/Ipratropium

6. Another name for Bactrim is:

   a) Bacitracin
   b) Baclofen
   c) Sulfamethoxazole/Trimethoprim
   d) Piperacillin/Tazobactam

7. Many dosage forms and medication delivery methods are considered suitable for nonprescription use. However, some are not available for nonprescription products. Which of the following is not available on a nonprescription basis?

   a) Inhalers
   b) Suppositories
   c) Enteric-Coated Tablets
   d) Injections
   e) Powders for Inhalation

8. Magnesium stearate is commonly used as what type of pharmaceutic ingredient in tablet preparation?

   a) Tablet Lubricant
   b) Tablet Disintegrant
   c) Tablet Opaquant
   d) Tablet Polishing Agent
   e) Tablet Glident

9. A 17-year-old sexually active gravida 0 para 0 presents with painful menstruation. This is accompanied by diarrhea, headache, nausea, and vomiting. She feels incapacitated for 48 to 72 hours during menstruation each period. She was tried on first line medication with side effects which she claims she could not tolerate. Doctor started her then on combination oral contraceptives.

   What is one of the effects of this medication?

   a) Osteoporosis
   b) Gallstone Formation
   c) Vaginal Dryness
   d) Increased cholesterol levels
   e) Blurry vision

10. A patient appearing to be aged in his 40s asks the pharmacist about a product to help his insomnia. He has only had it for 1 night, and thinks it may be caused by worry over an upcoming CPA exam. It may also be caused by the fact that his enlarged prostate causes him to have to urinate several times a night. He takes glyburide for diabetes. What should the pharmacist tell him?

    a) Insomnia for 1 night requires a physician appointment
    b) Nonprescription insomnia products are contraindicated with prostate enlargement
    c) Nonprescription products are not indicated for short-term insomnia
    d) Nonprescription insomnia products are contraindicated in patients with diabetes
    e) Nonprescription insomnia products interact with glyburide

11. Which agent is available in a rectal formulation for relief of constipation
    a) Bisacodyl
    b) Sorbitol
    c) Lubiprostone
    d) Methylcellulose
    e) Docusate Sodium

12. A 24-year-old woman is studying for final exams and wants to know what she can do about several small vesicles that have formed a crust on the upper margin of her lip. The lesions are painful and she would like to minimize discomfort in for an upcoming job interview.

    What most likely caused this infection?

    a) Fungal
    b) Viral
    c) Bacterial
    d) Candida
    e) Parasite

13. What is the appropriate needle gauge for a newly diagnosed diabetic patient requiring subcutaneous insulin?

    a) 25G, 1 inch
    b) 31G, 1 inch
    c) 33G, 5/16 inch
    d) 31G, 5/16 inch
    e) 25G, 5/16 inch

14. An 80-year-old patient comes to the pharmacy counter requesting assistance with choosing an appropriate medication to treat her cold symptoms. Her main symptom is nasal congestion. She is a routine customer in your pharmacy and is compliant with her blood pressure medications, glaucoma eye drops, and bisphosphonates for osteoporosis. Make a recommendation to treat this patient's cold symptoms

    a) Oral loratidine
    b) Nasal Spray Saline
    c) Oxymetazoline Nasal Spray
    d) Oral diphenhydramine
    e) Oral pseudoephedrine

15. A 17-year-old sexually active G1P1 female presents with white cheesy vaginal discharge. Speculum exam is performed visualizing adherent white and erythematous vaginal membranes. KOH smear - hyphae are seen. The patient is diagnosed with vaginal candidiasis and is prescribed fluconazole for treatment. She is allergic to penicillin and gets anaphylaxis.

   Which of the following is a side effect this patient should be counseled about?

   a) Potential for anaphylaxis due to cross reactivity
   b) Injection Site Reaction
   c) Nausea and Vomiting in conjunction with alcohol use
   d) Teeth discoloration
   e) Mild Nausea and Vomiting after a single pill use

   Use the following case for questions 16. And 17.

   A 20-year-old woman is studying for final exams and wants to know what she can do about several small vesicles that have formed a crust on the upper margin of her lip. The lesions are painful and she would like to minimize discomfort in for an upcoming job interview.

16. What OTC agent can be used to manage her condition?

   a) Carbamide peroxide 10%
   b) Benzocaine 20%
   c) Capsacin
   d) Oxybenzone
   e) Camphor 20%

17. Which one of the following is a trigger for reactivation of fever blisters?

   a) Shingles
   b) Chicken Pox
   c) Avobenzone
   d) Ultraviolet Radiation
   e) Sulfonamides

18.

Patient Profile

Name: Michael Jackson   Address: 46 TradePost Way, Wellpinit, WA

Age: 38   Sex: M   Race: NA   Height: 5'6"   Weight: 150 lbs

Allergies: Sulfa drugs   Diagnoses: Metabolic acidosis

Medications					
Date	Rx#	Prescriber	Drug	Quantity	Sig
01/19	7885	Dr. Qi, MD	Fentanyl Citrate	50 mcg	IM pre-op

Fentanyl Citrate Injection, USP is dispensed as a single dose in a syringe for use in surgery scheduled the same day the drug product is prepared. What would the appropriate storage conditions and beyond use date be for the dispensed product if it was prepared under ISO Class 5 conditions?

a) 14 days at cold temperature
b) 30 hours at controlled room temperature
c) 45 days in solid frozen state
d) 48 hours at controlled room temperature
e) 9 days at cold temperature

19. What dosage adjustment needs to be taken into consideration if a patient's phenytoin regimen needs to be changed from a capsule to a suspension?

a) The dose needs to be decreased by 8%
b) The dose needs to be increased by 8%
c) The dose needs to be increased by 50%
d) The dose needs to be decreased by 50%
e) The dose needs to be increased by 10%

20. A patient purchasing alli (orlistat) asks the pharmacist whether there are any special instructions he should follow. What should the pharmacist tell him?

   a) Take with a fiber supplement to prevent alli-induced constipation
   b) Take 4-6 capsules daily to reach maximal weight-loss potential
   c) Take a multivitamin once daily at bedtime
   d) Take along with an herbal weight loss product
   e) Ingest 1 serving of fat with each meal to counteract fat malabsorption

21. A 56-year-old male presents to the urologist with complaints of urinary frequency, urgency, hesitancy and nocturia. Upon examination, it is determined that the prostate is enlarged and weighs approximately 50 grams. His current medications include atorvastatin 40 mg once daily, lisinopril 20 mg once daily, aspirin 325 mg once daily, HCTZ 25 mg once daily, Humalog 7 units with meals, Lantus 50 units at night. Pertinent data: PSA 4.6 ng/mL, BP 120-130/74-80, fasting glucose 106, HgbA1c 6.2%. The physician decides to initiate terazosin.

   Which of the following patient education points will you address first regarding this medication with this patient?

   a) Monitor your blood pressure for additional decreases
   b) It is important that you monitor your PSA levels annually for efficacy
   c) Common side effects of this medication include nausea, headache, and stomach upset
   d) If you notice that you are starting to feel depressed or have thoughts of hurting yourself, seek help immediately
   e) Women of childbearing age should not handle this medication

22. A mother is asking for assistance. Her 6-year-old son has white bumps on his fingers that appear to be warts. The warts do not seem to bother him but he keeps injuring the warts.

   A child with warts on the hands should be counseled to use a nonprescription product that contains what concentration of salicylic acid?

   a) 10%
   b) 12%
   c) 17%
   d) 40%
   e) 35%

23.

Ingredient	Source
Cefazolin sodium	Cefazolin for Injection, USP Sterile Powder for Reconstitution, 500 mg vial
Thimerosal	Bulk thimerosal powder, non-sterile
0.9% Sodium chloride for injection, USP	0.9% Sodium Chloride for Injection, USP Sterile solution, 20 mL vial

The ingredients needed to prepare the formulation are listed in the table below. Based on this information, what USP <797> risk level and general associated beyond-use dating would you assign to this product?

a) High risk, 9 days refrigerated
b) High risk, 3 days refrigerated
c) Medium risk, 14 days refrigerated
d) Medium risk, 9 days refrigerated
e) Medium risk, 3 days refrigerated

24. A 21-year-old male presents to his primary care physician with urethritis, proctitis, urethral discharge, dysuria, and itching. The microscopic findings of the urethral discharge include C. trachomatis. The patient admits to unprotected intercourse approximately 10 days ago. His medical record indicates he is allergic to clarithromycin and penicillin. Which of the following is the most appropriate treatment option?

a) Acyclovir
b) Penicillin G
c) Doxycycline
d) Azithromycin
e) Cefdinir

25. This patient is prescribed the medication Latisse. When she comes to the pharmacy to get the prescription filled, she asks how the medication should be stored. The package insert for Latisse instructs the patient to store Latisse at 2° to 25°C. According to USP standards, which of the following environments is the best choice to recommend to this patient for storage of Latisse?

a) Cool
b) Cold
c) Frozen
d) Warm
e) Room Temperature

26. Which of the following is an SSRI that is marketed as an isomer rather than a racemate?

    a) Citalopram
    b) Fluoxetine
    c) Escitalopram
    d) Paroxetine
    e) Sertraline

27. A mother is asking for assistance. Her 6-year-old son has white bumps on his fingers that appear to be warts. The warts do not seem to bother him but he keeps injuring the warts. She is also afraid someone else in the family will "get these things."

    Salicylic acid for the nonprescription treatment of warts is contained in all of the following products except

    a) Compound W Freeze Off
    b) Occlusal-HP
    c) Dr. Scholl's Clear Away
    d) Wart-Off
    e) Compound Wart Strips

28. Omnipred® contains the following list of ingredients: prednisolone acetate 1%, benzalkonium chloride 0.01%, hypromellose, dibasic sodium phosphate, polysorbate 80, edatate disodium, glycerin, citric acid and/or sodium hydroxide, and purified water. What purpose does hypromellose serve in this formulation?

    a) Surfactant
    b) Viscous Vehicle
    c) pH adjuster
    d) Tonicity Adjuster
    e) Preservative

29. Which of the following is FDA-approved for treatment of infection C. difficile?

    a) Ciprofloxacin
    b) Metronidazole
    c) Vancomycin
    d) Streptomycin
    e) Clindamycin

30. Unless specified by a requirement in a USP monograph, in general the expiration date of a pharmaceutical product means that after that date, the product would lose what percentage of its original activity?

    a) 10%
    b) 20%
    c) 15%
    d) 5%
    e) 2%

31. Good oral hygiene is important to prevent a specific drug-related effect of which of the following drugs?

    a) Lamotrigine
    b) Phenytoin
    c) Phenobarbital
    d) Valproic acid
    e) Carbamazepine

32. A 46-year-old man inquires about quitting smoking. He currently smokes 9 cigarettes per day. He admits that he is a chronic gum chewer and he is concerned about weight gain upon quitting. His past medical history is significant for hypertension, depression, epilepsy, and seasonal allergies. He has tried nicotine patches in the past with limited success. What is the most appropriate treatment option for this patient?

    a) Clonidine 0.1 mg patch daily
    b) Nicotine 21 mg patch daily
    c) Bupropion 150 mg twice daily
    d) Nicotine gum 4 mg every week
    e) Nortriptyline 25 mg twice daily

33. The formula for 33 grams of coal tar ointment is: 0.33 g of crude coal tar, 0.165 g of polysorbate 80, and 32.505 g of zinc oxide paste. What equipment should be used to measure the required amount of coal tar?

   a) Stirring rod
   b) 10 mL cylindrical graduate
   c) oral or injectable syringe
   d) Spatula and electronic balance
   e) Spoon

34. Which of the following mathematical equations can be used to calculate the pH of an electrolyte solution?

   a) Henderson-Hasselbalch
   b) Arrhenius
   c) Cockcroft and Gault
   d) Michaelis-Menten
   e) Fundalis

35. Which of the following is an appropriate route for administration of heparin? (Select all that apply)

   a) Heparin flush
   b) Subcutaneous
   c) IV infusion administered intermittently
   d) Intramuscular administration
   e) Continuous IV infusion

36. A 64-year-old male is brought to ER by his spouse after she found him wandering in the back yard. He was spraying grass when he experiences stomach pain with cramping. He had episodes of diarrhea and vomiting. He is currently somewhat confused, his eyes are watery, pupils constricted, and skin is flushed. His spouse tells you that he has several different pills at home which he takes for different conditions. They include: verapamil, hydrochlorothiazide, lisinopril, cetirizine, warfarin, codeine syrup, allopurinol, vitamin D, St. John's wort, lansoprazole, and ibuprofen. He does drink about a 6-pack of beer per day. Vital signs include: T 37°C (98.6°F), BP 120/68, P 58, RR 14

Which of the following is likely to be effective in the treatment of this patient?

a) Naloxone
b) Physostigmine
c) 2PAM and atropine
d) Activated Charcoal
e) N-acetylcysteine

37. A 23-year-old woman with plaque psoriasis on the scalp asks the pharmacist to recommend a product. Which of the following is effective?

a) Head & Shoulders Intensive treatment
b) DHS tar shampoo (coal tar extract)
c) Nizoral A-D (ketoconazole)
d) Zinc Pyrithione
e) Lomalux Psoriasis Liquid

38. What is the most appropriate storage temperature for biologicals?

a) 85° C
b) 20° C
c) 2 to 10° C
d) 15° to 20° C
e) 2° to 8° C

39. Which of the following statements regarding the use of controlled-release analgesic formulations to provide longer-lasting analgesia is true?

a) The formulations have higher Cmax than immediate-release formulations
b) The formulations have shorter Tmax than immediate-release formulations
c) The formulations have higher bioavailability than immediate-release formulations
d) The formulations have same bioavailability as immediate-release formulations
e) The formulations are designed to break down in the stomach for optimal absorption

40. A 54-year-old male patient complains of a rash between the eyes, in the eyebrows, down the sides of the nose, and in the ear canals. He says it burns and itches. The pharmacist notes reddened areas of skin in a symmetric pattern with indistinct borders, and greasy yellowish scaling flakes. What condition is most likely?

a) Psoriasis
b) Contact Dermatitis
c) Miliaria
d) Tinea of the face
e) Soborrheic dermatitis

41. You receive a prescription for Crude Coal Tar ointment 33 grams. You have vials that contain triamcinolone acetonide suspension 40 mg/mL. What equipment would be most useful in compounding this preparation?

    a) Ointment Tile
    b) Stirring Rod
    c) Porcelain Mortar and Pestle
    d) Glass Mortar and Pestle
    e) Wood Mortar and Pestle

42. In an inpatient hospital pharmacy setting unit dose packaging refers to which of the following?

    a) Exact dose of the drug prescribed for the patient
    b) A specific route of administration for the drug
    c) The amount of the drug necessary for the patient's hospital course
    d) Half of the amount of the drug available in the pharmacy
    e) One dose of the drug to complete the entire patient regimen

43. With respect to drug entry into the CNS, the blood brain barrier

    a) Impearable to chloral hydrate
    b) Impearable to dopamine receptor antagonists
    c) Semi-permeable barrier of the brain only
    d) Semi-permeable barrer of the spine only
    e) Is more easily penetrated by lipophilic molecules

44. It is essential that patients use a metered-dose inhaler properly as drug effectiveness may be reduced considerably by poor technique. The recommended techniques for using a metered-dose inhaler to achieve maximum benefit include which of the following?

   a) Exhale. Place inhaler in mouth. Begin inhaling slowly. Activate inhaler while continuing to inhale then hold breath for 10 seconds and exhale
   b) If a spacer device is used, breathe normally into spacer while activating inhaler
   c) Exhale. Place inhaler in mouth. Activate inhaler, then inhale and hold breath for a few seconds
   d) Exhale. Hold inhaler 4 inches from mouth and inhale as inhaler is activated. Repeat 2 to 3 times to insure sufficient inhalation of drug
   e) Rinse mouth with water and swallow after use of a steroidal inhaler

45. After which phase of the new drug development process is a New Drug Application (NDA) submitted to the FDA?

   a) Phase I
   b) Phase II
   c) Phase III
   d) Phase IV
   e) Preclinical testing phase

46. A 20-year-old female presents to her gynecologist with a greenish vaginal discharge with a strong odor and vaginal itching. She also mentioned that the last time she and her boyfriend had intercourse, it was very painful and she bled afterward. Which of the following is this patient most likely experiencing?

   a) Trichomoniasis
   b) Gonorrhea
   c) Human Papilloma Virus
   d) Herpes Simplex Virus
   e) Syphillis

47. Which of these is a contraindication for Nicorette (nicotine) Gum?

   a) Renal dysfunction
   b) Vivid dreams
   c) Hepatic dysfunction

d) Skin eczema
e) Stomach ulcers

48. A 45-year-old woman presents to the clinic with a complaint of a runny nose, coughing, and chest congestion. She made a New Year's resolution to lose weight and is looking to you for advice. The patient has a past medical history of hypertension (6 months), arthritis in the knees (2 years), and asthma (5 years). The patient is 5'7, 165lbs, and has a waist circumference of 36 inches. The patient states she eats a light breakfast and lunch. She eats skinless chicken and a salad for dinner. She has been on this diet for 2 weeks. She does not like to exercise, but walks around the block twice a week. Which of the following is most appropriate to treat her weight concerns?

a) Healthy eating habits
b) Phentermine 37.5 mg daily
c) Begin jogging 30-45 minutes at least 5 days/week
d) Sibutramine 10 mg daily
e) Orlistat 60 mg twice daily

49. A patient ingested a month supply of amitriptyline 50 mg tablets in a suicide attempt. Her roommate found her approximately 2 hours after the ingestion and calls 911. When the patient arrives in the emergency room, the pharmacist is involved in the discussion of treatment options. Which of the following is most appropriate to treat this patient?

a) Activated charcoal
b) Syrup of ipecac
c) Gastric lavage
d) Hemodialysis
e) Hydrating execessively

50. Compared to the typical antipsychotic agents, the newer atypical antipsychotic drugs are less likely to cause which of the following side effects?

a) Orthostatic hypotension
b) Sedation
c) Akathisia
d) Weight gain
e) Agranulocytosis

51. What is the term for the inactive ingredient that holds the tablet together and provides stability and strength?

    a) Binder
    b) Lubricant
    c) Polymer
    d) Disintegrant
    e) Flavoring

52. Which of the following statements concerning FDA-approved manufactured drug products is/are correct? (Select **ALL** that apply.)

    a) FDA-approved and regulated drugs must have an approved NDA
    b) They must be produced under Good Manufacturing Practices (GMPs)
    c) They must have an expiration date that is provided to the pharmacy
    d) They must each have an NDC number
    e) They include compounded preparations

53. Which of the following statements concerning mortars, pestles and spatulas is correct?

    a) Wedgewood has a smoother surface than porcelain and is preferred for blending powders or pulverizing soft materials
    b) Porcelain is used for liquids and chemicals that are oily or will stain
    c) Bond paper should be used for weighing ointments and creams
    d) Generally large stainless steel spatula blades are used, except plastic spatulas are used for chemicals (e.g. iodine) that can react with stainless steel blades
    e) Glass mortars are best for triturating rough powders

54. Which of the following definitions describes a solution?

    a) A liquid preparation of soluble chemicals dissolved in solvents such as water, alcohol, or propylene glycol
    b) A solid dosage form used to deliver medicine into the rectum, vagina or urethra
    c) A semisolid dosage form used externally on the skin or mucous membranes
    d) A two-phase system of two immiscible liquids, one of which is dispersed through the other as small droplets
    e) A two phased-system of a finely divided solid in a liquid medium

55. Sorbitol has many uses in drug delivery. Which of the following represent viable uses for sorbitol? (Select **ALL** that apply.)

    a) Sweetener (sugar substitute)
    b) Thickening agent in liquids
    c) Plasticizer for gelatin capsules
    d) Treatment of GI distress in patients with IBS
    e) Suspending agent

56. Which of the following statements concerning compounded medications is/are correct? (Select **ALL** that apply.)

    a) Compounding is different from manufacturing since it is patient-specific (ordered by a prescriber for the patient)
    b) Compounded medications are regulated by the State Boards of Pharmacy
    c) Each compounded formula must be assigned a unique NDC number
    d) Compounds can only be prepared in specialty compounding pharmacies
    e) Prescriptions for compounded medications cannot be refilled

57. Which of the following is true?

    a) Creams have a higher percentage of oil than lotions
    b) Lotions have a higher percentage of oil than ointments
    c) Lotions are water in oil preparations
    d) Ointments wash off the skin easily
    e) Creams provide a stronger skin barrier than ointments

58. Which of the following correctly describes the use of *Tween* (polysorbate)? (Select **ALL** that apply.)

    a) It is used most commonly as a thickening agent
    b) *Tween* is a surfactant
    c) Surfactants are compounds with polar sides and nonpolar sides
    d) Surfactants are used as wetting agents
    e) Surfactants are used most often in ointments

59. Which of the following are used as ointments and can provide a protective barrier on the skin?

    a) Agar, carrageenan and gelatin
    b) Aquaphor, Aquabase, Eucerin, petrolatum
    c) Acacia
    d) Arlacel, Span, Myrj, Tween
    e) Dry gum

60. Which of the following medications used for rheumatoid arthritis are administered primarily as a self-injectable subcutaneous injection?

    a) Hydroxychloroquine
    b) Etanercept
    c) Sulfasalazine
    d) Leflunomide
    e) Minocycline

61. Which of the following criteria meet CMS' requirements for exemption for DMEPOS accreditation?

    a) The pharmacist in charge must take an additional 20 hours of annual continuing education (CE) credits
    b) All pharmacists working in the DME section must complete an additional 20 hours of annual continuing education (CE) credits
    c) The pharmacy must pay CMS a fee to avoid the accreditation process
    d) The pharmacist in charge must have been born prior to 1960
    e) The total billing for CMS is < 5% total of the pharmacy's total sales for the previous three years

62. Which of the following reasons can cause a patch to become loose from the skin, or fall off? (Select **ALL** that apply.)

    a) The patient applied *Lubriderm* after bathing and before applying the patch
    b) The patient applied *Nivea* to their skin after bathing and before applying the patch
    c) The patient did not press down on the patch for the required time during application
    d) The patient shaved prior to the patch application
    e) The patient cut the hair on the skin short prior to the patch application

63. If it is inconvenient to cut up patches and mix with a noxious substance, it is acceptable to flush the following patches down the toilet: (Select **ALL** that apply.)

   a) Butrans
   b) Neupro
   c) EMSAM
   d) Daytrana
   e) Duragesic

64. A pharmacy has an order for a glucose test meter and strips, and another order for a nebulizer to be used with budesonide *Respules*. Which of the following statements is correct?

   a) The nebulizer is billed under part B and the glucose meter and strips is Part D
   b) The nebulizer is billed under part D and the glucose meter and strips is Part B
   c) The nebulizer, glucose meter and strips are all billed under Part B
   d) The nebulizer, glucose meter and strips are all billed under Part D
   e) None of these are sold in the pharmacy; they are only sold by mail order

65. Application instructions for the hormone patches (estrogen, progestin and testosterone) include the following correct counselling points: (Select **ALL** that apply.)

   a) Do not let children or animals near used patches; dispose of safely
   b) Do not apply more than one patch at a time, or to broken or irritated skin
   c) Estrogen patches can be used if the women has had breast cancer, but the oral formulations cannot be used with this history
   d) Do not apply to the breasts or genitals
   e) Can be applied to the lower abdomen

66. If a drug has any of the following suffixes in the name he pharmacist should counsel the patient not to crush/chew the medication: (Select **ALL** that apply.)

   a) CR
   b) IR
   c) XL
   d) ER
   e) LA

67. A middle-aged man has paranoid schizophrenia. He has been in intensive therapy and states he is willing to use his antipsychotic. However, he is likely to forget to take a daily dose and may change his mind and decide not to use it. Which medications come in a long-acting injection that may be useful to improve adherence? (Select **ALL** that apply.)

    a) Abilify
    b) Seroquel
    c) Haldol
    d) Latuda
    e) Risperdal

68. Which of the following opioids comes in several sublingual formulations designed to provide faster onset of action (relative to oral gut absorption) for cancer patients requiring breakthrough pain medication?

    a) Oxycodone
    b) Morphine
    c) Fentanyl
    d) Buprenorphine/Naloxone
    e) Hydromorphone

69. A 30-year old man has migraines with dizziness, nausea and occasional vomiting. The migraines come on quickly and cause debilitating pain. Choose the drug and formulation that would be preferable:

    a) Frovatripan compressed tablet
    b) Maxalt-MLT
    c) Imitrex STATdose
    d) Duragesic injection
    e) Calcitonin nasal spray

70. Select the most accurate definition of durable medical equipment (DME):

    a) Long lasting items used for a medical condition kept in the patient's home
    b) Long lasting items kept in skilled nursing facilities labelled for patient's use
    c) Medical items designed to be disposed of after each use
    d) Medical items used for acute care conditions only
    e) Items such as oral medications, patches and injections

71. CMS routinely audits pharmacies providing DME. The most important requirement is documentation that can support DME-approved practices. Which of the following represents a DME-approved practice?

   a) Refills for supplies come only from the pharmacy
   b) "As-needed" orders are acceptable for monitoring, such as for test strips
   c) Delivery documentation should be kept for three years
   d) Refills for supplies come only from the patient or the patient's caregiver
   e) Transfers from one pharmacy to another do not require a new order; the transfer alone is acceptable to fill and bill for DME

72. Which of the following items are covered under DME? (Select **ALL** that apply.)

   a) Enteral nutrition
   b) Walkers
   c) Supplies to receive medications by the intravenous route at home
   d) Ostomy supplies
   e) OTC medications, such as the *Oxytrol* patch

73. Which of the following statements concerning durable medical equipment (DME) is accurate?

   a) DME does not require a prescription or order to be billed under the patient's insurance, but drugs do require a prescription for billing
   b) DME is paid for by CMS under Part D
   c) Nebulizers are covered by part D, as they are used with drugs
   d) Prosthetics are not covered under DME
   e) The patient will bring in an order for the DME, and the pharmacy will be paid by CMS under Part B

74. What is the primary purpose of using a glycerin suppository in a child or adult?

   a) To prevent constipation
   b) To treat constipation
   c) To prevent ileus
   d) To treat ileus
   e) To avoid the use of oral agents

75. A patient is using oxybutynin 5 mg TID. She often forgets to take her evening dose. She complains of incontinence and dry mouth. Choose the correct statement:

   a) It would be preferable for her to take the medication more frequently so that she can use smaller doses, such as 1 mg QID or 5 times daily
   b) She would have less dry mouth if she used a longer-acting formulation or the patch formulation
   c) She should be counseled to take the medication on an empty stomach to assist with the dry mouth
   d) Oxybutinin worsens urge incontinence episodes and should not be recommended in a patient with this pre-existing condition
   e) Oxybutinin does not cause dry mouth

76. Patients with cystic fibrosis require pancreatic enzymes are taken with meals and snacks to assist with food absorption. Which of the following statements concerning pancreatic enzymes are correct?

   a) These medications are not required if the child can limit their fat intake
   b) These can be mixed with foods with a high pH only, such as mashed peas
   c) These are taken only if the snack or meal is > 300 kcal
   d) Instruct the child not to chew the capsule contents
   e) They are taken 1/2 hour after the meal has been consumed

77. Which of the following sublingual medications is used for patients who have difficulty falling asleep when they go to bed in the evening?

   a) Intermezzo
   b) Fentora
   c) Bunavail
   d) Edluar
   e) Abstral

78. Which of the following drugs is available in an ODT formulation?
   a) Effexor
   b) Prozac
   c) Remeron
   d) Wellbutrin
   e) Nardil

79. Medicare requires that a new order be written for a DME item if any of the following conditions are met: (Select **ALL** that apply.)

    a) If the supplier of the DME item has changed.
    b) If it has been 60 days from the original order.
    c) If an item has been replaced, such as with a replacement glucose meter.
    d) When there is a change in the order (such as how often to use a nebulizer, or how often to check blood glucose).
    e) If it has been 90 days from the original order

80. Select the name of the glatiramer subcutaneous injection used for multiple sclerosis:

    a) Peg-Intron
    b) Rebif
    c) Evzio
    d) Copaxone
    e) Simponi

81. An investigational drug in early development has a high therapeutic index. What does this mean?

    a) The drug is eliminated by the kidney
    b) The drug is unlikely to have any significant adverse effects
    c) The drug has minimal entry to the brain
    d) The drug has plasma concentrations monitored
    e) The drug has minimal interactions with other drugs

82. What clinical trial is designed to show that a treatment is no less effective than an existing treatment?

    a) Noninferiority
    b) Superiority
    c) Equivalence
    d) Cohort
    e) Randomized

83. A patient presents to the pharmacy to refill prescriptions; she brings a grocery bag full of prescription medications, dietary supplements, and over-the-counter medications. She pulls 2 medications out of the bag and tells you that she received them from a relative in Spain. She would like to receive a similar medication if it is available in the United States.

    What reference would you consult for information about the imported medications?

    a) Remington
    b) Martindale
    c) USP
    d) Facts & Comparisons
    e) Micromedex

84. Which of the following is an appropriate statistic to describe the most common value in data distribution?

    a) Mean
    b) Median
    c) Mode
    d) Standard Deviation
    e) Central Tendency

85. What statement is true regarding the primary objective of different clinical studies in drug development?

    a) Phase 4 study is performed for determination of an appropriate dosage regimen to be used in a large number of patients
    b) Phase 3 study is performed for the purpose of post-marketing surveillance
    c) Phase 3 study is performed for evaluation of response in a large number of patients with the target disease
    d) Phase 2 study is performed for determination of the pharmacokinetic profile in a small number of healthy volunteers
    e) Phase 1 study is performed for determination of toxicity in a large number of patients

86. A multicenter randomized controlled phase III trial is designed to investigate whether a new drug, daclizumid, is better than placebo in the treatment of early breast cancer (stages I, II). Phase II trial has shown significant benefit over placebo in 42 women (open label trial) in overall response rates and recurrence rates. Women ages 34 to 65 will be enrolled if they have unilateral breast cancer, have not had any prior chemotherapy, have normal serum creatinine and liver function tests, as well as MUGA tests. Patients who are HER2/neu positive, have other prior cancers, or have any comorbidity will be excluded. Following treatment, ER/PR + cancer patients will be offered tamoxifen therapy for 5 years. Interim analysis performed in 2 years after opening of the study.

    What is the major limitation of this study?

    a) Interim analysis is performed too early
    b) Interim analysis needs to completed before the 1st year
    c) Tamoxifen administration may skew results
    d) Exclusion of HER2/neu patients from study
    e) Study is unethical

87. A pharmacist receives a new prescription for an isotonic eye solution. He would like to consult a reference about isotonicity before compounding the prescription; what reference should he consult?

    a) Remington
    b) Martindale
    c) USP
    d) Facts & Comparisons
    e) Micromedex

88. A patient wishes to attend a party tonight and ingest alcohol. However, he will have to drive home alone. He wishes to purchase a product he saw advertised as minimizing alcohol absorption to allow him to drive safely and also to prevent hangover. What advice should he be given?

    a) He should ingest syrup of ipecac after drinking. The emesis will reduce the load of alcohol reaching his bloodstream
    b) No nonprescription product can minimize or prevent hangover
    c) He should simply stop drinking about 30 minutes before he needs to drive home
    d) A nonprescription product containing herbal ingredients
    e) Activated charcoal will reduce absorption of alcohol

89. Which of the terms is appropriate for measuring the variability of a data set?

   a) Mean
   b) Median
   c) Mode
   d) Standard Deviation
   e) Range

90. A patient's bone mineral density (BMD) test revealed a T score of -2.7. Based on this result, the patient was diagnosed with osteoporosis. The World Health Organization (WHO) criteria for osteoporosis compare an individual's BMD to that of which of the following?

   a) Age and gender matched peers
   b) Postmenopausal women with previous fractures
   c) American woman at age 60
   d) Perimenopausal women with risk factors
   e) Young adult Caucasian women

91. During the counseling session with a patient Mark, he is encouraged to make lifestyle recommendations to reduce the likelihood of future gouty attacks. Which of the following dietary recommendations must be reviewed with this patient?

   a) Add more protein in the form of seafood
   b) Reduce purine-rich foods
   c) Decrease sodium intake
   d) Increase fructose intake
   e) Reduce fruit intake

92. What is the therapeutic target range for hemoglobin in patients receiving erythropoiesis-stimulating agent?

   a) 10 to 11 g/dl
   b) 10 to 13 g/dl
   c) 11 to 12 g/dl
   d) 12 to 13 g/dl
   e) 9 to 12 g/dl

93. Which of the following is an appropriate therapeutic target for erythropoietic therapy?

    a) Improved quality of life
    b) Improved cognitive function
    c) Increase in haemoglobin concentration from baseline
    d) Reduction in haemoglobin concentration from baseline
    e) Increased platelet count

94. A patient receiving warfarin 5 mg Mon/Wed/Fri and 3 mg all other days presents with an INR result of 3.7. His readings usually fall between 2.4 and 2.7. The patient was diagnosed with atrial fibrillation 6 months ago.

    When should the patient return for the next INR?

    a) 2 weeks
    b) 1 week
    c) 5 days
    d) 3 months
    e) 6 months

95. What laboratory test should be monitored in a patient taking allopurinol?

    a) Serum amylase
    b) Serum potassium
    c) Serum uric acid
    d) Blood glucose
    e) Serum Sodium

96. A patient presents for counseling and to initiate warfarin therapy. The patient is post-myocardial infarction with high risk for left ventricular thromboembolism requiring oral vitamin K antagonism.

    What is the most appropriate INR therapeutic range for this patient's therapy?

    a) 1.0-2.0
    b) 2.0-3.0
    c) 1.5-4.0
    d) 2.5-3.0
    e) 2.5-4.5

97. Which of the following antibacterial agents is judged to be "probably safe" and can be recommended for administration to a pregnant patient?

    a) Azithromycin
    b) Metronidazole
    c) Tetracycline
    d) Doxycycline
    e) Erythromicin estolate

98. What would be the desirable gastric pH that should be achieved with antacid administration?

    a) 4.5
    b) 3.5
    c) 2.5
    d) 6.5
    e) 5.5

99. Antimicrobial resistance is usually associated with which of the following factors?

    a) Increased use of broad-spectrum antibiotics
    b) Restriction of use imposed by formulary
    c) Decreased treatment failure
    d) Decreased use of antibiotics
    e) Increased costs of antibiotics

100. What risk factor(s)/lipid class combination most closely identifies the need to institute pharmacotherapy?

    a) An LDL cholesterol of >110; no history of coronary heart disease (CHD)
    b) An HDL cholesterol of >60; cigarette smoking
    c) An HDL of <40; age (men >45 yrs, women >55 yrs)
    d) VLDL of <100; diabetes
    e) A total cholesterol of <200; hypertension (BP >140/90)

101. The patient presents with a 36-hour history of excruciating pain in his right great toe. The patient admits to nonadherence to medications because he "just forgets to refill them". The patient received prescriptions for Zyloprim and Naprosyn EC the last time he had a similar episode, but he claims the medications did not seem to work. What is the most likely explanation?

a) Naprosyn EC is not indicated for treatment of an acute gouty attack
b) There is a drug-drug interaction between Zyloprim and another medication this patient is taking which results in decreased efficacy of Zyloprim
c) The patient has a history of nonadherence, so it is unlikely that he administered them correctly
d) Uricosurics such as Zyloprim are not effective in an acute gouty attack
e) Nonsteroidal anti-inflammatory drugs are not effective more than 24 hours after the start of an acute gouty attack

102. A 46-year-old male receives a prescription for fluoxetine 10 mg daily for his first episode of generalized anxiety disorder. He is reluctant to take medications but agrees to adhere to therapy if it will make him feel better. 3 months later, he returns and is in remission. How soon can he stop this medication?

a) Discontinue the medication today
b) Treatment is usually lifelong
c) Discontinue the medication in 2 years
d) Discontinue the medication in 1 year
e) Discontinue the medication in 3 months

103. A new patient presents to the pharmacist-run clinic for counseling and to initiate warfarin therapy. The patient recently underwent surgery for placement of a bileaflet mechanical valve in the mitral position. What is the most appropriate INR therapeutic range for this patient's therapy?

a) 3.0-4.0
b) 2.0-3.0
c) 2.5-3.5
d) 1.5-2.5
e) 1.0-2.0

104. A 54-year-old male presents for nonproductive cough, headache, runny nose, and chest pain. He was previously seen 2 weeks ago with the same symptoms. Physical exam at that time demonstrated coarse breath sounds. Chest X-ray demonstrated left lower lobe consolidation. CT scan showed ground glass pattern with centrilobular nodules. EKG was unremarkable. His final diagnosis upon discharge was Mycoplasma pneumonia pneumonia for which he was given a prescription for erythromycin 250 mg 4 times/day for 2 weeks.

Which of the following is the most likely explanation for persistence of patient symptoms?

a) Inadequate duration of treatment
b) Wrong drug
c) Antibiotic resistance
d) Wrong diagnosis
e) Non-compliance

105. A patient presents with c/o congestion, thick yellow nasal discharge, pain in sinus areas, and sore throat. She had a cold about 2 weeks ago, with symptoms still persisting. She is allergic to penicillin and she is currently taking ketoconazole. She is diagnosed with acute sinusitis. Which antibiotic of the following would be the best treatment option for this patient?

a) Amoxicillin
b) Ciprofloxacin
c) Bactrim
d) Telithromycin
e) Gentamicin

106. **Patient Profile**   **Patient Name:** JJJ   **Age:** 46   **Sex:** Male
    Race: Caucasian   **Height:** 5'6"   **Weight:** 70 kg
    Family history: None   **Allergies:** NKDA

ADMITTING DIAGNOSIS: Seizure, admitted to emergency department overdosed with phenytoin
PAST MEDICAL HISTORY: Diabetes, atrial fibrillation, peptic ulcer, gout
Phenytoin 300 mg qhs
Quinidine 300 mg qid (increased 1 week ago)
Cimetidine 200 mg qhs (increased 1 week ago)
Insulin NPH/Reg 20U/20U qam and 10U/15U qpm
Probenecid 500 mg bid

PE
VS: 120/86, 92 (regular), 39° C, 18   HEENT: Nystagmus on lateral gaze
COR: WNL   Chest: WNL   ABD: WNL
Neuro: Alert and oriented x 3, slight gait ataxia

All WNL except the 2 levels of phenytoin (45 and 34 mcg/L). The patient has an infection and sulfamethoxazole/trimethoprim (Septra) was prescribed 2 days ago based on culture & sensitivity results. Knowing the values of the 2 phenytoin concentrations (45 mcg/mL and 34 mcg/mL) and the exact time of sampling for the 2 blood samples.

What would be an appropriate target HbA1C level in patients with diabetes?

a) 7.5%
b) 6%
c) 6.5%
d) 7%
e) 8%

107. What drug has been shown to have a positive effect on mortality in patients with heart failure?

a) Furosemide
b) Hydrochlorothiazide
c) Diltiazem
d) Digoxin
e) Captopril

108. A 27-year-old female recently received prescriptions for lorazepam and paroxetine for treatment of generalized anxiety disorder. When counseling the patient, it is important to tell her that the full therapeutic effects of lorazepam will occur within:

a) 60 days
b) 43 days
c) 28 days
d) 7 days
e) 3 days

109. Which anti-Parkinson medications could be used for once-daily dosing?

a) Rasagline
b) Pramipexole
c) Amantadine
d) Carbidopa/Levodopa
e) Ropinirole

110. Before counseling a pregnant woman about the use of a medication that she has been prescribed, you should first check which of the following?

   a) The metabolism induced by CYP2E1 because she enjoys alcoholic drinks
   b) The metabolism induced by CYP1A2 because she is a smoker
   c) Whether it passes into breast milk
   d) Its teratogenic classification
   e) How the drug works

111. A patient comes in and asks you what his blood pressure goal should be. His past medical history includes hypertension, Type II diabetes, Angina, GERD, and hypercholesterolemia. What should you respond to this patient?

   a) <140/≤90 mm Hg
   b) <130/≤90 mm Hg
   c) <120/≤80 mm Hg
   d) <150/≤90 mm Hg
   e) <120/≤90 mm Hg

112. Which of the following drugs cannot be prescribed by a general practitioner?

   a) Schedule III
   b) Schedule I
   c) Schedule II
   d) Schedule IV
   e) Schedule V

113. A 55-year-old male patient with a past medical history of Type II diabetes, hyperlipidemia, and hypertension comes into your pharmacy. His past blood pressure reading is 142/93 mmHg. According to JNC 8 guidelines, what is the recommended blood pressure goal for this patient based on the information given?

   a) <150/90 mmHg
   b) <120/80 mmHg
   c) <140/90 mmHg
   d) <135/90 mmHg
   e) < 130/90 mmHg

114. Sara is a 54-year-old female patient with a past medical history of rheumatoid arthritis x 10 years (RA), hypertension, and dyslipidemia. She currently takes methotrexate 5 mg and folic acid 1 mg. During a recent visit with the rheumatologist, Sara reported a gradual increase in morning stiffness, joint pain, and swelling over the last 2 months. The rheumatologist would like to initiate combination therapy to help control her symptoms and prevent disease progression. Her current disease activity level is considered moderate. Which of the following is the most appropriate option to add to her current regimen?

a) Rituximab
b) Abatacept + etanercept
c) Sulfasalazine
d) Sulfasalazine + leflunomide
e) Infliximab

115. A patient presents for counseling and to initiate warfarin therapy. The patient recently experienced a DVT secondary to oral contraceptive therapy. What is the most appropriate INR therapeutic range for this patient's therapy?

a) 2.0 – 3.0
b) 2.5 – 3.5
c) 3.0 – 3.5
d) 2.5 – 3.0
e) 1.5 – 2.5

116. A father wishes to purchase NoDoz Maximum Strength (caffeine) for his 10-year-old daughter, who has perennial allergic rhinitis. The physician believes she has chronic fatigue due to a sleep disorder and requested further evaluation before prescribing any type of medication. The father only wants to use NoDoz until she can be seen by a sleep laboratory. What should the pharmacist advise him to do?

a) Recommend against its use, as caffeine is contraindicated with allergic rhinitis
b) Recommend against its use, as it is only for patients aged 12 and above
c) Ask the child to drink large quantities of caffeine-containing beverages
d) Use Vivarin (caffeine) instead, as it is labeled for her condition
e) Use NoDoz, but purchase the regular strength product instead

117. A new antibiotic for community-acquired pneumonia (CAP) was recently FDA-approved. The drug was presented at the Pharmacy and Therapeutics Committee meeting. The drug monograph included the following information:

Community-acquired pneumonia dosing (IV): 675 mg IV Q8H
Community-acquired pneumonia dosing (PO): 675 mg PO TID

What hospital policy/protocol should this drug be added to?

  a) CAP Policy
  b) Antibiogram Protocol
  c) Therapeutic Interchange Protocol
  d) Pharmacokinetic Policy
  e) High Risk Medication Protocol

118. Which of the following defines pharmacodynamics?

  a) What the kidney does to the drug
  b) What the liver does to the drug
  c) What the body does to the drug
  d) What the drug does to the body
  e) What the drug does to the microorganism

119. A patient has been using phenytoin 100 mg three times daily for 6 months. A steady state phenytoin level was taken and found to be 9.8 mcg/mL. She recently had a seizure, so the prescriber increased the dose to 100 mg with breakfast and lunch, and 200 mg with dinner. The prescriber calculated that if 300 mg/day provided a level of 9.8 mcg/mL, then 400 mg/day would increase the level to approximately 13 mcg/mL. After the dosage change, the patient started to slur her words, felt fatigued and returned to the medical office office. The level was retaken and found to be 18.7 mcg/mL. At both visits, her serum albumin level was 4.2 g/dL. What is the most likely reason for the phenytoin level?

  a) Phenytoin exhibits increased metabolism with higher doses
  b) Phenytoin exhibits Michaelis-Menten kinetics
  c) Phenytoin has reduced protein binding at higher doses
  d) Patient non-compliance
  e) The patient did not take with food

120. A patient has overdosed on phenytoin and is experiencing symptoms of phenytoin toxicity. The prescriber asks how much drug the patient has consumed because he wishes to calculate how long it will take the patient to clear the drug. The pharmacist offers the following correct advice: (Select **ALL** that apply.)

   a) Phenytoin exhibits Michaelis-Menten elimination
   b) Once the metabolizing enzymes are saturated, phenytoin elimination follows zero-order elimination. The elimination will not correlate in a linear fashion with the amount of drug consumed
   c) With significant overdose the patient will display extreme irritability, anxiety and difficulty sleeping and concentrating
   d) With significant overdose the patient will exhibit CNS depressant effects
   e) Phenytoin initially follows first-order elimination

121. A drug that exhibits Michaelis-Menten kinetics will display the following properties: (Select **ALL** that apply.)

   a) A linear relationship between dose and serum level until the metabolizing enzymes are saturated
   b) Improved distribution
   c) A nonlinear relationship between dose and serum level
   d) Saturable kinetics
   e) Poor bioavailability

122. What is the primary pathway of drug degradation in the gut?

   a) Oxidation
   b) Phase II conjugation reactions
   c) Hydrolysis
   d) Proteolysis
   e) P-glycoprotein efflux drug transportation

123. Which of the following defines pharmacokinetics?

   a) What the kidney does to the drug
   b) What the drug does to the body
   c) What the body does to the drug
   d) What the liver does to the drug
   e) What the drug does to the microorganism

124. Choose the pharmacokinetic term used to describe the process by which the body breaks down drugs into compounds that can be more readily eliminated:

   a) Dissolution
   b) Absorption
   c) Distribution
   d) Metabolism
   e) Excretion

125. A chemist wishes to increase the rate of gut dissolution of a new tablet formulation. Which of the following would be the most useful option to consider for most medications?

   a) Decreasing the surface area of the tablet
   b) Increasing the surface area of the tablet
   c) Adding an emulsifying agent
   d) Instructing the patient to take thirty minutes after the morning dose of a proton pump inhibitor
   e) Instructing the patient to take thirty minutes after the morning dose of an antacid

126. Which formula is used to describe the rate of drug dissolution (or the rate at which the drug dissolves)?

   a) Michaelis-Menten
   b) Noyes-Whitney
   c) Henderson-Hasselbach
   d) Remington's Coefficient
   e) Stimmel's

127. A pharmacy student asks why most drugs are weak acids or weak bases. Which of the following points are correct and could be included in the explanation?

   a) If the drug dissolves in the gut fluid, it will not get absorbed
   b) If the compound is charged it cannot interact with the cell receptors
   c) Weak acids are highly charged compounds in physiological pH
   d) Weak bases are highly charged compounds in physiological pH
   e) Charged compounds dissolve more easily in water than uncharged compounds

128. Choose the statements that describe elimination half-life (t½): (Select **ALL** that apply)

   a) The half-life is the time for the plasma concentration of the drug to decrease by 50%
   b) If a drug is eliminated via zero order kinetics, the half life is always the same
   c) The half-life is the time it takes for half of dose to be absorbed by the gut lining
   d) After approximately 5 half-lives, the elimination is considered to be nearly complete
   e) The half-life can be calculated if you know the elimination rate constant, k_e

129. When a drug is administered IV, which of the following does not occur?

   a) Absorption
   b) Distribution
   c) Metabolism
   d) Excretion
   e) All of the steps (absorption, distribution, metabolism and excretion) occur when a drug is administered intravenously

130. A drug that exhibits first-order kinetics will display the following properties:

   a) A linear relationship between dose and serum level
   b) A nonlinear relationship between dose and serum level
   c) A Michaelis-Menten relationship
   d) As the concentration increases the AUC decreases in a corresponding manner
   e) Short half-life and increased bioavailability

131. Large changes in drug distribution can be caused by small changes in:

   a) Release of parathyroid hormone
   b) Release of growth hormone
   c) Protein binding
   d) Protein consumption
   e) Protein absorption

132. How many half-lives are required to reach steady state (assuming a one compartment model and no loading dose)?

   a) Approximately 2
   b) Approximately 5
   c) Approximately 8
   d) Approximately 12
   e) Steady state is reached after 2 days of continuous drug administration

133. A clinical trial is conducted on a new drug, FresKI. FresKI is found to reduce serum sodium to 135 mEq/L, with a 95% confidence interval of 128.7 mEq/L to 135.3 mEq/L. What is the correct interpretation of this 95% confidence interval?

   a) There is a 95% chance that the interval contains the true population value
   b) When using this drug in a larger population, one can expect that 95% of the patients will have a serum sodium between 128.7 to 133.3 mEq/L
   c) When using this drug in a larger population, one can say with 95% confidence that the serum sodium will be 131 mEq/L
   d) There is a 5% chance that the true population mean is within the stated range
   e) There is a 5% chance that the results of this study are rejected in error

134. What is the definition of a Type II error?

   a) The clinical trial was not large enough to detect a meaningful difference between treatment groups
   b) The null hypothesis is true, but is rejected in error
   c) The null hypothesis is false, but it is rejected in error
   d) The null hypothesis is false, but is accepted in error
   e) The null hypothesis is true, but it is accepted in error

135. Over 35,000 nurses were studied in a longitudinal study based in Framingham, Massachusetts. Each year, the nurses were followed up and asked to report on any incidence of heart disease. Describe this type of study:

   a) Controlled clinical trial
   b) Meta analysis
   c) Case control trial
   d) Cohort study
   e) Crossover analysis

BACKGROUND: Angiotensin-converting-enzyme inhibitors improve the outcome among patients with left ventricular dysfunction, whether or not they have heart failure. We assessed the role of an angiotensin converting-enzyme inhibitor, ramipril, in patients who were at high risk for cardiovascular events but who did not have left ventricular dysfunction or heart failure.

METHODS: A total of 9,297 high-risk patients who had evidence of vascular disease or diabetes plus one other cardiovascular risk factor and who were not known to have a low ejection fraction or heart failure were randomly assigned to receive ramipril or matching placebo for a mean of five years. The primary outcome was a composite of myocardial infarction, stroke, or death from cardiovascular causes.

RESULTS: A total of 4,645 patients were assigned to receive ramipril 10 mg daily and 4,652 were assigned to receive placebo. Of the patients taking ramipril, 650 patients reached the primary endpoint as compared with 826 patients who were assigned to receive placebo ($p < 0.001$). Treatment with ramipril reduced the rates of death from cardiovascular causes (6.1% vs. 8.1% in the placebo group, < 0.001), myocardial infarction (9.9% vs. 12.3%, $p < 0.001$), stroke (3.4% vs. 4.9%, $p < 0.001$) and death from any cause (10.4% vs. 12.2%, $p = 0.005$).

CONCLUSION: Ramipril significantly reduces the rates of death, myocardial infarction, and stroke in a broad range of high-risk patients who are not known to have a low ejection fraction or heart failure

136. From the abstract above, calculate the absolute risk reduction of the composite primary endpoint of myocardial infarction, stroke, or death from cardiovascular causes. (Round to the nearest tenth. Put your answer in percentage form. Do not include the percentage sign when you type in the number.)

137. From the abstract above, calculate the relative risk of the primary endpoint in the Ramipril group compared to the placebo group.

138. What is the definition of a Type I error?

   a) The degree to which a study accurately reflects or assesses the specific concept that the researcher is attempting to measure but misses the mark
   b) The null hypothesis is true, but is rejected in error
   c) The study was not large enough to detect a meaningful difference between treatment groups
   d) The null hypothesis is false, but is accepted in error
   e) A clinical trial with too many confounding variables

139. Choose the name of the assertion that a clinical trial is designed to disprove which states there is no difference between two groups.

   a) The assertive hypothesis
   b) The null hypothesis
   c) The alternative hypothesis
   d) Type II error
   e) The disclaimer

140. A pharmacy intern has been asked by his preceptor to gather 200 discharged patient charts from the chart room. He has been told that half the charts should be patients who received proton pump inhibitor (PPI) therapy while hospitalized. The other half should be patients with similar conditions and length of stay but who did not receive PPI therapy. The pharmacist wishes to conduct a study to see if there is any difference in the incidence of nosocomial infection in the PPI group versus the non-PPI group. Which of the following describes this type of study?
(Select **ALL** that apply.)

   a) Cohort study
   b) Meta analysis
   c) Case control study
   d) Controlled clinical study
   e) Observational study

141. A pharmaceutical company wished to show that their antiplatelet agent worked better than placebo. They enrolled 12,000 patients at many different research sites. They worked with the physicians to ensure that the patients were randomly assigned to the antiplatelet agent or to a placebo. The physicians did not know which of their patients received the active drug. Describe this type of trial:

a) Open-label clinical trial
b) Controlled clinical trial
c) Crossover trial
d) Cross sectional trial
e) Propensity matching study

142. A clinical trial evaluated the effects of a chemotherapeutic given to patients with osteosarcoma. The trial duration was three months. During this time, there were two deaths among patients receiving placebo and one death among patients receiving active drug. It could be stated that the drug decreased the risk of death by 50%. The "relative risk" of death in the placebo group was 2, or twice the amount in the drug group. The benefit sounds great, but in reality the benefit was very small. Choose the correct statements: (Select **ALL** that apply.)

a) The relative risk can be used to make a small benefit appear larger than is warranted
b) Relative risk is also called the risk ratio
c) Relative risk tells you little about the actual risk outside the trial
d) A relative risk > 1 means that the event is less likely to occur in the group with the intervention compared to the control group
e) A relative risk < 1 means that the event is less likely to occur in the group with the intervention compared to the control group

143. In biostatistics, what is meant by the median of a group of values?

a) The relative risk reduction
b) The value in the middle of the list
c) The average
d) The variance squared
e) The value that occurs most frequently

144. A researcher gathered all vitamin E studies from the past ten years. Vitamin E was used for a variety of conditions. The populations studied as well as the vitamin E formulations and doses were all different. However, the researcher did the best he could and compared the incidences of cardiovascular-related mortality in those taking vitamin E supplements versus those that did not. Describe this type of study:

a) Observational study
b) Case control study

c) Cohort study
d) Controlled clinical trial
e) Meta analysis

145. A very large study has measured the body weight of everyone living west of the Mississippi River. If the values of all the weights were plotted, the graph would resemble this shape:

a) A bell-shaped curve
b) A parabola
c) A quadrilateral
d) A bell-shaped curve skewed to the left
e) A bell-shaped curve skewed to the right

146. In a small, randomized, double-blind trial of a new treatment in patients with acute myocardial infarction, the mortality in the treated group was half that in the control group, but the difference was not significant. We can conclude that:

a) The treatment is useless
b) There is no point in continuing to develop the new treatment
c) The reduction in mortality is so great that we should introduce the treatment immediately
d) Cases should be added to the trial until the Normal test for comparison of two populations is significant
e) The clinical trial may not have enough power

147. A pharmacist is considering which beta blocker should be preferred at his institution. He has narrowed his search down to two agents. Each drug provides similar health benefits, has similar tolerability and is dosed once daily. The pharmacist will base his decision on the drug that can be purchased at the lower cost. He will use the following analysis to choose the beta blocker:

a) A cost minimization analysis
b) A cost effectiveness analysis
c) A cost control analysis
d) A meta analysis
e) A cost utility analysis

148. Marital status (married, single, divorced) can be described as this type of data:

a) Ordinal
b) Nominal
c) Continuous
d) Random
e) Interval

149. Blood pressure, hemoglobin A1C and LDL cholesterol can each be described as this type of data:

a) Ordinal
b) Nominal
c) Continuous
d) Random
e) Discrete

150. A cardiologist will select a group of patients with atrial fibrillation and a group without atrial fibrillation. He will review the medical records of both groups looking for exposure to zolpidem. What type of study design does this trial represent?

a) Cross-sectional study
b) Case series
c) Case-control study
d) Cohort study
e) Case report

151. A pharmacist is considering which intravenous vasodilator should be preferred at her institution. She has narrowed her search down to two agents. Each drug provides similar health benefits and similar tolerability. The pharmacist will base her decision on drug acquisition, administration, and monitoring costs. The pharmacist should use the following analysis to decide which intravenous vasodilator should be added to her institution:

a) Cost-utility analysis
b) Cost-minimization analysis
c) Cost-effectiveness analysis
d) Cost-benefit analysis
e) Cost-optimization analysis

152. A pharmacy administration resident will conduct a study to evaluate the fluoroquinolone IV to oral interchange program at her institution. The goals of the study are to assess the impact of the program: including cost to maintain and staff the program, antimicrobial expenditures and length of stay. Choose the type of analysis the pharmacy resident should perform:

a) Cost-Minimization Analysis
b) Cost-Benefit Analysis
c) Cost-Effectiveness Analysis
d) Cost-Utility Analysis
e) ECHO Model Analysis

BACKGROUND: Although low-density lipoprotein (LDL) lowering has been the mainstay of therapy for primary and secondary cardiovascular (CV) prevention, the data have been primarily for statins. Other nonstatin agents such as fibrates, niacin, and high-density lipoprotein (HDL)-raising agents have failed to show a clinical benefit when added to statins. The current trial sought to study the safety and efficacy of ezetimibe/simvastatin compared with simvastatin alone in reducing CV events in patients at high risk.

METHODS: Patients with recent ACS were randomized in a 1:1 fashion to either ezetimibe 10 mg/simvastatin 40 mg or simvastatin 40 mg in this placebo-controlled, randomized, double-blinded parallel study.

RESULTS: A total of 18,144 patients were randomized at 1,158 sites in 39 countries, 9,067 to ezetimibe/simvastatin and 9,077 to simvastatin alone as part of the intention-to-treat group. Baseline characteristics were fairly similar between the two arms. Presentation was ST-segment elevation MI (STEMI) in 29%, NSTEMI in 47%, and unstable angina (UA) in 24%. Nearly 88% underwent diagnostic angiography and 70% underwent percutaneous coronary intervention. Premature discontinuation was observed in 42% of patients in both arms. Baseline LDL cholesterol (LDL-C) levels were 95 mg/dL in both arms; the median follow-up average was 53.7 mg/dL versus 69.5 mg/dL in the ezetimibe/simvastatin and simvastatin arms, respectively. LDL lowering was observed as early as 1 month, and appeared sustained over the duration of follow-up. At 1 year, triglycerides were also lowered by 16.7 mg/dL in the combination arm, while HDL was increased by 0.6 mg/dL. The primary endpoint of CV death/MI/UA/coronary revascularization beyond 30 days/stroke was lower in the ezetimibe/simvastatin arm compared with the simvastatin arm over the duration of follow-up (32.7% vs. 34.7%, p = 0.016). Other endpoints including MI (13.1% vs. 14.8%, p = 0.002), stroke (4.2% vs. 4.8%, p = 0.05), ischemic stroke (3.4% vs. 4.1%, p = 0.008), and CV death/MI/stroke (20.4% vs. 22.2%, p = 0.003) were all lower in the ezetimibe/simvastatin arm; no differences were noted for all-cause mortality (15.4% vs. 15.3%, p = 0.78), CV mortality (6.9% vs. 6.8%, p = 0.99) and need for coronary revascularization (21.8% vs. 23.4%, p = 0.11). Per protocol analysis confirmed and further embellished the primary intention-to-treat analyses; the primary endpoint was significantly reduced in the ezetimibe/simvastatin arm compared with placebo (29.8% vs. 32.4%, p = 0.012).

153. In the trial above, what is the hazard ratio of the primary endpoint in the intention-to-treat population?

    [   ]

154. Which of the following statements regarding specificity are true? (Select **ALL** that apply.)

    a) The percentage of time a test is negative when disease is not present
    b) The percentage of time a test is positive when disease is not present
    c) The percentage of time a test is negative when disease is present
    d) The percentage of time a test is positive when disease is present
    e) It is equal to 1 – type I error

155. Although trends in the prevalence of obesity and obesity-attributable deaths have been examined, little is known about the resultant burden of disease associated with obesity. This study examined trends in the burden of obesity by estimating the obesity-related quality-adjusted life years (QALYs) lost—defined as the sum of QALYs lost due to morbidity and future QALYs lost in expected life years due to premature deaths—among U.S. adults along with differences by gender, race/ethnicity, and state.

    What type of pharmacoeconomic analysis is this?

    a) Cost-Minimization Analysis
    b) Cost-Benefit Analysis
    c) Cost-Effectiveness Analysis
    d) Cost-Utility Analysis
    e) ECHO Model Analysis

156. A new diagnostic test detects a certain genetic marker linked to the development of breast cancer. The test has 79% sensitivity and 94% specificity. Which of the following statements are correct? (Select **ALL** that apply.)

a) Test will be positive 79% of the time in patients who have breast cancer marker
b) Test will be positive 94% of the time in patients who have breast cancer marker
c) Test will be negative 79% of the time in patients who have breast cancer marker
d) Test will be negative 94% of the time in patients who have breast cancer marker
e) Test will be able to detect 94% of the breast cancer cases in the United States

157. A patient has received pharmacogenomic testing and has been identified lacking the CYP 2C19 enzyme due to a single-nucleotide polymorphism. Which of the following statements is correct?

   a) The patient is at risk for bleeding if clopidogrel is used
   b) The patient should be instructed not to use any 2C19 inhibitors, such as omeprazole or fluoxetine
   c) The patient would be expected to have a very good response to clopidogrel since he is lacking the enzyme that metabolizes this drug
   d) The patient would experience an increased INR if clopidogrel is administered
   e) The patient should not receive clopidogrel

158. A female with breast cancer has received pharmacogenomic testing. She is positive for the HER2/neu oncogene. Select the correct statement/s. (Select **ALL** that apply.)

   a) This testing is an example of using pharmacogenomics to ascertain benefit (rather than toxicity) from the use of a drug; pharmacogenomics is used for both purposes
   b) The patient would likely receive benefit with the use of trastuzumab
   c) The patient would likely receive benefit with the use of Lupron
   d) The patient would likely receive benefit with the use of Herceptin
   e) There is currently no accepted pharmacogenomic testing for cancer drugs

159. A patient has tested positive for the HLA-B*5701 allele. Which of the following statements is correct?

   a) The patient can receive Epzicom
   b) The patient cannot be dispensed abacavir
   c) The patient can receive Trizivir
   d) The patient would be expected to launch an aggressive immune response against HIV
   e) The patient is not at risk for hypersensitivity reactions with any of the HIV medications

160. A child is a rapid metabolizer of the CYP 2D6 enzyme. Which of the following statements are correct? (Select **ALL** that apply.)

   a) Codeine, a partial pro-drug of morphine, would be rapidly converted to the potent opioid if used by this patient
   b) The child will produce less morphine and receive reduced analgesia
   c) It is unsafe to dispense Tylenol #3 to this patient
   d) The child will have reduced opioid side effects
   e) If Tylenol #3 is dispensed to this patient it is likely that the patient will experience tachycardia, very high blood pressure and agitation; seizures are possible

161. Warfarin does not have required pharmacogenomic testing but it can be used to identify at-risk patients. Which of the following is correct? (Select **ALL** that apply.)

   a) The S isomer is more potent than the R isomer and is metabolized by CYP 2C9 enzyme
   b) The VKORC1 gene SNP is also important in response to warfarin
   c) A person with less expression of CYP 2C9 enzyme will be at higher risk for clotting
   d) If a patient produces less VKORC1, they require a higher dose of warfarin
   e) Checking for these genetic variations can help clinicians choose an appropriate starting dose of warfarin in their patients

162. A 42-year-old female received codeine with acetaminophen after a dental extraction. She developed dizziness and shortness of breath and went to the emergency room. Since this incident, she is very cautious about any medications. Which of the following medications would not cross react with codeine?

   a) Norco
   b) Lortab
   c) Duragesic
   d) Percocet
   e) Lorcet

163. Marlo has such a severe allergy to peanuts that he and his mother must carry an EpiPen. Which of the following medications are in a soy base and must be avoided in patients with a peanut allergy? (Select **ALL** that apply.)

   a) Albuterol inhaler
   b) Cleviprex
   c) Diprivan
   d) Precedex
   e) Morphine

164. Which of the following are symptoms unique to a true (anaphylactic) allergic reaction (as opposed to an intolerance)? (Select **ALL** that apply.)

   a) Mild rash
   b) Swollen face, lips or tongue
   c) Tendency to burn more quickly when in the sun
   d) Trouble breathing
   e) Large drop in blood pressure

165. Jamie developed hives and got a swollen face from using sulfamethoxazole. Which of the following drugs should be avoided? (Select **ALL** that apply.)

   a) Sulfasalazine
   b) Sulfisoxazole
   c) Zonisamide
   d) Celecoxib
   e) Morphine sulfate

166. Jason has a peanut allergy. His aunt will need to be instructed about an anaphylactic reaction. Choose the correct instructions: (Select **ALL** that apply.)

   a) If Jason has an anaphylactic reaction, he will need to receive epinephrine
   b) If Jason has an anaphylactic reaction, he should wait 1 hour before going to the ED
   c) If he is just wheezing slightly, you can give him some loratadine
   d) Swollen airways can be quickly fatal
   e) Jason should receive the EpiPen if he has difficulty breathing

167. Natalie has poorly controlled asthma. She finds that if she uses aspirin she cannot breathe easily. Which of the following drugs is the safest option for mild pain relief in this patient?

   a) Ibuprofen
   b) Acetaminophen
   c) Sulindac
   d) Indomethacin
   e) Naproxen

168. If a patient has a true allergy to penicillin, they may have a similar reaction to which of the following drugs? (Select **ALL** that apply.)

   a) Zosyn
   b) Augmentin
   c) Keflex
   d) Primaxin
   e) Zithromax

169. Which of the following is an incorrect statement in using the EpiPen?

   a) Grasp the epinephrine shot injector in one fist with the tip pointing down. Do not touch the tip. With the other hand, pull off the cap
   b) There is no need to remove the pants in order to use the pen
   c) Swing and jab the black tip into your outer thigh. The injector should be at a 90-degree angle to your thigh (straight down). Keep the injector in your outer thigh while you slowly count to five
   d) Remove the injector and rub the area where the medicine entered the skin. Look at the tip: If the needle is showing, the dose was received. If not, repeat the above steps
   e) After the shot, press the needle against a hard surface to bend the needle back. Put the injector back in its case, needle first

170. What is the name of the FDA's adverse event reporting system program?

   a) ISMP
   b) MedCoAlert
   c) MedWatch
   d) MedAware
   e) MedAction

171. Whenever Kelly dispenses a new prescription to one of her patients, Kelly counsels the patient. Kelly understands that the use of patient counseling has these benefits: (Select **ALL** that apply.)

   a) Counseling ensures that the drug will cure the patient's condition
   b) Counseling can ensure that the patient knows any monitoring required for the drug - the physician might not order the proper monitoring, such as renal or liver function tests
   c) Counseling can ensure the patient is aware of safety concerns with the use of the drug
   d) Counseling makes the patient aware of treatment goals - the patient should be assisting in the measurement of the drug's efficacy
   e) Counseling can ensure that the patient is getting a drug for their condition (and not for a wrong indication, or for a wrong patient)

172. What is the name of the accreditation body for more than 21,000 health care organizations and programs in the U.S. including hospitals, health care networks, long term care facilities, home care organizations, office-based surgery centers and independent laboratories?

   a) Institute of Medicine
   b) The Joint Commission
   c) Institute for Safe Medication Practices
   d) National Institutes of Health
   e) Food and Drug Administration

173. Dr. Davis wrote this prescription: *1.0 teaspoonful of oral suspension. UAD*
The pharmacist wanted to verify the dose, but neither the child's age nor weight was provided. What are possible sources of medication errors found in this prescription? (Select ALL that apply.)

   a) Using "as directed" for patient instructions
   b) Not providing the route of administration
   c) Using a "teaspoonful" to indicate the dose
   d) Not providing the patient's weight to verify the dose, or the indication
   e) Use of a trailing zero

174. Choose the correct statement/s regarding practices to help ensure the sterility in a laminar flow hood: (Select ALL that apply.)

   a) Do not interrupt the flow of air by placing items in the hood all lined up across the front of the hood; items should be placed in a straight line behind one another
   b) Use of a mask that covers the nose and mouth is required for regular hoods, but not for laminar flow hoods
   c) Preparation should be at least six inches into the hood
   d) Items such as pens and calculators should remain outside the hood
   e) Laminar flow hoods should be cleaned at least at the start of each shift, but more frequently depending on use

175. A hospital pharmacist dispensed the wrong vaccine for an infant, who then had to be re-inoculated. The same pharmacist pulled the wrong type of insulin from the refrigerator to send to the floor. Which of the following represents the most reasonable method to help the pharmacist avoid this type of error in the future?

   a) Indications for use on the prescription
   b) Placing the medications in high-risk bins, with notations on the front of the bins regarding name-mix-ups and other relevant alerts
   c) Having the pharmaceutical companies present more information on their drugs at grand rounds
   d) The use of standardized protocols
   e) Patient discharge education

176. A pharmacist works in a small city hospital that has a medical doctor who is an orthopedist. He does several hip replacements and several knee replacements at this hospital per month. The pharmacist hopes to implement patient-controlled analgesic (PCA) devices for the orthopedic patients. However, the medical staff at the hospital is overburdened and the head of the nursing team is not interested in changing to a new system. Communication between healthcare professionals is lacking. Choose the primary reason why PCA devices may not be appropriate in this setting:

   a) PCAs cannot be used in small hospitals
   b) PCAs require an educated, coordinated health care team
   c) PCAs are not used in orthopedic surgeries due to higher-than-normal DVT risk
   d) PCAs are only used in outpatient clinics
   e) The use of a PCA would increase costs too much for a small hospital to manage

177. Which of the following represents a common cause of hospital-acquired (nosocomial) infections?

   a) UTIs, due to the use of broad-spectrum antibiotics
   b) UTIs, due to enlarged prostates
   c) UTIs, due to the use of parenteral nutrition and "PICC" lines
   d) UTIs, due to uterine prolapse
   e) UTIs, due to indwelling catheters

178. One of the largest causes of needlestick infections is due to the use of glucose meters in healthcare settings that are used to test many patients. Another cause of needlestick infections is due to vials of medicine, such as insulin, that are used in more than one patient. Choose the correct statement/s: (Select **ALL** that apply.)

   a) If a glucose meter travels from room-to-room, the nursing staff must replace the lancet tip prior to testing each patient
   b) If the same injection vial will be used for multiple patients, it is imperative never to re-insert a needle that has already been used on a patient into the vial
   c) It is preferable to avoid the use of multi-use vials in different patients; it is preferable to label the multi-use vial with one patient's name only
   d) The ISMP recommends using insulin pens to avoid contamination from using insulin in multiple patients
   e) Glucose meters should not be used in the hospital; blood sugar can be tested with the daily labs

179. Which of the following are High-Alert drugs per ISMP?

   a) Hypertonic saline and fosphenytoin
   b) Vancomycin and potassium chloride injection
   c) Potassium chloride injection and hypertonic saline
   d) Vancomycin and gentamicin
   e) Insulin and 0.45% sodium chloride

180. Doris is admitted to the hospital for treatment of atrial fibrillation. While hospitalized, she receives IV diltiazem. When Doris returns home she continues on oral diltiazem she was given at discharge and her previous blood pressure medication amlodipine. Which of the following medication error-reduction programs would most likely have helped to avoid this duplication of therapy?

a) Barcoding
b) CPOE
c) Medication Reconciliation
d) High-Risk Drug Protocols
e) Staff In-services

181. What is the purpose of the FDA REMS program?

    a) To ensure that the benefits of dangerous drugs outweigh the risks
    b) To help control drug costs
    c) To get unsafe OTC drugs off the market
    d) To educate patients about herbals and other natural products
    e) To employ more government workers

182. A local skilled nursing facility (SNF) has an automated drug dispensing cabinet for the daily medications needed by the residents. The use of ADCs in skilled nursing or transitional care facilities is safest if this requirement/s is met: (Select **ALL** that apply.)

    a) A pharmacist must have reviewed all medication orders and the patient's profile prior to drugs being removed for any patient
    b) The stocking of the automated drug delivery system should be done by a pharmacist
    c) If a pharmacist is not available, the medical director of the facility may fill the cabinet, but not nursing staff
    d) The override function is limited to true emergencies
    e) Look-alike, sound-alike medications are stored in different locations within the ADC

183. What is the primary purpose of Phase III studies?

    a) To determine safety, efficacy and dose-response relationships in the population
    b) To put the drug manufacturing system in place and ready for FDA approval
    c) To determine the profit potential of the drug
    d) To evaluate safety after the drug has been approved and released for sale
    e) To rate the drug against a panel of known drug inducers and inhibitors

184. Which of the following designations describes equivalence between two products?

   a) BC
   b) BX
   c) AX
   d) AB
   e) ABC

185. A community pharmacist reports that a new drug has caused an unexpected adverse reaction in a patient. This information can be assessed under this phase of the drug approval process:

   a) There is no corresponding phase once the drug is released
   b) Phase I
   c) Phase II
   d) Phase III
   e) Phase IV

186. What is the primary purpose of Phase II studies?

   a) To find the treatment dose
   b) To evaluate side effects
   c) To determine efficacy
   d) To determine the drug's profit potential
   e) To review the marketing approach

187. Which organization is responsible for the drug approval process in the United States?

   a) Institute of Medicine
   b) Joint Commission
   c) Institute for Safe Medication Practices
   d) National Institutes of Health
   e) The Food and Drug Administration's (FDA) Center for Drug Evaluation and Research (CDER)

188. Select the agents that are used for anxiety: (Select **ALL** that apply.)

   a) Garlic
   b) Chamomile tea
   c) Lemon balm
   d) Ginseng
   e) Valerian root

189. A patient with recently-diagnosed active tuberculosis was prescribed isoniazid, rifampin, pyrazinamide and ethambutol. Which vitamin is recommended?

   a) Vitamin B1
   b) Vitamin B12
   c) Vitamin B2
   d) Vitamin B3
   e) Vitamin B6

190. Select the correct vitamin name and abbreviation match. (Select **ALL** that apply.)

   a) Vitamin B6-Pyridoxine
   b) Vitamin B1-Riboflavin
   c) Vitamin B12-Cobalamin
   d) Vitamin B3-Thiamine
   e) Vitamin A-Retinol

191. It's a priority to increase folic acid intake among women of child-bearing age. Why is this important?

   a) To reduce the risk of low bone density in young women
   b) To reduce the risk of serious birth defects in children born to women with low folic acid intake
   c) To reduce the risk of ovarian cancer in young women
   d) To reduce the risk of endometrial cancer in young women
   e) To make money for the manufacturer of folic acid

192. Mary developed a UTI and received a 3-day course of an antibiotic. She tells the pharmacist that she used to get diarrhea when she took antibiotics but does not expect this to happen now because she uses a probiotic. What should you say?

a) Do not use the probiotic during the 3 days you are using antibiotic; wait until the therapy is complete
b) If you take the antibiotic in the morning and at night, take the probiotic in the middle of the day
c) It would be best to replace the probiotic with lycopene
d) It would be best to replace the probiotic with saw palmetto
e) It would be best to replace the probiotic with comfrey

193. A patient brings in a prescription for orlistat. Which of the following vitamins should the pharmacist recommend the patient take? (Select **ALL** that apply.)

   a) Vitamin A
   b) Vitamin B6
   c) Vitamin D
   d) Vitamin E
   e) Vitamin K

194. Which natural products can be useful for migraine headache prophylaxis? (Select **ALL** that apply.)

   a) Feverfew
   b) Saw palmetto
   c) Ginger
   d) Magnesium
   e) Riboflavin

195. Which calcium supplement is absorbed better in an acidic environment and is taken with meals?

   a) Calcium citrate
   b) Citracal
   c) Oscal
   d) Citrucel
   e) None of these should be taken with food

196. A product labeled as homeopathic is supposedly useful for sleep and anxiety. It contains an inert filler and an active ingredient labeled as *Anxol*. A patient using it regularly develops liver damage. Select the correct statement:

a) Homeopathic products may not be homeopathic but labeled as such to sound pleasing to the patient
b) Homeopathic products generally cause liver damage and are not recommended, for this reason, by competent pharmacists
c) Homeopathic products are regulated strictly by the FDA and must be produced according to Good Manufacturing Principles
d) Homeopathy is based on the belief that giving an illness to healthy patients will produce an immune response if the patient is infected at a later date
e) Homeopathic products are not sold in most pharmacies

197. A patient does not consume dairy products and needs 1,000 mg calcium daily. She has purchased calcium carbonate 500 mg elemental per tablet. What is the best way to take the two tablets she needs each day?

a) For the best adherence, take both with breakfast
b) For help sleeping, take both with at bedtime with a light snack
c) Take one with breakfast and the other with dinner
d) Take both with the largest meal of the day
e) For help sleeping, take both at bedtime with a fatty meal

198. Which of the following agents is required for calcium absorption?

a) Folic acid
b) Vitamin C
c) Vitamin D
d) Vitamin E
e) Vitamin K

199. Which agent is a precursor to androgens (male sex hormones)?

a) GABA
b) Lysine
c) Chondroitin
d) SAMe
e) DHEA

200. Choose the correct statement concerning vitamin D supplements:

a) 50,000 units of vitamin D (the large green capsules), taken daily, is acceptable for most patients

b) Vitamin D intake is acceptable in most patients in the United States
c) Vitamin D2 should not be recommended
d) Vitamin D3 should not be recommended
e) Cholecalciferol is vitamin D3 and is the preferred source

201. A patient presented with poor muscle coordination, confusion and vision changes. He was diagnosed with Wernicke's encephalopathy. Select the correct statement:

    a) The patient has a vitamin B6 deficiency
    b) This condition is mostly common caused by a lack of intrinsic factor
    c) This condition can lead to permanent cognitive deterioration, and cause psychosis
    d) The patient has a vitamin B9 deficiency
    e) The patient has a vitamin A deficiency

202. Olga is a 51 year-old pharmacist with night sweats. Due to having difficulty sleeping, she is moody at work and the pharmacist interns are quite unhappy. Olga is in the peri-menopause. What supplement/s are used by some to possibly provide a mild benefit? (Select **ALL** that apply.)

    a) Saw palmetto
    b) Willow bark
    c) Ginseng
    d) Estroven
    e) Black cohosh

203. A patient brings the pharmacist a bottle of "natural pain pills" that he ordered off a late-night TV show. The name of the manufacturer listed on the bottle is "*Magic Cure-All*." The pharmacist conducts an internet search and cannot locate that this company exists. Choose the correct statement regarding the "natural pain pills":

    a) Natural products are always manufactured according to Good Manufacturing Processes (GMPs), according to FDA regulations passed in 1984
    b) The dietary supplement manufacturer must have proved the product's safety and effectiveness
    c) Pharmacists have easily accessible sources to check for drug interactions and safety concerns with natural products
    d) This product has been approved by the FDA
    e) This product was obtained illegally

204. Jerry has high cholesterol. Which of the following agents can help improve cholesterol values? (Select **ALL** that apply.)

   a) St. John's wort
   b) Plant stanols/sterols
   c) Ginseng
   d) Statins
   e) Red yeast rice

205. The use of metformin can cause a depletion of which of the following nutrients that may need to be supplemented?

   a) Thiamine
   b) Niacin
   c) Vitamin B6
   d) Vitamin B12
   e) Vitamin C

206. Choose the correct statements concerning vitamin supplementation for breast-fed babies: (Select **ALL** that apply.)

   a) Breast-fed babies need 1 mg/kg of iron daily from 4-6 months old and until consuming iron-rich foods
   b) Breast-fed babies need calcium supplementation
   c) Formula-fed babies need iron supplementation
   d) Exclusively breastfed infants or babies drinking less than 1 liter of baby formula need 400 IU of vitamin D daily
   e) Formula-fed babies need vitamin D supplementation

207. Which calcium supplement is absorbed well on either an empty stomach or with food?

   a) Tums
   b) Citracal
   c) Oscal
   d) Rolaids
   e) Caltrate

208. Jamie recently became involved in a sexual relationship. She went to the clinic and was prescribed *Loestrin Fe* 1/20. She believes in natural healing and takes a handful of supplements daily: a fish oil capsule, a B vitamin complex, a multivitamin, a vitamin E 400 IU capsule, St. John's wort, kava and a probiotic supplement. She uses melatonin when she has trouble sleeping. Despite strict adherence with her birth control pill regimen, Jamie became pregnant. What was the most likely cause of the pregnancy?

   a) Concurrent use of birth control pills and fish oils
   b) Concurrent use of birth control pills and St. John's wort
   c) Concurrent use of birth control pills and lactobacillus
   d) Concurrent use of birth control pills and melatonin
   e) Concurrent use of birth control pills and high-dose vitamin E

209. Mary uses *Imitrex* for migraines 2-4 times each month. Recently she began to use *Sarafem* 10 mg daily for premenstrual dysphoric disorder. In addition, she uses meperidine once or twice daily for headache relief. Mary is at risk for the following symptoms: (Select **ALL** that apply.)

   a) Tremor, agitation, confusion, hallucinations
   b) Tachycardia, sweating
   c) Diarrhea
   d) Muscle rigidity, shivering
   e) Acute bradycardia

210. Drug A is a substrate of 2C9 and a potent 3A4 inhibitor. Drug B is a substrate of 2D6 and 1A2 as well as a potent inhibitor of 2C19. Drug C is a substrate of 3A4 and a potent inhibitor of 2D6. If all three drugs were given together, what would the expected levels of each drug to do?

   a) Drug A levels would stay the same, Drug B levels increase, Drug C levels increase
   b) Drug A levels would increase, Drug B levels decrease, Drug C levels increase
   c) Drug A levels would decrease, Drug B levels decrease, Drug C levels increase
   d) Drug A levels would increase, Drug B levels stay the same, and Drug C levels decrease
   e) Drug A, B, and C levels would all increase

211. Mart uses ibuprofen for pain. Mart has hypertension. He takes two over-the-counter ibuprofen tablets twice daily on work days. Lately, he has noticed his blood pressure is elevated more than usual. Which of the following would be safe options that would not elevate his blood pressure? (Select **ALL** that apply.)

   a) Advil or Aleve
   b) ThermaCare Activated Heat Wraps
   c) Acetaminophen
   d) A topical menthol analgesic patch, such as BenGay
   e) Aspirin

212. Which of the following statements concerning drug interactions are correct? (Select **ALL** that apply.)

   a) If a compound is a P-gp pump inhibitor, it can cause the levels of P-gp substrates to decrease if given concurrently
   b) If a compound is a P-gp pump inducer, it can cause the levels of P-gp substrates to decrease if given concurrently
   c) Inducers cause more metabolism of drugs that are substrates of the enzymes
   d) Inhibitors reduce or knock out the ability of the enzyme to work; this increases metabolism of the substrates
   e) Tacrolimus is a substrate of the P-gp efflux pump

213. A patient is at risk for atrial fibrillation; she has had this atrial fibrillation in the past. The medical team has asked the pharmacist to check for drugs on her profile which can increase her risk of arrhythmia. The pharmacist should include the following medication:

   a) Xolair
   b) Lamictal
   c) Ziprasidone
   d) Proscar
   e) Xalatan

214. Sandra is about to get on the waiting list for a kidney transplant. She has a creatinine clearance of 16 mL/min and experiences frequent bouts of hyperkalemia. She cannot use any medicines that elevate potassium because in this patient even small increases in potassium trigger an arrhythmia. Which medications elevate potassium and would put Sandra at risk for arrhythmia? (Select **ALL** that apply.)

a) Altoprev
b) Dyazide
c) Inspra
d) Aldactone
e) Yasmin

215. Ann lives in Florida and occasionally eats grapefruit. Choose the correct statement/s concerning grapefruit-drug interactions: (Select **ALL** that apply.)

   a) Do not use grapefruit with cyclosporine
   b) Do not use grapefruit with buspirone
   c) If a drug interacts with grapefruit, use a long gut separation period, such as taking the grapefruit two hours before or four hours after the interacting drug
   d) Do not use grapefruit with rivaroxaban
   e) Do not use grapefruit with valproate

216. A patient is using digoxin. If he is prescribed the following drug, the digoxin dose will need to be decreased:

   a) Diazepam
   b) Phenytoin
   c) Cyclosporine
   d) Carbamazepine
   e) Cancidas

217. A 76-year-old woman had been taking metoprolol extended-release 100 mg daily and warfarin 4 mg daily (both for atrial fibrillation) and amitriptyline 50 mg QHS (for migraine prophylaxis) for several years. Shortly after the death of her spouse, she experienced very sad mood swings. Initially she was prescribed citalopram 40 mg daily. When this was not very effective, the physician added on paroxetine 10 mg daily (as he did not wish to increase the citalopram dose). What is this patient at risk for due to the drug combinations?

   a) Increased bleeding risk but decreased risk of arrhythmia
   b) Increased risk of clotting but decreased risk of bleeding
   c) Increased risk of bleeding and increased risk of arrhythmia
   d) Increased risk of worsening depression
   e) Worsening depression and increased clotting risk

218. Choose the correct statements concerning lithium: (Select **ALL** that apply.)

   a) Lithium is a safe drug in elderly patients if the serum creatinine is below 1 g/dL
   b) Lithium is not considered serotonergic and can be mixed safely with meperidine
   c) Increased salt intake increases serum lithium levels
   d) If a drug has a high degree of nephrotoxicity it will likely not be a safe option in a patient using chronic lithium therapy
   e) Lithium is not metabolized; it is excreted renally

219. A patient is taking immediate release niacin 1 gram three times daily and atorvastatin 40 mg daily. Choose the correct statements of concomitant statin and niacin therapy. (Select **ALL** that apply.)

   a) Niacins and statins taken together have a lower risk of muscle toxicity
   b) Niacins and statins taken together have increased risk of muscle toxicity
   c) Niacins and statins used concurrently enable the patient to use lower statin doses, resulting in lower risk of muscle damage
   d) Niaspan is contraindicated with any of the statins
   e) If a patient uses both niacin and a statin it would be expected that both the LDL and the triglycerides would be lowered more than with the use of either agent alone

220. Amiodarone is both a substrate and an inhibitor of CYP 450 2C9, 2D6, and 3A4. The pharmacist is aware that these medications must have their doses reduced when dispensing amiodarone: (Select **ALL** that apply.)

   a) Quinidine
   b) Warfarin
   c) Lithium
   d) Pravastatin
   e) Digoxin

221. Thomas is using simvastatin and requires another agent to lower his triglycerides. He cannot afford Lovaza or Vascepa. Of the following agents, which has the highest risk for additive toxicity when added to the statin therapy?

   a) Trilipix
   b) Triglide
   c) Antara
   d) Lopid
   e) Tricor

222. Blanca uses *Kariva* estrogen-progestin birth control pills. The pills would be expected to have reduced efficacy if she uses the following medication:

a) The drug of choice for infective endocarditis prevention in a patient with no known drug allergies
b) The "RIPE" regimen for treating active tuberculosis
c) The drug of choice for infective endocarditis prevention in a patient with penicillin drug allergy
d) The drug of choice for initial treatment of mild-to-moderate *C. difficile* infection
e) The drug of choice for initial treatment of a rickettsial infection

223. Choose the correct statements concerning tetracycline and doxycycline. (Select **ALL** that apply.)

a) Separate tetracycline, but not doxycycline, from compounds containing aluminum, calcium, magnesium and iron-including antacids, supplements and dairy products
b) Separate doxycycline, but not tetracycline, from compounds containing aluminum, calcium, magnesium and iron-including antacids, supplements and dairy products
c) Both doxycycline and tetracycline must be separated from compounds containing aluminum, calcium, magnesium and iron-including antacids and dairy products
d) The tetracycline class works by reversibly binding to the 30S ribosomal subunit, which prevents protein transcription
e) Tetracyclines cause photosensitivity; patients should be counseled on sunscreen

224. Which of the following statins has the lowest risk of drug interactions?

a) Atorvastatin
b) Pravastatin
c) Lovastatin
d) Simvastatin
e) Fluvastatin

225. Sara has been using a monoamine oxidase inhibitor. Which of the following drugs can be dispensed to Sara and will not cause concern? (Select **ALL** that apply.)

a) Prempro
b) Boniva

c) Zolmitriptan
d) Xalatan
e) Sumatriptan

226. Fera is a patient with severe renal insufficiency and moderate heart failure. She has been using levofloxacin for the past five weeks in an attempt to treat osteomyelitis. Her other medications include methadone and amitriptyline 150 mg QHS for neuropathic pain. Which agents could cause the QT interval to be increased and put the patient at risk for torsades de pointes? (Select **ALL** that apply.)

a) Levofloxacin
b) Methadone
c) Mupirocin
d) Cascara
e) Amitriptyline

227. The antifungal agents itraconazole, ketoconazole and voriconazole have safety issues that the pharmacist must address. These include the following: (Select **ALL** that apply.)

a) All are CYP 450 3A4 inhibitors; the dose of 3A4 substrates may need to be lowered
b) Itraconazole and ketoconazole have pH-dependent absorption; avoid use with drugs that raise pH, such as antacids
c) Voriconazole is an enzyme substrate and is subject to many drug interactions
d) Voriconazole metabolism is initially first-order, but can become zero-order with higher doses, and toxicity can result
e) With severe renal impairment it is safer to use IV voriconazole only, rather than the oral formulation, due to the excipients in the tablets and oral suspension

228. The phosphodiesterase inhibitors, such as tadalafil, cannot be used safely with nitrates. What is most likely to happen if a pharmacist missed this interaction?

a) QT prolongation
b) Hypertensive crisis
c) Cerebrovascular accident
d) Acute drop in blood pressure
e) Serotonin syndrome

229. Which of the following drugs can cause hearing damage? (Select **ALL** that apply.)

   a) Demadex
   b) Amikacin
   c) Tobramycin
   d) Lasix
   e) Adalimumab

230. A patient with atrial fibrillation has been using warfarin for nine months. The INR is stable around 2.3. The patient is having a return of major depressive disorder, which she has had in the past. Which of the following agents would not increase bleeding risk in this patient and could be used for a suitable trial? (Select **ALL** that apply.)

   a) Bupropion
   b) Effexor
   c) Pristiq
   d) Lexapro
   e) Cymbalta

231. Select the correct statements concerning the drug interaction between valproic acid and lamotrigine. (Select ALL that apply.)

   a) Valproic acid inhibits lamotrigine metabolism
   b) This interaction increases the risk for a severe lamotrigine-induced rash
   c) This interaction increases the risk for severe valproate-induced pancreatitis
   d) When using these two medications concurrently, the *Lamictal Dose Titration* pack cannot be used; lower doses will be required
   e) This interaction increases the risk for severe valproate-induced hepatotoxicity

232. Martin has been using a monoamine oxidase inhibitor to help control his depression for many years. He is careful to check that other drugs and foods do not interact with his medicine. Which of the following drugs can be dispensed to Martin and will not cause concern with the concurrent use of his antidepressant? (Select ALL that apply.)

   a) Bupropion
   b) Meperidine

c) Toprol XL
d) Pseudoephedrine
e) Alprazolam

233. Jess worries that she will have a hip fracture. Which of the following agents increase the risk of the patient having a fall? (Select **ALL** that apply.)

a) Flexeril
b) Remeron
c) Nuvigil
d) Bactrim
e) Restoril

234. A patient with non-small cell lung cancer is receiving cisplatin as part of the treatment regimen. Select the lab test that should be ordered to monitor for myelosuppression:

a) BMP
b) CMP
c) CBC
d) PMN
e) Bands

235. RM is a 48 year-old female patient who is hospitalized with chest pain. She uses many drugs, including *Cozaar, Coumadin, Coreg, Lasix* and *Micro-K*. An INR is taken and is reported as a critical lab value. At this hospital the critical value for warfarin is an INR ≥ 4. Select the best definition of a critical:

a) A value that can be life-threatening if corrective action is not taken quickly
b) A value that can cause the patient to suffer physical or psychological harm
c) A value that has to be acted on within 6 hours
d) A value that has to be acted on within 8 hours
e) A value that has to be acted on within 2 hours

236. A patient has G6PD-deficiency. What will occur if the patient receives primaquine for malaria prophylaxis?

a) The patient will be at higher risk of catching malaria
b) The patient will be at higher risk of developing primaquine-induced neurotoxicity

c) The patient will be at risk for serious internal bleeding
d) The patient will have increased renal excretion of electrolytes
e) The patient will develop leukopenia

237. TG, a 72 year-old Hispanic male is hospitalized with a pulmonary embolism. He is receiving unfractionated heparin initiated at a rate of 1000 units/hour. The control value at this hospital is 22-38 seconds. Select the correct test and an appropriate treatment level for this patient:

a) INR, 2 - 3
b) aPTT, 18 seconds
c) INR, 2.5 - 3.5
d) aPTT, 44 seconds
e) Platelets, above 50

238. A child is receiving enoxaparin. The clinical team in the pediatric unit is not sure if the medication is being dosed correctly due to the child's age and body weight. Which test should be ordered?

a) INR
b) aPTT
c) Platelets
d) BNP
e) Anti-Xa

239. A 34-year-old male with a history of non-Hodgkin's lymphoma received several cycles of chemotherapy. The patient received the CODOX-M/VAC regimen (cyclophosphamide, doxorubicin, methotrexate, etoposide, and cytarabine). During the hospitalization she developed sepsis which was positive for *Streptococcus viridans* and was treated with levofloxacin 500 mg IV Q daily. The patient is found to have decreased serum folate levels. The clinical pharmacist participating in the medical rounds is asked if any of the inpatient medications could have contributed to the low folate levels. Select the best response:

a) The most likely drug contributing to the decrease in folate is levofloxacin
b) The most likely drug contributing to the decrease in folate is cytarabine
c) The most likely drug contributing to the decrease in folate is cyclophosphamide
d) The most likely drug contributing to the decrease in folate is methotrexate
e) The most likely drug contributing to the decrease in folate is doxorubicin

240. A male is hospitalized with a pulmonary embolism. He is receiving unfractionated heparin for VTE treatment. Which of the following lab values would indicate heparin-induced thrombocytopenia?

WBC: 13.5 (3.5-12)   HGB: 16.1(13.4-17.7)
HCT: 48.2 (40-53)   MCV: 93 (80-97)
PLT: 73 (150-420)   BUN: 22 (6-23 mg/dL)
Creatinine: 1.9 (0.7-1.6 mg/dL)

a) The hemoglobin
b) The hematocrit
c) The glucose
d) The platelets
e) The CBC

241. What lab values will be present in a patient with a metabolic acidosis?

a) Low pH, low serum bicarbonate
b) Low pH, high serum bicarbonate
c) High pH, low serum bicarbonate
d) High pH, high serum bicarbonate
e) Low pH, low alkaline phosphatase

242. A patient presents with a butterfly-shaped rash on her face and achey joints. The patient's chronic medications include *Klor-Con, Lasix, Toprol XL, BiDil, Atacand* and *Inspra*. Which of the daily medication is most likely contributing to this presentation?

a) Lasix
b) Toprol
c) BiDil
d) Atacand
e) Inspra

243. Select the name of the lab test used to distinguish between a microcytic and a macrocytic anemia:

a) RDW
b) MCH
c) MCV

d) MCHC
e) TIBC

244. An 82 year-old male with COPD, has difficulty breathing and finds little relief from daily *Advair Diskus* and *Spiriva*. Which condition is most likely in this patient?

a) Respiratory acidosis
b) Respiratory alkalosis
c) Anion gap acidosis
d) Lactic acidosis
e) Diabetic ketoacidosis

245. Sam has a creatinine clearance of 38 mL/min. Which of the following statements are accurate concerning this degree of renal impairment? (Select **ALL** that apply.)

a) This is classified as severe renal insufficiency
b) This is defined as Stage 3 CKD
c) The patient may need to have the erythropoetin level checked if anemic
d) ACE inhibitors or Angiotensin Receptor Blockers should be initiated if there are no contraindications to use
e) The blood pressure should be controlled to less than 110/70 mmHg with this degree of impairment

246. A patient who was receiving enalapril and spironolactone develops renal insufficiency. An ECG is obtained in the emergency department which demonstrates electrolyte changes consistent with hyperkalemia. What should be administered to this patient to reverse the effects of hyperkalemia on the heart?

a) Albuterol
b) Sodium bicarbonate
c) Dextrose
d) Calcium chloride
e) Kayexalate

247. Tom has end stage renal disease and uses many medications, including *Renagel*. Previously he was using *PhosLo*. What is a possible reason that Tom needed to stop using *PhosLo*?

a) Cost; *Renagel* is less expensive than *PhosLo*
b) Higher calcium levels
c) Lower calcium levels
d) Hyperphosphatemia
e) Lower efficacy

248. Which of the following statements concerning bone metabolism abnormalities in chronic kidney disease (CKD) is correct?

a) Initially, bone metabolism abnormalities are caused by a rise in calcium
b) Hyperphosphatemia causes an increase in the release of parathyroid hormone
c) A benefit of hyperphosphatemia is improved bone health
d) To counteract the increase in phosphate levels, it is necessary to give injectable phosphate binders
e) Treatment of secondary hyperparathyroidism is restricting dietary calcium

249. Sam has lupus-related renal disease. Her serum creatinine today is 2.7 g/dL and the potassium is 6.2 mEq/L. The physician has prescribed sodium polystyrene sulfonate. Choose the correct statement concerning sodium polystyrene sulfonate:

a) The brand name is Gabitril
b) This drug is a cation exchange resin that binds potassium in the gut
c) This drug may stabilize cardiac tissue to reduce arrhythmia risk
d) The potassium should be lowered to 3.2 mEq/L
e) SPS increases appetite

250. A pharmacist will provide information on treatment options for hyperthyroidism during pregnancy. (Select **ALL** that apply.)

a) Propylthiouracil is Pregnancy Category D and is used during the first trimester
b) Methimazole is Pregnancy Category D and is used during the first trimester
c) Methimazole is Pregnancy Category D and is used after the first trimester
d) Methimazole has a higher risk of hepatotoxicity than propylthiouracil
e) Both agents can cause serious liver damage

Practice NAPLEX® Exam

This section will consist of a 250 question practice exam. You should consider this the real deal and time yourself as if you are taking the actual exam. We have tried our best to ensure this practice exam reflects highly on the actual NAPLEX® exam. It is advised to provide yourself 6 hours to take this exam to allow for 30 minutes as a "buffer zone". So please consider only providing yourself 6 hours to take this exam. The actual NAPLEX® exam provides 6.5 hours but note this includes all breaks and bathroom breaks so time is continuously ticking when you are taking the real exam. Good luck!

2017 NAPLEX Practice Exam: 250 Questions, 6 hours

1. Choose the correct statement/s concerning lithium and drug interactions: (Select **ALL** that apply.)

   a) Lithium is a relatively safe drug in elderly patients if the serum creatinine is below 1 g/dL
   b) Lithium is not considered serotonergic and can be mixed safely with meperidine, but not with tramadol
   c) Increased salt intake increases serum lithium levels
   d) If a drug has a high degree of nephrotoxicity it will likely not be a safe option in a patient using chronic lithium therapy
   e) Lithium is not metabolized; it is excreted renally

2. Amiodarone is both a substrate and an inhibitor of CYP 450 2C9, 2D6, and 3A4. The pharmacist is aware that these medications must have their doses reduced when dispensing amiodarone: (Select **ALL** that apply.)

   a) Quinidine
   b) Warfarin
   c) Lithium
   d) Pravastatin
   e) Digoxin

3. A major drug interaction can occur with the use of grapefruit juice and which of the following medications?

   a) Atorvastatin and amiodarone
   b) Celecoxib and felodipine
   c) Lovastatin and lithium
   d) Levetiracetam and topiramate
   e) Duloxetine and mirtazapine

4. Elaine is beginning amiodarone therapy. She is easily stressed and worried about having another "racing heart and dizziness" or what her doctor said was an "arrhythmia". Elaine uses furosemide and has had hypokalemia in the past. She has been told that her potassium and magnesium need to be within normal limits to keep her heart at a normal rhythm, and that she should try to relax. The physician has decided that she wants to check magnesium and potassium and orders a Basic Metabolic Panel (BMP). Select the correct statement:

   a) The physician should also order the potassium level; this is not included in the BMP
   b) The physician should order the magnesium level; this is not included in the BMP
   c) The potassium level has no effect on the risk of arrhythmia
   d) The magnesium level has no effect on the risk of arrhythmia
   e) The physician should also order the sodium level; this is not included in the BMP

5. Which drugs exhibit sorption issues? (Select **ALL** that apply.)

   a) Regular human insulin
   b) Tacrolimus
   c) Paclitaxel
   d) Nitroglycerin
   e) Etoposide

6. Ash has a history of atrial fibrillation and is picking up moxifloxacin. He is currently taking atorvastatin, amiodarone, *Januvia*, *Byetta*, and metformin,. Which of the following can be caused by potential drug interactions? (Select **ALL** that apply.)

a) QT prolongation
   b) Impaired absorption of moxifloxacin
   c) Hypoglycemia or hyperglycemia
   d) Peripheral edema, fluid retention due to quinolone addition
   e) Additive nephrotoxicity

7. Select the correct section of the US Pharmacopoeia (USP) National Formulary that includes standards for sterile compounding:

   a) USP Chapter 790
   b) USP Chapter 795
   c) USP Chapter 797
   d) USP Chapter 875
   e) USP Chapter 890

8. Select the correct section of the US Pharmacopoeia (USP) National Formulary that includes standards for non-sterile compounding:

   a) USP Chapter 790
   b) USP Chapter 795
   c) USP Chapter 797
   d) USP Chapter 875
   e) USP Chapter 890

9. What is the brand for olanzapine?

   a) Zyprexa
   b) Zygonda
   c) Zyloprim
   d) Zylox
   e) Zyzez

10. What is the generic for Calan and it's mechanism of action?

    a) Losartan; Angiotensin Receptor Blocker
    b) Lisinopril; Angiotensin Converting Enzyme Inhibitor
    c) Verapamil; Calcium Channel Blocker
    d) Amlodipine; Calcium Channel Blocker
    e) Diltiazem; Calcium Channel Blocker

11. What is the generic name of Tradjenta and it's mechanism of action?

   a) Linagliptin; DPP-4 inhibitor
   b) Saxagliptin; DPP-4 inhibitor
   c) Sitagliptin; DPP-4 inhibitor
   d) Alogliptin; DPP-4 inhibitor

12. What is the generic name of Onglyza and it's mechanism of action?

   a) Linagliptin; DPP-4 inhibitor
   b) Saxagliptin; DPP-4 inhibitor
   c) Sitagliptin; DPP-4 inhibitor
   d) Alogliptin; DPP-4 inhibitor

13. What is the generic name of Januvia and it's mechanism of action?

   a) Linagliptin; DPP-4 inhibitor
   b) Saxagliptin; DPP-4 inhibitor
   c) Sitagliptin; DPP-4 inhibitor
   d) Alogliptin; DPP-4 inhibitor

14. A patient is picking up a prescription for erythromycin ethylsuccinate (E.E.S.) oral suspension. Choose the correct statement:

   a) This medication cannot be used if the patient has a penicillin allergy
   b) This medication should not be administered with food
   c) This medication is a major inhibitor of cytochrome P450 2C9
   d) This medication is effective for treating the flu
   e) This medication should be refrigerated

15. Of the following oral suspension antibiotics, which one should not be refrigerated?

   a) Augmentin
   b) Pen VK
   c) Ceftin
   d) Keflex
   e) Biaxin

16. Which of the following IV agents are not refrigerated? (Select **ALL** that apply.)

    a) Ceftriaxone
    b) Cefazolin
    c) Moxifloxacin
    d) Phenylephrine
    e) Bactrim

17. Which of the following statements concerning IV medications are correct? (Select **ALL** that apply.)

    a) Furosemide and metronidazole IV bags are not refrigerated
    b) Phenytoin IV requires a filter due to the potential for precipitation
    c) Sulfamethoxazole/trimethoprim and phenytoin IV are diluted with NS only
    d) Phenytoin IV has a maximum infusion rate of 50 mg/min
    e) Metronidazole IV does not require protection from light

18. Which of the following statements is correct regarding linezolid? (Select **ALL** that apply.)

    a) Linezolid is associated with bone marrow suppression
    b) Linezolid is part of the streptogramin class of antibiotics
    c) Linezolid should be dose adjusted in renal impairment
    d) Linezolid is a weak MAO inhibitor
    e) Linezolid oral suspension should not be refrigerated

19. What is the rationale of combination therapy with hydralazine and isosorbide dinitrate in management of patients with heart failure?

    a) Isosorbide dinitrate relieves chest pain, hydralazine reduces preload
    b) Isosorbide dinitrate decreases afterload, hydralazine reduces preload
    c) Isosorbide dinitrate and hydralazine both decrease preload
    d) Isosorbide dinitrate and hydralazine both decrease afterload
    e) Isosorbide dinitrate decreases preload, hydralazine decreases afterload

20. Which of the following anticonvulsants is the drug of choice for treatment of trigeminal neuralgia?

    a) Valproate
    b) Primidone

c) Phenobarbital
d) Diazepam
e) Carbamazepine

21. Which of the following anti-retroviral drugs can be used in pediatric patients?

    a) Amprenavir
    b) Atazanavir
    c) Emtricitabine
    d) Raltegravir
    e) Tipranavir

22. Which is used in a bronchial challenge test (bronchoprovocation)?

    a) Acetylcholine
    b) Bethanacol
    c) Carbachol
    d) Plasma cholinesterases
    e) Methacholine

23. A patient has tested positive for the HLA-B*5701 allele. Which of the following statements is correct?

    a) The patient can receive *Epzicom*
    b) The patient cannot be dispensed *Ziagen*
    c) The patient can receive *Trizivir*
    d) The patient would be expected to launch an aggressive immune response against HIV
    e) The patient is not at risk for hypersensitivity reactions

24. Nucleoside reverse transcriptase inhibitors (NRTIs) are used for treatment of both HIV and for hepatitis. Which of the following statements are correct concerning NRTIs? (Select **ALL** that apply.)

    a) Ribavirin can increase the level of the NRTIs
    b) A patient using *Epivir* should be counseled to monitor for nausea with feelings of incredible muscle weakness (feeling like they can't move their arms and legs.)
    c) *Epivir HBV* and *Epivir* are interchangeable
    d) Entecavir must be taken with food

e) Common side effects with this class of drugs includes headache, fatigue, nausea, diarrhea, stomach pain and possible skin rash

25. Which of the following is correct regarding the need to test for HIV before starting HBV therapy? (Select **ALL** that apply.)

    a) Anti-virals used for HBV can have activity against HIV
    b) Anti-virals used for HBV use higher doses of drug than are needed for HIV activity
    c) HIV resistance can occur if HIV is unrecognized
    d) HIV resistance can occur if HIV is untreated
    e) HIV and HBV share similar routes of transmission

26. Which of the following statements concerning Yellow Fever are correct? (Select **ALL** that apply.)

    a) HIV patients with a CD4+ count less than 200/mm3 should not receive the yellow fever vaccine
    b) Patients using at least 5 mg of prednisone-equivalent daily for at least 7 days should not receive the yellow fever vaccine
    c) Patients using steroid inhalers at medium or high doses for asthma should not receive the yellow fever vaccine
    d) Patients with a hypersensitivity to eggs should not receive the yellow fever vaccine
    e) Patients receiving *Enbrel, Humira* or *Remicade* should not receive the yellow fever vaccine

27. What is the generic of Reyataz and it's mechanism of action?

    a) Abacavir; NRTI
    b) Atazanavir; protease inhibitor
    c) Atonavir; protease inhibitor
    d) Nelfinavir; entry inhibitor
    e) Darunavir; protease inhibitor

28. What is the generic of Complera?

    a) Efavirenz/emtricitabine/tenofovir DF
    b) Rilpivirine/emtricitabine/tenofovir DF
    c) Elvitegravir/cobcistat/emtricitabine/tenofovir alafenamide

d) Elvitegravir/cobcistat/emtricitabine/tenofovir DF
e) Dolutegravir/abacavir/lamivudine

29. Refer to the case question below:

History of Present Illness: KS is a 30 y/o female who comes to the ER today for worsening shortness of breath and cough. She is out of her albuterol inhaler. She occasionally lives on the street, but has been staying in the local homeless shelter for 3 nights. She reports fatigue, but denies night sweats and hemoptysis. Her cough is nonproductive. KS has mild right lower extremity cellulitis extending from right ankle to right calf. Patient states she scraped her leg on a fence and it has not healed.

Allergies: NKDA
Past Medical History: HIV x 5 years, PCP pneumonia 5 years ago when she was diagnosed with HIV, asthma, and dyslipidemia
Medications: *Truvada* 1 tablet daily, *Tivicay* 50 mg once daily, albuterol inhaler 1 puff 3-4 times daily as needed, *Flovent Diskus* 100 mcg BID, simvastatin 20 mg QHS

Physical Exam / Vitals:
Height: 5'2" Weight: 105 pounds
BP: 122/72 mmHg HR: 71 BPM RR: 18 BPM Temp: 103.2°F Pain: 3/10
General: Pleasant ill appearing female
Lungs: decreased breath sounds bilaterally – right worse than left. Mild wheezing
Ext: Mild right lower extremity cellulitis with some purulence

Labs:
Na (mEq/L) = 129 (135 – 145)   WBC (cells/mm3) = 10.4 (4 – 11 x 10^3)
K (mEq/L) = 3.5 (3.5 – 5)   Hgb (g/dL) = 13.4 (13.5 – 18 male, 12 – 16 female)
Cl (mEq/L) = 103 (95 – 103)   Hct (%) = 40.1 (38 – 50 male, 36 – 46 female)
AST (IU/L) = 62 (10 – 40)   ALT (IU/L) = 58 (10 – 40)
Albumin (g/dL) = 3.1 (3.5 – 5)

Plan: Obtain CD4+ count and viral load. Admit for IV antibiotics and additional diagnostic work-up.

Question: Based on chest Xray, KS will be treated empirically for PCP. An order is received for *Bactrim* 20 mg/kg/day IV divided Q6H. What is the correct dose for KS?

a) Bactrim 26 mg IV Q6H
b) Bactrim 160 mg IV Q6H
c) Bactrim 240 mg IV Q6H
d) Bactrim 300 mg IV Q6H
e) Bactrim 950 mg IV Q6H

30. Jeesy is a 41 year old male who is HIV positive and has reduced renal function with a CrCl of 24 ml/min who is on hemodialysis. He is currently taking Genvoya with Prezista. Which of the following is false? (Select **ALL** that apply.)

a) The patient cannot take Genvoya and needs to switch to an alternative agent
b) The patient can be switched to Truvada
c) The patient can continue his Genvoya and Prezista regimen
d) The patient can be switched to Atripla
e) Cobicistat in Genvoya should not be given less than 70 ml/min

31. What is the generic name for Selzentry and what is the binding target and host?

a) Maraviroc; CCR4/CXCR4 on Human CD4 cells
b) Maraviroc; CCR5 on Human CD4 cells
c) Maraviroc; CCR5 on HIV virus
d) Maraviroc; CCR4/CXCR4 on HIV virus
e) Maraviroc; CCR6 on HIV virus

32. What is the benefit of adding Norvir to an HIV regimen? (Select **ALL** that apply.)

a) Blocks first pass metabolism
b) Leads to higher concentrations of other HIV medications in regimen
c) Blockage of GLUT4 insulin-regulated transporter
d) At high doses, it can enhance other protease inhibitors
e) It inhibits the major P450 enzymes 3A4 and 2D6

33. A patient is prescribed *Atripla*. What are the components of *Atripla*?

a) Efavirenz, etravirine, delavirdine
b) Efavirenz, elvitegravir, rilpivirine
c) Emtricitabine, rilpivirine, tenofovir
d) Emtricitabine, efavirenz, tenofovir
e) Emtricitabine, tenofovir

34. Which of the following statements are true about HIV pre-exposure prophylaxis? (Select **ALL** that apply.)

   a) An individual who does not have HIV can take one *Truvada* tablet daily to reduce his risk of becoming infected.
   b) An individual who has HIV can take one *Atripla* tablet daily to reduce his risk of transmitting the virus
   c) The individual must be at a very high risk for acquiring HIV in order to be a candidate for pre-exposure prophylaxis
   d) The HIV test must be taken weekly when using pre-exposure prophylaxis therapy
   e) Once treatment is initiated, the individual no longer needs to follow safe sex practices

35. Which of the following HIV drugs needs to be refrigerated? (Select **ALL** that apply.)

   a) Fuzeon once mixed
   b) Norvir liquid
   c) Epivir liquid
   d) Aptivus + norvir before opening package
   e) Norvir capsules

36. A patient in the critical care unit is receiving *Precedex* for sedation. Which of the following statements concerning *Precedex* is correct?

   a) It is reconstituted in dextrose solutions only
   b) *Precedex* should only be given if a patient is also receiving a paralytic
   c) *Precedex* is an alpha2-adrenergic antagonist
   d) The maximum infusion duration is 48 hours
   e) Patients are more easily arousable and alert when stimulated, compared to propofol

37. What is the formulation of propofol?

   a) Oil-in-water emulsion
   b) Water-in-oil emulsion
   c) Suspension
   d) Water-soluble prodrug
   e) Solubilized in cremophor EL

38. A pharmacist is preparing an IVIG infusion. Which of the following statements is incorrect?

   a) If the patient experiences side effects such as nausea or a drop in blood pressure during the infusion, slowing the infusion rate may be helpful
   b) IVIG may come already in solution, or it may come as a powder that is reconstituted with diluent
   c) The IVIG dose is based on the Ideal Body Weight (IBW)
   d) If particles are present, the pharmacist should shake well to dissolve the particles prior to the infusion
   e) Certain patients respond to one IVIG brand better than another

39. You have a vial that contains 5 grams of drug and the chart to the right for mixing the drug for use. Nurses want to mix the vial so that it comes out with 200 mg per ml and ask you how much diluent they should add to make that concentration?

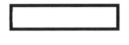

Diluent added	Concentration Resulting
9.6 mL	500 mg per mL
19.6 mL	250 mg per mL
49.6 mL	100 mg per mL

40. A bottle is labeled 0.89 PPM of Drug X. How many liters of this solution will contain 5 mg of Drug X? Round to the nearest tenth. Enter the number only. Do not enter units or commas.

41. A patient with recently-diagnosed active tuberculosis was prescribed isoniazid, rifampin, pyrazinamide and ethambutol. Which vitamin supplement is recommended with this regimen?

   a) Vitamin B1
   b) Vitamin B12
   c) Vitamin B2
   d) Vitamin B3
   e) Vitamin B6

42. What condition may be caused by a lack of vitamin B12 defiency?

    a) Microcytic anemia
    b) Macrocytic anemia
    c) Pernicious anemia
    d) Fanconi anemia
    e) Myelophthisic anemia

43. What is Benzyl Alcohol used for compounding?

    a) Preservative
    b) Binding agent
    c) Stabilizer
    d) Antioxidant
    e) Distillant

44. Click and select where a male patient may apply testosterone gel:

45. Application instructions for the hormone patches (estrogen, progestin and testosterone) include the following correct counseling points: (Select **ALL** that apply.)

a) Do not let children or animals near used patches; dispose of safely
b) Do not apply more than one patch at a time. Do not apply to broken/irritated skin
c) Estrogen patches can be used if the women has had breast cancer, but the oral formulations cannot be used with this history
d) Do not apply to the breasts or genitals
e) Can be applied to the lower abdomen

46. "Low T" is commonly treated in older men. Which of the following testosterone formulations is applied to the upper body as a gel? (where a t-shirt would cover)?

    a) Fortesta
    b) Androderm
    c) AndroGel
    d) Striant
    e) Testopel

47. A 78 year-old 135-pound male is hospitalized with a deep vein thromboembolism (DVT). He is receiving unfractionated heparin for DVT treatment. What does should he receive?

    a) Administer 4900 units IV bolus, then 1100 units/hour continuous infusion
    b) Administer 5000 units IV bolus, then 1300 units/hour continuous infusion
    c) Administer 5000 units SC every 8 to 12 hours
    d) Administer 7500 units SC every 12 hours
    e) Administer 8000-10,000 units IV initially, then 50-70 units/kg Q4-6 hours

48. Aslie is a four-year-old who is 37 pounds and 39.5 inches. She has a congenital ventricular septal defect and absence seizures, with breakthrough episodes on ethosuximide. She will be started on valproic acid at an initial dose of 15 mg/kg/day. Her parents will sprinkle the *Depakote Sprinkle* 125 mg capsules on food twice daily, with breakfast and with dinner. Which of the following counselling statements should be provided? (Select **ALL** that apply.)

    a) This drug may cause very bad and sometimes deadly liver problems. This most often happens within the first 6 months of using this drug. Call your child's doctor if your child has dark urine, is feeling tired, is not hungry, has an upset stomach, is throwing up, or has yellowing of the skin or eyes

b) This drug may cause very bad and sometimes deadly pancreas problems (pancreatitis). This could happen in children at any time during care. Symptoms of pancreatitis include tummy pain, upset stomach, throwing up, or not feeling hungry
c) This drug comes with an extra patient fact sheet called a Medication Guide
d) This drug may cause very bad birth defects if your child takes it while your child is pregnant. It can also cause the baby to have a lower IQ. Do not give this drug to prevent migraine headaches if your child is pregnant
e) It is important to chew the medicine thoroughly or not enough of the medicine will get into the child's body and the medicine may not work well

49. Select the correct statements concerning the drug interaction between valproic acid and lamotrigine. (Select **ALL** that apply.)

a) Valproic acid inhibits lamotrigine metabolism
b) This interaction increases the risk for a severe lamotrigine-induced rash
c) This interaction increases the risk for severe valproate-induced pancreatitis
d) When using these two medications concurrently, the *Lamictal Dose Titration* pack cannot be used; lower doses will be required
e) This interaction increases the risk for severe valproate-induced hepatotoxicity

50. A patient with COPD and seizures has been using theophylline and valproate for many years. Recently, the neurologist took the patient off valproate and started phenytoin due to an increase in seizure activity. The patient has been under a lot of stress lately and took up smoking again. She uses about 15 or 20 cigarettes daily. Which of the following statements are correct? (Select **ALL** that apply.)

a) The phenytoin will decrease the theophylline level and the patient may have impaired asthma control
b) The smoking will decrease the theophylline level and the patient may have impaired asthma control
c) The smoking will increase theophylline and the patient may experience toxicity
d) Smoking is a potent enzyme inhibitor
e) Smoking has little effect on theophylline levels but has a significant effect on clozapine levels

51. Which of the following statements concerning IV medications are correct? (Select **ALL** that apply.)
    a) Furosemide and metronidazole IV bags are not refrigerated
    b) Phenytoin IV requires a filter due to the potential for precipitation
    c) Sulfamethoxazole/trimethoprim and phenytoin IV are diluted with NS only
    d) Phenytoin IV has a maximum infusion rate of 50 mg/min
    e) Metronidazole IV does not require protection from light

52. What are possible complications with long-term phenytoin therapy? (Select **ALL** that apply.)

    a) Hirsutism
    b) Skin thickening (children)
    c) Shrinkage/atrophy of dental gum tissue
    d) Osteoporosis
    e) Hypertension

53. Which of the following anti-retroviral drugs would need dosage adjustment in patients with renal impairment?

    a) Tipranavir
    b) Raltegravir
    c) Emtricitabine
    d) Atazanavir
    e) Amprenavir

54. Which of the following is the most potent inhibitor of CYP2D6?

    a) Fluoxetine
    b) Paraoxetine
    c) Fluvoxamine
    d) Quinidine
    e) Ketoconazole

55. Which of the following enzymes or transporters is implicated in drug interactions with raltegravir?

    a) CYP3A4
    b) UGT1A1

c) P-GP
d) N-Acetyltransferase
e) Glutathione transferase

56. Which of the following antimicrobial agents is a useful alternative to vancomycin in treatment of MRSA infection?

    a) Clindamycin
    b) Metronidazole
    c) Penicillin
    d) Azithromycin
    e) Linezolid

57. Which of the following drugs can be used to reverse apnea and coma in a patient with opioid toxicity?

    a) Codeine
    b) Naloxone
    c) Methadone
    d) Pentazocine
    e) Nucynta

58. **Patient Name:** AJG   **Age:** 28   **Sex:** Male   **Race:** Caucasian   **Height:** 5' 10"
Weight: 76 kg   **Family history:** None   **Allergies:** NKDA

PMH: 5 year standing diagnosis of Bipolar disorder, Relapse of Bipolar disorder
MEDICATIONS: None upon admission

Patient arrived amidst a severe depressive episode. Patient self-discontinued use of paroxetine and lithium due to the side effects, as well as the need for therapeutic drug monitoring

Which of the following is appropriate dosage regimen for each of the listed medications?

    a) Lithium 3000 to 4000 mg per day
    b) Valproic acid 300 to 600 mg per day
    c) Lamotrigine 150 to 400 mg per day

d) Risperidone 30 to 60 mg per day
e) Topiramate 1000 to 2000 mg per day

59. A 68-year-old man with chronic lymphocytic leukemia was asymptomatic up until 3 months ago, when he started to develop increasing night sweats, fatigue, and weight loss. He also complained of easy bruising. Current labs include Hb 8 g/dL and platelets of 50,000/dL. His past medical history is significant for hypertension, which is treated with diltiazem and hydrochlorothiazide, and benign prostatic hypertrophy, which is treated with tamsulosin. His doctor is about to start this patient on alemtuzumab.

Which medication(s) is/are indicated in prophylaxis of infections caused by this agent?

a) Trimethoprim/sulfamethoxazole and famcyclovir
b) Trimethoprim/sulfamethoxazole, fluconazole, and acyclovir
c) No prophylaxis required
d) Gancyclovir and levofloxacin
e) Gancyclovir and fluconazole

60. A 23-year-old white female who is sexually active with multiple partners presents after noticing postcoital vaginal bleed. Her last pap smear was performed 3 years ago and it was normal. A mass lesion is visualized on the cervix. Further workup and cone biopsy of this lesion demonstrated locally advanced cervical cancer.

Which vaccine that is currently available could have prevented this patient's condition?

a) HSV vaccine
b) DTaP vaccine
c) Yellow fever vaccine
d) HPV vaccine
e) Flu vaccine

61. Which of the following statements describing pertinent pharmacokinetic and pharmacodynamic measures for different antibacterial agents is true?

a) AUC:MIC ratio is an appropriate measure for macrolides
b) Time > MIC is an appropriate measure for beta-lactams
c) AUC:MIC ratio is an appropriate measure for beta-lactams
d) Time > MIC is an appropriate measure for aminoglycosides

e) Time > MIC is an appropriate measure for azalides

62. DS is a 76-year-old male with a prior history of HTN and hyperlipidemia admitted yesterday to the CCU following a large anterior-wall MI. Current medications include: ASA 325mg po daily, nitroglycerin 0.4mg SL prn, metoprolol 50mg po BID, ramipril 5mg po daily, and atorvastatin 20mg po daily. Overnight, DS began experiencing runs of PVCs at a ventricular rate of 80 bpm despite his current therapy. A previous echo estimates an LVEF of 50%. The medical intern rotating through the CCU asks if metoprolol should be switched to sotalol to control PVC's.

DS converts to normal sinus rhythm. Approximately 1 hour later the team observes a party streamer-like wave-pattern on the EKG. What is now the drug of choice for DS?
a) Magnesium 2 g IV bolus
b) Epinephrine 1 mg IV bolus
c) Warfarin 5 mg PO daily
d) Amiodarone 300 mg IV bolus
e) Sotalol 50 mg PO daily

63. Which of the following is the regimen of choice for treatment of infection caused by Clostridium difficile?

a) Intravenous vancomycin 1 gm q 12 hr
b) Oral loperamide 4 mg 4 times daily
c) Oral vancomycin 125 mg 4 times daily
d) Oral metronidazole 500 mg 3 times daily
e) Intravenous vancomycin 1 gm q 6 hr

64. Which of the following medications can interact with vitamin D?

a) Aspirin
b) Orlistat
c) Vitamin C
d) Digoxin
e) Lidocaine

65. A patient is diagnosed with anxiety disorder and complains of the inability to fall asleep at night. Which hypnotic drug is most appropriate for this patient?

a) Triazolam
b) Zolpidem
c) Flurazepam
d) Ramelteon
e) Diphenhydramine

66. The antifungal agent ketoconazole is sometimes combined with cyclosporine to achieve which of the following therapeutic goals?

a) Increase cyclosporine levels
b) Reduce cyclosporine exposure
c) Reduce White blood cell count
d) Reduce infection potential
e) Reduce cyclosporine-related GI toxicity

67. A patient is receiving high-dose methotrexate and the nurse is about the start administering leucovorin rescue therapy. What is important to know regarding the administration of leucovorin:

a) Leucovorin should be administered concurrently with methotrexate
b) Leucovorin should not be administered at a rate >160 mg/min
c) Leucovorin should not be given with high-dose methotrexate (only low dose)
d) Leucovorin can be given with 72 hours of methotrexate
e) Leucovorin may increase the side effects of methotrexate

68. The physician is unable to obtain CSF after multiple attempts. Based on clinical findings, the team believes that the 13-day-old former 35-week gestational age baby may have meningitis. What is the best empirical therapy to begin in this baby before sending her to a pediatric hospital?

a) Ampicillin and gentamicin
b) Ceftriaxone and gentamicin
c) Vancomycin and cefotaxime
d) Ampicillin and ceftriaxone
e) Cephalexin and ampicillin

69. Jamie is a 20-year-old female patient who received kidney transplantation 3 months ago. She fills her prescription for tacrolimus, mycophenolate sodium, and prednisone at your pharmacy.

Which of the following represents two adverse effects specific to corticosteroids Jamie may experience?

a) Diarrhea and leukopenia
b) Alopecia and hyperglycemia
c) Water retention and osteoporosis
d) Hirsutism and nephrotoxicity
e) Blood in urine and bruising

70. The physician decides to start the 66-year-old woman on vancomycin, ampicillin, and ceftriaxone, but the patient has a history of difficult IV access. Which of the following is an appropriate plan for treatment of this patient's bacterial meningitis?

a) Attempt immediate IV line placement and administer antibiotics IV for the duration of therapy
b) Administer antibiotics orally for the duration of therapy
c) Administer antibiotics intramuscularly for the duration of therapy
d) Immediately insert an external ventricular drain into the brain and administer antibiotics intraventricularly for the duration of therapy
e) Administer antibiotics rectally for the duration of therapy

71. Select the medications that should be given to a patient before receiving paclitaxel.

a) Colony stimulating factors (eg, Filgrastim)
b) Diphenhydramine, dexamethasone, ranitidine
c) Amifostine
d) Dexrazoxane
e) Neulasta

72. F Which of the following combinations of antiretrovirals should be avoided? (Select **ALL** that apply.)

a) Rilpivirine and tenofovir
b) Efavirenz and nevirapine
c) Lamivudine and zidovudine
d) Fosamprenavir and ritonavir
e) Truvada and Atripla

73. Select the antineoplastic that may cause a disulfiram-like reaction when a patient drinks alcohol:

   a) Cisplatin
   b) Methotrexate
   c) Procarbazine
   d) Hydroxyurea
   e) Fluorouracil

74. A treatment experienced patient receiving atazanavir therapy should avoid the addition of which of the following medications? (Select **ALL** that apply.)

   a) Omeprazole
   b) Metronidazole
   c) Pravastatin
   d) Metoprolol
   e) Pantoprazole

75. JL is a 47-year-old Caucasian man who reports to his primary care physician complaining of a 2-week history of fatigue and fever. A CBC with differential reveals an elevated WBC (35,000 U/L) and profound thrombocytopenia (platelets 30,000 U/L). The patient is diagnosed with acute myeloid leukemia (AML-M4). Initial induction therapy should consist which of the following:

   a) Mitoxantrone
   b) Cytarabine + idarubicin
   c) Cytarabine + imatinib
   d) Asparaginase
   e) Avastin

76. The diagnostic criterion for which of the following opportunistic infections is seropositive for immunoglobulin G (IgG)?

   a) Candidiasis
   b) Toxoplasmosis
   c) MAC
   d) PCP
   e) IgE

77. Ryan is an HIV patient on the following medications: simvastatin, pantoprazole, TMP/SMZ, and as needed ibuprofen. Because his CD4 count has decreased, he is to be placed on MAC primary prophylaxis. Which of the following medications may be utilized for MAC prophylaxis? (Select **ALL** that apply.)

    a) Azithromycin
    b) Clarithromycin
    c) Clindamycin
    d) Clotrimazole
    e) Metronidazole

78. A 4-year-old girl with no significant past medical -history is admitted for suspected bacterial meningitis and started on empirical therapy with ceftriaxone and -vancomycin. What is the purpose of adding vancomycin to this empirical regimen for bacterial meningitis?

    a) To provide coverage against resistant *Listeria monocytogenes*
    b) To provide coverage against resistant *Neisseria meningitidis*
    c) To provide coverage against resistant *Streptococcus pneumoniae*
    d) Vancomycin is not needed in a 4-year-old with bacterial meningitis because *Staphylococcus aureus* is unlikely
    e) This patient needs *C. Difficile* coverage

79. A 70-year-old man presents with fever, nausea, vomiting, severe headache, and extreme photophobia. CSF results: WBC 2500 cells/mm3, 87% neutrophils, glucose 37 mg/dL, and protein 240 mg/dL. What type of CNS infection is considered based upon the information provided?

    a) Bacterial meningitis
    b) Aseptic meningitis
    c) Viral meningitis
    d) HSV encephalitis
    e) Viral meningitis

80. A 12-year-old boy presents to his pediatrician for a routine follow-up visit. The patient denies having any complaints. Physical exam, vital signs, and laboratory values are all within normal limits. Which of the following vaccinations should the patient receive today as part of routine care for a healthy adolescent?

a) PPSV23
   b) PPSV15
   c) MPSV4
   d) MCV4
   e) PCV13

81. A 70-year old patient with bacterial meningitis has a penicillin allergy but no signs of shortness of breath or respiratory distress. How would you treat this patient?

   a) Vancomycin
   b) Vancomycin and ceftriaxone
   c) Vancomycin, ceftriaxone, and ampicillin
   d) Ampicillin and ceftriaxone
   e) None of the above

82. BT is a 54-year-old African American man recently diagnosed with nonischemic cardiomyopathy. His past medical history is notable for moderate asthma since childhood and hypertension. Current medications include salmeterol 50 mcg, one inhalation twice daily; fluticasone 88 mcg, one inhalation twice daily, inhaled twice daily; furosemide 80 mg twice daily; enalapril 20 mg twice daily; and spironolactone 25 mg daily.

    Which of the following medication changes may provide further mortality benefit for BT once stabilized on β-blocker therapy?

   a) Digoxin 0.125 mg daily
   b) Combination hydralazine 25 mg and isosorbide dinitrate 10 mg TID
   c) Valsartan 160 mg twice daily
   d) Amlodipine 5 mg daily
   e) Entresto 5 mg daily

83. BT is a 54-year-old African American man recently diagnosed with nonischemic cardiomyopathy. His past medical history is notable for moderate asthma since childhood and hypertension. Current medications include salmeterol 50 mcg, one inhalation twice daily; fluticasone 88 mcg, one inhalation twice daily, inhaled twice daily; furosemide 80 mg twice daily; enalapril 20 mg twice daily; and spironolactone 25 mg daily.

Which of the following β-blockers is the best option to treat BT's heart failure and minimize aggravating his asthma?

a) Carvedilol
b) Metoprolol succinate
c) Propranolol
d) Atenolol
e) Nadolol

84. Select all that apply for the correct counselling for a patient picking up Orlistat:

a) Take vitamin supplements at least 2 hours before or after Orlistat
b) A nutritionally balanced diet should be maintained with 30% of calories from fat
c) Take a multivitamin with fat-soluble vitamins
d) If taking levothyroxine, administer at least 4 hours apart from Orlistat
e) The brand name of Orlistat is Xeniteel

85. What is Adcirca used to treat?

a) Erectile Dysfunction
b) Pulmonary Arterial Hypertension
c) Hyperlipidemia
d) Diabetes
e) Asthma

86. What is the preferred treatment option for a 48-year-old man with the diagnosis of asthma? Current complaints are wheezing in morning that gets better as day progresses. One episode of cough in last month and has required three courses of oral steroids within the last year. Current FEV1 = 55%.

a) Medium-dose inhaled corticosteroid (ICS)
b) Low-dose ICS and LABA
c) Medium-dose ICS and LABA
d) Theophylline
e) Brovana

87. What are the components of Symbicort?

a) Flucticasone/Salmeterol
b) Budesonide/Formoterol
c) Flucticasone furoate/vilanterol
d) Mometasone/Formoterol
e) Budesonide/Salmeterol

88. What drugs are used to treat pinworm? (Select **ALL** that apply.)

a) Pyrantel pamoate
b) Mebendazole
c) Metronidazole
d) Albendazole
e) Pantoprazole

89. What is another name of Phytonadione?

a) Vitamin K1
b) Vitamin B12
c) Vitamin E
d) Vitamin K3
e) Vitamin K2

90. Jamie is a 37-year-old female coming into your pharmacy to pick up Pylera. What condition does Jamie most likely have?

a) Heartburn
b) Upset stomach
c) H. Pylori
d) Flu
e) Common Cold

91. What are side effects of Erythropoiesis-stimulating agents (ESAs)? (Select **ALL** that apply.)

a) High blood pressure
b) Swelling
c) Pyrexia
d) Dizziness
e) Pain at injection site

92. What is the pathophysiology of Alzheimer's disease? (Select **ALL** that apply.)

    a) Plaques and tangles are present in the neurons of brain tissue
    b) Neuron signaling is interrupted and shortened
    c) Neurotransmitters are altered (i.e. decrease acetylcholine)
    d) Blood brain barrier presents with gaps and crevices
    e) The fluid and white matter in the brain become dry

93. Kara has a presentation coming up soon and she is under a lot of anxiety. Her main complaint is helping her sleep until she's done with the presentation. What benzodiazepine do you recommend to help Kara in the short term for a few days? (Select **ALL** that apply.)

    a) Temazepam
    b) Triazolam
    c) Flurazepam
    d) Estazolam
    e) Alprazolam

94. RA is taking Risperdal Consta for his bi-polar disorder. How often does his doctor need to administer his medication?

    a) Every two weeks
    b) Every four weeks
    c) Every day
    d) Once a week
    e) Every other day

95. What is the brand name of ziprasidone and olanzapine, respectively?

    a) Zyprexa, Geodon
    b) Geodon, Zyprexa
    c) Zyprexa, Seroquel
    d) Seroquel, Zyprexa
    e) Seroquel, Geodon

96. What is the active ingredient medication in Plan B?

    a) Levonorgestrel 1.5 mg
    b) Levonorgestrel 5 mg

c) Ulipristal acetate 30 mg
d) Ulipristal acetate 15 mg
e) Mifepristone 5 mg

97. What diagnostics are used to measure thyroid function? (Select **ALL** that apply.)

    a) Thyroid-Stimulating Hormone (TSH)
    b) Free thyoxine
    c) Free T4
    d) Total or free triiodothyronine
    e) Total or free T3

98. A patient is picking up Synthroid, what are counseling points to recommend? (Select **ALL** that apply.)

    a) The generic name is levothyroxine and may be cheaper
    b) Take Synthroid on an empty stomach 30-60 minutes before eating anytime during the day at changing intervals of morning and night
    c) Partial hair loss may occur in the first few months of therapy
    d) Drug should not be administered within 4 hours of iron, calcium supplements or antacids
    e) Notify your doctor if you have a rapid heartbeat, chest pain, or SOB

99. Select all of the following with the correct strengths and colors for warfarin:

    a) 1 mg Green
    b) 5 mg Peach
    c) 10 mg White
    d) 2 mg Blue
    e) 7.5 mg Yellow

100. Amitriptyline is structurally similar to what other medications? (Select **ALL** that apply.)

    a) Desipramine
    b) Cyclobenzaprine
    c) Doxepin
    d) Nortriptyline
    e) Imipramine

101. What counseling points should you give to a patient who is taking ibandronate? (Select **ALL** that apply.)

    a) You must sit upright or stand for at least one full hour after administration
    b) Take ibandronate first thing in the morning 1 hour before eating or drinking or taking any other medication
    c) Take ibandronate with a full glass (6-8 ounces) of mineral water
    d) If you develop signs of bone loss in the jaw, report to your doctor
    e) Ibandronate is used to treat or prevent osteoporosis in woman after menopause

102. Which of the following need to be turned into prodrugs? (Select **ALL** that apply).

    a) Clopidogrel
    b) Plavix
    c) Brillinta
    d) Effient
    e) Ticagrelor

103. What is a recommended drug reference for immunizations and injectables, respectively?

    a) CDC pink book, Trissels handbook
    b) CDC yellow book, Trissels handbook
    c) Briggs drugs, Remington's
    d) Trissels, CDC pink book
    e) Stafford guide, National Library of Medicine (NLM)

104. What is the mechanism of action of pramipexole?

    a) Norepinephrine agonist
    b) Serotonin agonist
    c) Norepinephrine and dopamine agonist
    d) Dopamine agonist
    e) Dopamine antagonist

105. Select all of the following medications used to treat relapsing-emitting multiple sclerosis?

a) Fingolimod
b) Teriflunomide
c) Amantadine
d) Pemoline
e) Glatiramer acetate

106. CR is a 1-year-old boy who was recently prescribed montelukast. What is the recommended dose, mechanism of action, and brand name respectively?

a) Montelukast 4 mg, leukotriene receptor antagonist, Singulair
b) Montelukast 10 mg, leukotriene receptor antagonist, Singulair
c) Montelukast 5 mg, leukotriene receptor antagonist, Accolate
d) Montelukast 1 mg, 5-lipoxygenase inhibitor, Zyflo
e) Montelukast 4 mg, 5-lipoxygenase inhibitor, Zyflo

107. JR is a new patient in your pharmacy. He brings in a few notes from his doctor stating, "ADHD with aggressive behavior" and is taking risperidone. What is risperidone used to treat? (Select **ALL** that apply).

a) ADHD
b) Aggressive behavior
c) Schizophrenia
d) Bipolar I Disorder
e) Irritability with autistic disorder

108. A 72-year-old male comes into your pharmacy asking for what vaccinations he needs to get to be "up-to-date". You review his profile and he received a shingles vaccine 5 years ago. What vaccines do you recommend? (Select **ALL** that apply).

a) Flu vaccine
b) Td/Tdap
c) PCV13
d) PPSV23
e) Zoster

109. A 26-year-old female comes into your pharmacy. She has a past medical history of HIV and is immunocompromised with a CD4 count less than 200. What vaccines should she avoid? (Select **ALL** that apply).

a) Zoster
b) Td/Tdap
c) MMR
d) Varicella
e) LAIV

110. Natalie comes into your pharmacy with her first born 18-month infant, Jeffe. She asks you what vaccines her Jeffe needs and states she never gave a vaccine to her child. What do you recommend? (Select **ALL** that apply).

a) HepB
b) DTaP
c) HiB
d) PCV13
e) MMR

111. Natalie comes back in with Jeffe again, her 18-month infant. It's flu season and she sees your pharmacy is advertising like crazy so she comes in to get a flu vaccine for Jeffe. She tells you Jeffe has an allergy to peanuts and what flu vaccine is okay to give to him. What vaccine do you recommend? (Select **ALL** that apply).

a) FluMist Quadrivalent vaccine
b) Flublok
c) Fluzone Intradermal flu vaccine
d) Fluzone Quadrivalent vaccine
e) FLUAD

112. James is a 64-year old male who has end stage renal disease on dialysis three times weekly. His provider ran labs and it has shown the following:
Calcium: 12.5 mg/dL
Phosphate: 6.5 mg/dL

What medication (s) do you recommend to the attending for Mr. James and for what condition, respectively? (Select **ALL** that apply).

a) Sevelamer; hyperphosphatemia
b) Renagel; hypercalcemia
c) Pamidronate; hyperphosphatemia
d) Fosamax; hyperphosphatemia
e) Sensipar; hypercalcemia

113. Which of the following affects the steady state plasma drug concentration for a constant infusion drug? (Select **ALL** that apply).

    a) Half-life
    b) Clearance
    c) V_d
    d) Infusion rate
    e) Dose

114. JR is an African American 64-year-old female who is currently taking metformin 500 mg by mouth twice daily and glyburide 5 mg once daily with a past medical history of diabetes. Her CrCl is 59 ml/min, SCr 1.4 mg/dL, eGFR 45 ml/min/1.73 m² and her A1c is 8.5%. She does not want insulin and refuses needle sticks. What would you recommend to JR's primary care physician? (Select **ALL** that apply).
    a) Discontinue metformin
    b) Double metformin from 500 mg to 1000 mg by mouth twice daily
    c) Increase glyburide frequency to glyburide 5 mg by mouth twice daily
    d) Recommend Novolin N/R
    e) Switch from glyburide to glimepiride 4 mg by mouth twice daily

115. Sammy is a 46-year-old male who was recently diagnosed with MRSA. What drugs listed below do NOT treat for MRSA?

    a) Doycycline
    b) Vancomycin
    c) Cefepime
    d) Oxacillin
    e) Daptomycin

116. Kelly is a 22-year-old pregnant female who comes into your pharmacy with her allergies acting up again. She asks you what she can take that would be non-drowsy as she has to get to work quickly. What do you recommend?

    a) Allegra
    b) Claritin
    c) Desloratadine
    d) Zyrtec
    e) Chlorpheniramine

117. Which insulin(s) can be stored outside of the refrigerator for up to 28 days only and not more? (Select **ALL** that apply).

   a) Levemir
   b) Novolin N
   c) Lantus
   d) Toujeo
   e) Novolin R

118. Which insulin provides a long, non-peak release?
   a) Glargine
   b) Levemir
   c) Novolin N
   d) Apidra
   e) Novolin R

119. Which antipsychotic comes in a sprinkle capsule formulation release?

   a) Topiramate
   b) Carbamazepine
   c) Lamotrigine
   d) Levetiracetam
   e) Primidone

120. You perform a medication therapy management call for a 67-year-old female patient. She has a part medical history of congestive heart failure (CHF), hypertension, depression, and COPD. Her current medication regimen is lisinopril, nitrostat PRN, ProAir, and Symbicort. She says her doctor wants to start her on a beta blocker medication and was wondering which one she should avoid due to her history of depression. What do you recommend for her to avoid?

   a) Propranolol
   b) Labetalol
   c) Carvedilol
   d) Atenolol
   e) Nadolol

121. JR is a 12-year-old male with a past medical history of bipolar disorder and ADHD. He recently tried Concerta but is failing treatment and doesn't like taking pills. His parents are requesting any recommendations to try something else. What do you recommend?

   a) Ritalin
   b) Focalin
   c) Adderall
   d) Daytrana
   e) Intuniv

122. What is the benefit of digoxin in patients with atrial fibrillation?

   a) Increased mortality benefit
   b) Restoring normal heart rate control
   c) Restoring normal sinus rhythm control
   d) Repairing leaky heart valves
   e) Increased mortality benefit in ventricular fibrillation

123. MC is a 45-year-old male with Schizophrenia and bipolar disorder. He also has congestive heart failure and atrial fibrillation. He asks you what medications he should avoid for something his doctor called, "QT Prolonging". What medications should you advise this patient to avoid? (Select **ALL** that apply).

   a) Abilify
   b) Seroquel
   c) Risperdal
   d) Zyprexa
   e) Invega

124. MR is a 54 year old male with a history of Hepatitis C. He has lots of anxiety in starting his new Harvoni treatment and hoping it "cures" him from his Hepatitis C. He asks you if he should try Kava. What do you recommend?

   a) Kava has shown benefit for anxiety and MR can take this herb
   b) Kava is like a benzodiazepine so it should provide fast relief
   c) Kava is safe and has not been linked to deaths for long-term use
   d) Kava is not safe due to hepatotoxicity and should be avoided
   e) Try Valerian instead of Kava due to less liver toxicity

125. MS is a 33-year-old nurse who complains of migraines. She is looking for an herb to help her with her migraines. What do you recommend?

   a) Kava
   b) Valerian
   c) Ginger
   d) Feverfew
   e) Coenzyme Q10

126. A frantic mother bursts into your pharmacy with her 4-year-old son who is autistic. Her doctor keeps asking her to get her son up to date on vaccinations but she wants to consult you as her trusty pharmacist for the evidence. What do you say to her?

   a) MMR vaccines have shown to cause autism
   b) Thimerosal-containing vaccines cause autism
   c) There is no association between vaccines and autism
   d) The antigens from vaccines cause autism
   e) Preservatives in vaccines cause autism

127. Brock, a 25-year-old male, suffered from a car accident recently. Otherwise he was a perfectly normal young adult. His current medical history is severe back pain and has no history of taking any medications. The prescriber prescribed Brock a fentanyl patch to help with the pain. What should you recommend to this patient?

   a) Fentanyl is a strong pain medication that will help provide relief
   b) Fentanyl should not be dispensed as Brock is opioid naïve and be at a high risk of respiratory depression and possibly death
   c) Fentanyl is a safe non-addictive choice for long-term pain relief
   d) Fentanyl should be dispensed as Brock is opioid naïve and will be at a low risk of respiratory depression and possibly death
   e) Fentanyl should be dispensed as it is a patch and Brock hates taking pills

128. Click on the body where low molecular weight heparins such as enoxaparin can be administered to a patient:

129. Which antipsychotics have lowest potential to worsen movement disorders? (Select **ALL** that apply).

   a) Chlorpromazine
   b) Fluphenazine
   c) Haloperidol
   d) Perphenazine
   e) Olanzapine

130. Timmy is a 64-year-old male who gets readmitted to your hospital and is on a tracheostomy. The nurse asks what she should use to clean his intra-tracheal tube to prevent pneumonia. What medication do you recommend?

   a) Bactrim
   b) Metronidazole
   c) Chlorhexidine
   d) Normal Saline and hydrogen peroxide
   e) Normal Saline

131. What is a major side effect of Sorbitol?

   a) Diarrhea
   b) Constipation
   c) Bleeding
   d) Bruising
   e) Sore throat

132. James had a recent heart attack and is placed on clopidogrel. His current medication history is: Clopidogrel, aspirin, metoprolol, nitrostat, pantoprazole, and fish oil. He presents a prescription with omeprazole, what counseling point do you recommend for Mr. James?

   a) It is safer to take omeprazole with your clopidogrel versus pantoprazole
   b) Evidence has shown it is safe to coadminister clopidogrel and PPIs
   c) Clopidogrel does interact with PPIs but it only applies to pantoprazole
   d) Clopidogrel does interact with PPIs but it only applies to omeprazole
   e) Pantoprazole has a major inhibitory effect on CYP2C19

133. A patient is a 67-year-old man weighing 246 lbs and standing 5'9 tall. What is this patient's body surface area?

134. A patient is a 23-year-old woman weighing 146 lbs and standing 5'3 tall. What is this patient's body surface area?

135. Kate, a recent pharmacist grad, is trying to find a good resource where she can find drug recalls. What resource do you recommend?

   a) CDC
   b) NIH
   c) FDA
   d) CMS
   e) NLM

136. Samantha is a 27-year-old female who comes into your pharmacy to pick up amoxicillin and fluticasone nasal spray. Her past medication history is Zyrtec and pseudoephedrine. What is the possible condition this patient has?

   a) Acute Sinusitis
   b) Allergic Rhinitis
   c) Bronchitis
   d) Lower Respiratory Tract Infection
   e) Sleep apnea

137. Jaris was recently diagnosed with gonorrhea and was prescribed aqueous procaine penicillin G 5 M units IM. What other condition may he have?

   a) Herpes
   b) Chlamydia
   c) Syphilis
   d) Urethritis
   e) HIV

138. Which of the following agents is a surfactant?

   a) Psyllium
   b) Docusate
   c) Senna
   d) Bisacodyl
   e) Milk of magnesia

139. What HIV medication can also be used to treat for Hepatitis B?

   a) Lamivuidine
   b) Efavirenz
   c) Abacavir
   d) Dolutegravir
   e) Rilpivirine

140. What medication can also be used to treat for Hepatitis C and HIV co-infection without regard for drug interactions?

   a) Daclatasvir
   b) Ledipasvir-Sofosbuvir
   c) Ombitasvir-Paritaprevir-Ritonavir
   d) Tenofovir alafenamide
   e) Ribavirin

141. How are interferons such as Pegasys administered in a patient?
   a) SQ
   b) IM
   c) IV
   d) Oral
   e) Rectal

142. TF is a 10-year-old female recently diagnosed with active tuberculosis. Her other medications include: methylphenidate 10 mg twice daily. She is HIV negative. Which medication should not be included in her regimen for TB?

   a) Isoniazid
   b) Rifampin
   c) Pyrazinamide
   d) Ethambutol
   e) Ribavirin

143. JK is a 32-year-old HIV-negative patient presenting to your clinic. He receives a Mantoux skin test that returns positive 2 days later. He was born in the United States and works as a prison guard. He injects heroin on a regular basis. His chest x-ray comes back normal, he has no symptoms of tuberculosis, and his smear culture is negative. What type of drug therapy would be appropriate for this patient?

   a) Isoniazid 300 mg daily x 9 months
   b) Rifampin 100 mg daily x 4 months
   c) No drug therapy needed
   d) Isoniazid 300 mg and rifampin 600 mg x 6 months
   e) Isoniazid, rifampin, ethambutol, and pyrazinamide

144. Which of the following is true regarding acid-fast bacteria?

   a) They retain their stained color even with acid-alcohol washes
   b) Cultures of acid-fast bacteria grow faster than other bacteria
   c) Mycobacterium tuberculosis is the only type of acid-fast bacteria
   d) They cause the majority of bacterial infectious diseases in the US
   e) They do not retain their stained color with acid-alcohol washes

145. SF is a 57-year-old male patient with a latent TB infection. He had a positive IGRA result and TST reaction of greater than 5 millimeters. He also has a past medical history of HIV but wants to wait before getting treated. How long can SF wait before getting treatment for his latent TB infection?

   a) 6 months
   b) 9 months
   c) 12 months
   d) Immediately; do not wait for treatment
   e) 3 months

146. Jamie is a 46-year-old female weighing 246 lbs and is 5'3". She has congestive heart failure, hypertension, and hyperlipidemia. She recently got a deep vein thrombosis in her left arm and was discharged on warfarin 5 mg daily. What is her INR target?

   a) INR 2.0 - 3.0
   b) INR 1.5 - 2.5
   c) INR 2.5
   d) INR 2.0
   e) INR 1.0 - 2.0

147. Jamie is a 46-year-old female weighing 246 lbs and is 5'3". She has congestive heart failure, hypertension, and hyperlipidemia. She comes back into the ER with another DVT in her left leg. What is the emergent treatment?

   a) Enoxaparin SQ 112 mg every 12 hours
   b) Enoxaparin SQ 52 mg every 12 hours
   c) Enoxaparin SQ 76 mg every 12 hours
   d) Xarelto 20 mg twice daily with food for 21 days
   e) Pradaxa 150 mg daily after parenteral anticoagulation

148. What is the mechanism of action of ropinirole?

   a) Direct replacement of dopamine in the central nervous system
   b) Inhibition of the enzymatic breakdown of dopamine in the CNS
   c) Inhibition of the enzymatic breakdown of dopamine in the periphery
   d) Direct stimulation of postsynaptic dopamine receptors
   e) Activation of enzymatic breakdown of dopamine in the periphery

149. Your long-term patient with Parkinson disease, WO, is complaining of hallucinations. She has no recent additions to her medication regimen or changes in medication doses. Her symptoms include visual hallucinations which are frightening to her. The decision is to initiate antipsychotic therapy. Which medication is the best initial treatment of Parkinson disease–associated psychosis?

   a) Chlorpromazine
   b) Haloperidol
   c) Olanzapine
   d) Alprazolam
   e) Quetiapine

150. SP was diagnosed with Parkinson disease 7 years ago. Originally, she was taking carbidopa/levodopa 25/100 mg po tid, which has since been increased to 50/250 mg po qid. Nonmotor symptoms include constipation and insomnia, and she also has arthritis for which she takes acetaminophen 650 mg po tid. Assuming another medication is to be added at this time, which medication would you suggest avoiding based on her history of present illness?

   a) Selegine
   b) Ropinirole
   c) Rasagiline
   d) Pramipexole
   e) Sinemet

151. Which drug should be dosed simultaneously with levodopa?

   a) Rasagiline
   b) Pramipexole
   c) Entacapone
   d) Amantadine
   e) Selegine

152. TS lives in a rural community where there is no neurology practice. For the last several years, he has been experiencing tremors, rigidity, and bradykinesia that began on his left side, but has since migrated and become bilateral, though his left side is still affected more than his right. He is diagnosed with Parkinson disease, and his motor symptoms are graded as moderate (tremor and bradykinesia) and moderate to severe (rigidity). What is the most appropriate order for the initiation and progression for his treatment?

   a) Carbidopa/levodopa, rotigotine, rasagiline
   b) Ropinirole, levodopa/carbidopa, tolcapone
   c) Pramipexole, entacapone, carbidopa/levodopa
   d) Benztropine, rasagiline, carbidopa/levodopa
   e) Rasagiline, rotigotine, carbidopa/levodopa

153. What is the concern of using Sinemet long-term?

   a) Taking Sinemet over time loses its efficacy
   b) Sinemet is effective for many years and its loss of efficacy is due to the progression of the disease than with duration of treatment

c) Taking Sinemet over time increases side effects and will cause more nausea
   d) Carbidopa will shift from blocking levodopa breakdown inside the CNS
   e) Taking Sinemet over times increases its efficacy

154. JR is a 45-year-old male with a history of an MI back in 2015. He had a bare metal stent placed to help prevent more blockages, is taking atorvastatin 40 mg daily and metoprolol 25 mg daily. What other medications should JR be on to help his stents last longer? (Select **ALL** that apply).

   a) Warfarin
   b) Aspirin
   c) Clopidogrel
   d) Xarelto
   e) Pradaxa

155. Rank in order the correct donning procedures per USP 797 for sterile compounding. (**ALL** options must be used.) Left-click the mouse to highlight, drag, and order the answer options.

   a) Perform hand hygiene, Wash hands
   b) Sanitize the gloves with 70% isopropyl alcohol and allow gloves to dry
   c) Don sterile powder-free gloves
   d) Place surgical scrub solution into palm and rub nails then work way to elbows. Pump again into other hand and repeat until both hands are sanitized. Ensure to sanitize hands using an ABHR and allow hands to dry
   e) Don shoe covers, hair and beard covers, and a face mask
   f) Don gown, fastened securely at the neck and wrists

156. Sammie is a 67-year-old male who has recently been diagnosed with osteoarthritis. His kidney function is poor with a CrCl of 30 ml/min. He comes to your pharmacy asking what he should take to help with the pain. What do you recommend?

   a) Ibuprofen
   b) Excedrin
   c) Advil
   d) Tylenol
   e) Naproxen

157. Sovanie is a 69-year-old female who has terrible GERD and heartburn. She is considering an NSAID to help with her pain. What NSAID would have the lowest risk of worsening her GERD?

   a) Etodolac
   b) Celebrex
   c) Mobic
   d) Nabumetone
   e) Indomethacin

158. Nancy is a 59-year-old female who has a past medical history of diabetes. Her most recent HbA1c is 7.1%. She has terrible foot callouses and is wondering how to treat them. What do you recommend?

   a) Use a butter knife to gentle remove the callus
   b) Use well-fitted walking shoes and inserts in addition to a pumice stone
   c) Use hydrogen peroxide and bleach to flake off the dead cells
   d) Use a Callus Chemical remover and soak foot in isopropyl alcohol
   e) Use Dr. Scholl's Salicyclic Acid and don't wear 100% cotton socks

159. DeeDee is a 57-year-old female with Sjogren's syndrome. She is complaining of dry mouth and hasn't tried anything yet to treat. What do you suggest as an initial option?

   a) Artificial Saliva
   b) Pilocarpine
   c) Cevimeline
   d) Chewing gum
   e) Tea

160. Celebe is a 29-year-old female who is taking Paroxetine, mirtazapine, and Adderall. She comes to your pharmacy concerned about serotonin syndrome. The nurse stated that she should be cautious to report these symptoms. What medications increase the risk of developing serotonin syndrome?

   a) Tramadol
   b) Percocet
   c) Mirtazapine
   d) Bupropion
   e) Cyproheptadine

161. What is the mechanism of action of how risperidone causes gynecomastia?

   a) Histaminergic receptor antagonist
   b) Norepinephrine receptor antagonist
   c) Serotonin receptor antagonist
   d) GABA receptor antagonist
   e) Dopamine receptor antagonist

162. What is aluminum acetate used for in compounding medications?

   a) Surfactant
   b) Preservative
   c) Topical astringent and antiseptic
   d) Wetting agent
   e) Plasticizer

163. Which inhalers need to be washed and how often? (Select **ALL** that apply).

   a) HFA inhalers, once a week
   b) Asthmaneprine, once a week
   c) Dry Powder inhalers, once a month
   d) CFC inhalers, once a month
   e) Actuator, once a week

164. What is the generic of Cardura and what is its mechanism of action?

   a) Terazosin, alpha 1 adrenergic receptor blocker
   b) Prazosin, alpha 2 adrenergic receptor blocker
   c) Tamsulosin, alpha 2 adrenergic receptor blocker
   d) Alfuzosin, alpha 2 adrenergic receptor blocker
   e) Doxazosin, alpha 1 adrenergic receptor blocker

165. A woman would like you to make a product selection to help her in case she experiences motion sickness and nausea on a deep sea fishing trip she plans to take during her summer vacation. What herbal do you recommend?
   a) Kava
   b) Valerian
   c) Ginger
   d) Emetrol
   e) Chocolate

166. A 17-year-old male cocaine addict develops substernal chest pain and is rushed to the emergency room by his friends. They reveal that he had been smoking 'crack' when the symptoms developed. An ECG is consistent with anterior wall myocardial ischemia. This effect on the heart is attributed to the drug. What is the mechanism of this effect?

   a) Direct inhibition of beta-adrenergic receptors
   b) Indirect stimulation of alpha-adrenergic receptors
   c) Direct stimulation of adenosine receptors
   d) Direct stimulation of beta-adrenergic receptors
   e) Indirect inhibition of alpha-adrenergic receptors

167. Ondansetron is commonly given to patients who exhibit nausea and vomiting associated with chemotherapy. The mechanism of the antiemetic effect of ondansetron is blocking which of the following central receptors?

   a) Dopamine receptors
   b) Histamine receptors
   c) Muscarinic cholinergic receptors
   d) Serotonin receptors
   e) Norepinephrine receptors

168. Select the genitourinary adverse reaction associated with cyclophosphamide.

   a) Cardiomyopathy
   b) Myelosuppression
   c) Ototoxicity
   d) Xerostomia
   e) Hemorrhagic cystitis

169. Select the chemoprotectant that is used to prevent nephrotoxicity and xerostomia.

   a) Leucovorin
   b) Mesna
   c) Amifostine
   d) Dexrazoxane
   e) Folic Acid

170. Which antineoplastic is associated with causing tinnitus?

   a) Cytarabine
   b) Cisplatin
   c) Cyclophosphamide
   d) Dactinomycin
   e) Ifosfamide

171. Select the antineoplastic that may cause a disulfiram-like reaction when a patient drinks alcohol:

   a) Cisplatin
   b) Methotrexate
   c) Hydroxyurea
   d) Procarbazine
   e) Ifosfamide

172. Using the diagram below, identify where in the HIV life-cycle maraviroc exerts its mechanism of action. (Select the **text** response, and left-click the mouse. To change your answer, move the cursor, select alternate **text** response, and click.)

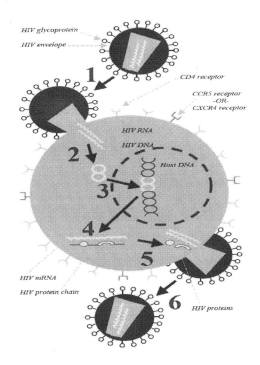

173. A patient is receiving doxorubicin. What major side effect should this patient be aware of and not be alarmed about?

   a) Nails turning bright orange or red
   b) Urine may appear red, dark brown, or orange
   c) Eyes drying
   d) Hirsutism
   e) Diarrhea

174. Using the diagram below, identify where in the HIV life-cycle efavirenz exerts its mechanism of action. (Select the **text** response, and left-click the mouse. To change your answer, move the cursor, select alternate **text** response, and click.)

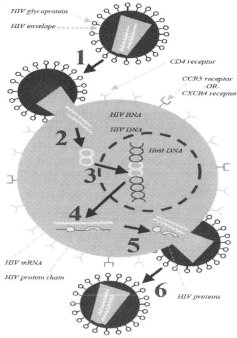

175. Using the diagram below, identify where in the HIV life-cycle raltegravir exerts its mechanism of action. (Select the **text** response, and left-click the mouse. To change your answer, move the cursor, select alternate **text** response, and click.)

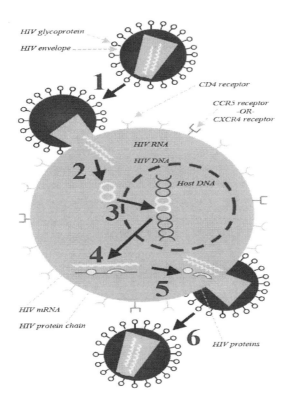

176. Using the diagram below, identify where on the cell platelet Clopidogrel exerts its mechanism of action. (Select the **text** response, and left-click the mouse. To change your answer, move the cursor, select alternate **text** response, and click.)

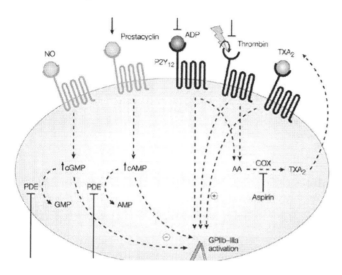

177. Using the diagram below, identify where on the cell platelet Eptifibatide exerts its mechanism of action. (Select the **text** response, and left-click the mouse. To change your answer, move the cursor, select alternate **text** response, and click.)

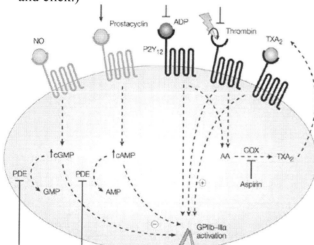

178. What is the maximum dose of Imodium per day?

   a) 5 mg
   b) 10 mg
   c) 16 mg
   d) 15 mg
   e) 20 mg

179. What is albuterol HFA and what type of device?

   a) Autohaler
   b) Handihaler
   c) Flexihaler
   d) Inhaler
   e) Nebulizer

180. What are the types of Risperdal formulations? (Select **ALL** that apply).

   a) Tablet
   b) Orally Dissolving Tablet
   c) Oral Solution
   d) Suspension IM Injection
   e) IV injection

181. Which bisphosphonate comes in IV injectable form? (Select **ALL** that apply).

   a) Boniva
   b) Fosamax
   c) Actonel
   d) Reclast
   e) Prolia

182. Which of the following has intrinsic sympathomimetic activity? (Select **ALL** that apply).

   a) Pindolol
   b) Nadolol
   c) Labetalol
   d) Acebutolol
   e) Metoprolol

183. What are the current market tablet doses of Allegra? (Select **ALL** that apply).
    a) 30 mg
    b) 60 mg
    c) 180 mg
    d) 50 mg
    e) 20 mg

184. Simps is a 36-year-old male picking up Welchol from your pharmacy. What are some counseling points for this medication? (Select **ALL** that apply).

    a) Welchol should be separated by 4 hours from other medications such as calcium, iron, and cholestyramine
    b) This medication is recommended for patients with greater than 500 mg/dL of serum triglyceride concentrations and patients using insulin
    c) Take a multivitamin at least 4 hours before Welchol
    d) Take fat-soluble vitamins A, D, E, and K at least 4 hours before Welchol
    e) A major side effect of Welchol is diarrhea

185. Which of the following are category X drugs? (Select **ALL** that apply).

    a) Warfarin
    b) Xanax
    c) Crestor
    d) Trexall
    e) Allegra

186. What are the side effects of trexall? (Select **ALL** that apply).

    a) Hirsutism
    b) Alopecia
    c) Thrombocytopenia
    d) Stomatitis
    e) Bleeding

187. What can be taken with Colyte? (Select **ALL** that apply).
    a) Pepsi
    b) Orange juice
    c) Clear broth
    d) Apple juice
    e) White grape juice

188. IO is 31 years old and starting a new job in a dental clinic. She wishes to quit smoking before she starts her new job because the clinic does not allow employees to smoke during their shift. However, she would also like to quit to preserve her lung health. She smokes approximately 15 cigarettes daily and has her first one in the car on the way to work (about 95 minutes after waking). She wishes to use the lozenges for her quit attempt. What product would you suggest that IO use?

   a) Nicotrol 4 mg
   b) Commit 2 mg
   c) Commit 4 mg
   d) Nicotrol 2 mg
   e) Commit 5 mg

189. LK is a 62-year-old woman with osteoporosis, chronic allergic rhinitis, and a 50-pack-year history of smoking cigarettes. At a recent trip to the dentist, she was told that due to poor oral hygiene and tooth decay, she needs her teeth removed and fitted for dentures. He also recommends that she quit smoking during this time period as it most likely contributed to her current predicament. Which agent listed below would be the best agent for LK to choose?

   a) Nicotine transdermal patch
   b) Nicotine nasal spray
   c) Nicotine lozenge
   d) Nicotine polacrilex gum
   e) Vapor cigarettes

190. JE is a 72-year-old man smoking one pack per day for the last 40 years of smoking history. He has never attempted to quit smoking, but wants to try after being hospitalized for pneumonia. While he was in the hospital he was given a nicotine patch to wear and change daily until discharge. Upon discharge, he was not given the nicotine patch, but wants to continue using it. What dose of the patch should JE start?

   a) 7 mg/d patch
   b) 14 mg/d patch
   c) 21 mg/d patch
   d) 30 mg/d patch
   e) He does not smoke enough to qualify for NRT with a patch

191. TY is a 40-year-old obese man with a medical history significant for hypertension and dyslipidemia. He also smokes cigarettes and has smoked 1.5 packs per day for the last 16 years. His most recent blood pressure was 161/94 mm Hg. His physician is convinced that if TY were to lose weight and quit smoking, many of his medical issues would be easier to manage. Which of the following medications would be the best choice for TY?

   a) Bupropion
   b) Catapres
   c) Nicotine polacrilex gum
   d) Nicotine patch
   e) Varenicline

192. Wernicke-Korsakoff syndrome is caused by what vitamin deficiency?

   a) Vitamin B1
   b) Vitamin B2
   c) Vitamin B12
   d) Riboflavin
   e) Pyridoxine

193. Dr. Smith calls your pharmacy and wants to know what to prescribe for his patient with primary early Lyme disease. The patient is a 33-year-old male. Which of the following agents would you recommend?

   a) Amoxicillin 500 mg PO TID x 14 days
   b) Itraconazole 400 mg PO BID x 14 days
   c) Fluconazole 400 mg PO daily x 14 days
   d) Ciprofloxacin 500 mg PO BID x 14 days
   e) Doxycycline 100 mg PO BID x 14 days

194. Dr. Smith calls your pharmacy again and wants to know what to prescribe for his patient with late Lyme neurologic disease. The patient is a 23-year-old female who got a tick bite a year ago. Which of the following agents would you recommend?

   a) Ceftriaxone 2 grams IV twice daily x 28 days
   b) Cefuroxime 500 mg PO daily x 14 days
   c) Ceftriaxone 2 grams IV once daily x 28 days
   d) Ciprofloxacin 500 mg PO BID x 14 days
   e) Doxycycline 100 mg PO BID x 14 days

195. Mark is a 49-year-old male who was recently diagnosed with mild-moderate *Clostridium difficile* and was treated with metronidazole 2 weeks ago. He now has his first recurrence of the same severity. What treatment should he receive now?

    a) Flagyl 500 mg IV Q6H
    b) Flagyl 500 mg PO TID
    c) Vancomycin 125 mg PO QID
    d) Vancomycin 500 mg PO QID
    e) Fidaxomicin 200 mg PO BID

196. Which of the following are high emetic drugs? (Select **ALL** that apply).

    a) Cisplatin
    b) Bleomycin
    c) Anthracycline
    d) Lomustine
    e) Bortezomib

197. What are the major side effects and toxicity of Cisplatin? (Select **ALL** that apply).

    a) Peripheral neuropathy
    b) Chemotherapy induced Nausea and Vomiting
    c) Nephrotoxicity
    d) Ototoxicity
    e) Anemia

198. Mary comes into your pharmacy with a prescription for amiodarone. She states how her friends say this is a "scary" drug and what her doctor needs to check to make sure she will be okay. What monitoring labs do you recommend? (Select **ALL** that apply).

    a) Hearing exams
    b) Ophthalmic exams
    c) Thyroid panel tests
    d) ECG and rhythm monitoring
    e) Liver function tests

199. JR is a frequent flyer in your pharmacy. He is taking amiodarone 800 mg daily and presents new prescriptions for simvastatin and lovastatin from two different prescribers. What are the max doses of simvastatin and lovastatin, respectively with amiodarone?

   a) Simvastatin 80 mg/day, lovastatin 20 mg/day
   b) Simvastatin 40 mg/day, lovastatin 40 mg/day
   c) Simvastatin 20 mg/day, lovastatin 20 mg/day
   d) Simvastatin 20 mg/day, lovastatin 40 mg/day
   e) Simvastatin 40 mg/day, lovastatin 80 mg/day

200. The American College of Cardiology (ACC) and American Heart Association (AHA) developed a staging classification of heart failure based on disease progression and risk factors. An asymptomatic patient with structural heart disease would be classified into which of the following stages?

   a) Stage A
   b) Stage B
   c) Stage C
   d) Stage D
   e) Stage E

201. Which of the following medical terms refers to the time until maximal level of anticancer drug-related toxicity on white blood cells or absolute neutrophil counts?

   a) Threshold
   b) Onset of effect
   c) Nadir
   d) Suppression time
   e) Time to maximum concentration

202. When differentiating Cushing syndrome and idiopathic Addison's disease, both can exhibit elevated levels of adrenocorticotropic hormone (ACTH). Additionally, Cushing's syndrome exhibits _____ levels of cortisol and Addison's disease exhibits _____ levels of cortisol

a) Elevated; decreased
b) Elevated; elevated
c) Decreased; elevated
d) Decreased; decreased
e) Cushing syndrome usually has a reduced level of ACTH

203. Patient Name: Sal
Age: 66   **Sex:** Male   **Race:** Caucasian   **Height:** 5'10"
Weight: 75 kg   **Family history:** None   **Allergies:** None
DIAGNOSES: Seizure, diabetes, mild obesity
MEDICATIONS: Phenytoin 400mg q hs, Phenobarbital 120 mg q hs, Insulin NPH/Reg 20U/10U q am and 10U/10U q pm
Gen: Mildly obese WM complaining of swelling and drainage from left foot
VS: 150/96, 85(regular), 38C, 14
HEENT: Nystagmus on lateral gaze
Neuro: Alert and oriented x 3, slight gait ataxia

LAB/DIAGNOSTIC TESTS

Na	138	Phenobarbital	25
BUN	22	Cl	99
WBC	17K	Hgb	15
Phenytoin	16	FBS	140
K	4.5	HCO3	24
SCr	1.5	Hct	45
Plts	300 K	Alb	2.5

Based on the information provided, what is the primary medical problem with respect to the phenytoin regimen?

a) Phenytoin-induced renal dysfunction
b) Phenytoin-induced hyperglycemia
c) Phenytoin-induced obesity
d) Phenytoin toxicity
e) Phenytoin-induced infection

204. Patients with heart failure have been traditionally classified into different New York Heart Association (NYHA) classes based on their presenting symptoms. A patient with symptoms associated with ordinary exertion would be classified into what NYHA category?
   a) Class I
   b) Class II
   c) Class III
   d) Class IV
   e) Class V

205. Choose the correct interpretation of the following arterial blood gas result: pH=7.6; pCO2=normal; HCO3=39mEq/L

   a) Metabolic acidosis
   b) Mixed acidosis
   c) Respiratory alkalosis
   d) Respiratory acidosis
   e) Metabolic alkalosis

206. What class of organisms appears purple on a Gram stain?

   a) Gram-positive organisms
   b) Gram-negative organisms
   c) Fungal organisms
   d) Atypical organisms
   e) Viral organisms

207. A TPN solution contains 750 mL of D5W. If each gram of dextrose provides 3.4 kcal, how many kcals would the TPN solution provide?

208. How many 60 mg tablets of codeine sulfate should be used to make this cough syrup?

Codeine SO4 30 mg/teaspoon
Cherry Syrup qs ad 150 mL
Sig: 1 teaspoonful every 6 hours as needed for cough

209. If 10 mL of a diluent is added to an injectable containing 0.5 g of a drug with a final volume of 7.3 mL, what is the final concentration of the parenteral solution in mg/mL?

210. An inhalant solution contains 0.025% w/v of a drug in 5 mL. Calculate the number of milligrams in this solution.

211. How many milliequivalents of potassium are in 240 mL of a 10% solution of KCL? The gram molecular weight is 74.5 g (K+ 39 atomic weight; Cl 35.5 atomic weight)

212. How many millimoles of HCl are contained in 130 mL of a 10% solution? Molecular weight = 36.5.

213. A medication order of a drug calls for a dose of 0.6 mg/kg to be administered to a child weighing 31 lb. The drug is to be supplied from a solution containing 0.25 g in 50 mL bottles. How many milliliters of this solution are required to fill this order?

214. How many milliliters of a 17% solution of benzalonium chloride are required to prepare 350 mL of a 1:750 w/v solution?

215. A solution contains 2 mEq of KCl/mL. If a TPN order calls for the addition of 180 mg of K+, how many milliliters of this solution should be used to provide the potassium required. Atomic weight of K = 39 and the atomic weight of Cl = 35.5

216. How many milliosmoles of sodium chloride are there in 1 L of a 0.9% solution of normal saline solution? Molecular weight of NaCl = 58.5

217. If 120 mL of a cough syrup contains 0.4 g of dextromethorphan, how many milligrams are contained in 1 teaspoonful?

218. How many milligrams of a drug would be contained in a 10 mL container of a 0.65% w/v solution of a drug?

219. Interferon injection contains 5 million U/mL. How many units are in 0.65 mL?

220. What is the percentage concentration (w/v) of a 250 mL solution containing 100 mEq of ammonium chloride? Molecular weight of NH_4Cl is 53.5

221. 437.5 grains equal how many ounces?

222. A study is evaluating the cost associated with anxiety due to an illness. What type of cost would anxiety represent? (Select **ALL** that apply).

a) Direct Medical
b) Direct nonmedical
c) Indirect
d) Intangible
e) Indirect nonmedical

223. What type of pharmacoeconomic analysis assumes the outcomes are equal?

a) Epidemiologic study
b) Parametric analysis
c) Cost-minimization
d) Retrospective study
e) Cost-effectiveness

224. A medical center located in the Northeast part of the United States is dealing with resistant bacterial organisms at their institution. Specifically, they are over whelmed with cases of extended spectrum β-lactamase gram negative rods. The medical center director charges pharmacy service with comparing different types of treatment to optimize clinical cure outcomes. Which of the following types of pharmacoeconomic evaluations should be conducted?

a) Cost-minimization analysis
b) Cost-benefit analysis
c) Cost-effectiveness analysis
d) Cost-utility analysis
e) Cost-maximization analysis

225. Which of the following pharmacoeconomic models evaluated adjusted life years?

a) Cost-minimization analysis
b) Cost-benefit analysis
c) Cost-effectiveness analysis
d) Cost-utility analysis
e) Cost-maximization analysis

226. The infusion rate of theophylline established for an infant is 0.08 mg/kg/h. How many milligrams of drug is needed for a 12-hour infusion bottle if the body weight is 16 lb?

227. What flow rate must be programmed into the PCA unit to obtain the desired amount of morphine per minute?

Dosing to start at 08:00 AM tomorrow
Morphine sulfate 500 mg in a 100-mL PCA unit to deliver 0.05 mg/min

228. You prepare a solution of ^{99m}Tc (40 mCi/mL) at 06:00 AM. If the solution is for administration at 12:00 PM at a dose of 20 mCi, how many milliliters of the original solution is needed? The half-life of the radioisotope is 6 hrs

229. Based on the below values, what is the sensitivity of this test?
Number of subjects ($n = 910$)

Results	Disease Present	Disease Not Present
Testing positive	80	20
Testing negative	10	800

230. Dopamine (intropin) 200 mg in 500 mL normal saline at 5 g/kg/min is ordered for a 155-lb patient. At what rate (mL/min) should the solution be infused to deliver the desired dose of 5 g/kg/min?

231. How many milliliters of normal saline should be mixed in a syringe with 1 mL of a 1:1,000 strength solution in order to obtain a 1:2,500 dilution?

232. What is the decay constant (k) of the radioisotope ^{32}P if its half-life is 14.3 days? Assume that radiopharmaceutical decay follows first-order kinetics.

233. View case below:

Parenteral admixture order   For: Alex Sanders, Room: M 704

Cefazolin sodium 400 mg in 100 mL normal saline   Infuse over 20 min q6h ATC for 3 days

Available in the pharmacy are cefazolin sodium 1-g vials with reconstitution directions of "addition of 2.5 mL SWFI will give 3.0 mL of solution." What infusion rate in mL/min should the nurse establish for each bottle?

234. A vial containing 1,000 units of an expensive drug powder is labeled "add 9 mL SWFI to obtain 100 units/mL." How many milliliters of diluent is needed if the nursing staff requests a concentration of 120 units/mL?

235. Based on the below values, what is the prevalence of disease in population tested?

Number of subjects ($n = 910$)

Results	Disease Present	Disease Not Present
Testing positive	80	20
Testing negative	10	800

236. If a Lantus insulin pen contains 100 units/mL, how many mLs would you need for a 20-unit dose?

   a) 2 mL
   b) 0.2 mL
   c) 0.5 mL
   d) 2.5 mL
   e) 3.0 mL

237. What is the minimum amount of a potent drug that may be weighed on a prescription balance with a sensitivity requirement of 6 mg if at least 95% accuracy is required?

   a) 6 mg
   b) 120 mg
   c) 180 mg
   d) 200 mg
   e) 300 mg

238. An ICU order reads "KCl 40 mEq in 1-liter NS. Infuse at 0.5 mEq/min". How many minutes will this bottle last on the patient?

   a) 20
   b) 500
   c) 1000
   d) 80
   e) 2000

239. The usual dose of sulfamethoxazole/trimethoprim (Bactrim®) is 150 mg TMP/m2/day in divided doses every 12 hours for PCP prophylaxis. What would be the usual dose for SG who is a 2-year-old male (Wt = 12 kg, Ht = 34")?

   a) 5 mg
   b) 10 mg
   c) 40 mg
   d) 80 mg
   e) 20 mg

240. After 1 month of therapy, all of the patients listed using the following data had a systolic blood pressure reduction of 10 mm with a standard deviation (SD) of ±5 mm. What percentage of patients had a reduction between 5 and 15 mm?

Patient	1	2	3	4	5
B.P.	140/70	160/84	180/88	190/90	150/70

241. A hospital pharmacy technician adds by syringe 20 mL of a concentrated sterile 2% w/v dye solution to a 250-mL commercial bag of sterile normal saline. A very accurate assay of the solution will probably result in the solution being which of the following?

a) Slightly stronger than calculated
b) Significantly stronger than calculated
c) Exactly as calculated
d) Significantly lower than desired
e) Slightly weaker than desired

242. Which of the following drugs may be an amphetamine type drug?

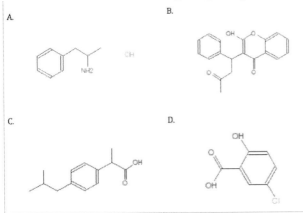

a) Drug D
b) Drug C
c) Drug B
d) Drug A
e) None of the above

243. Which of the following drugs may be sulfamethaoxazole?

A.

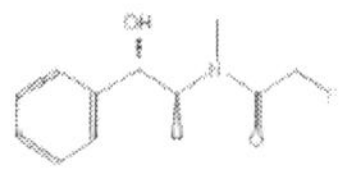

B.

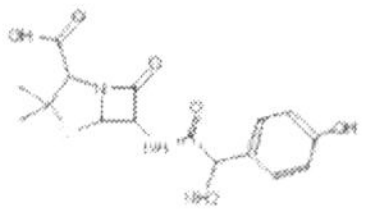

C.

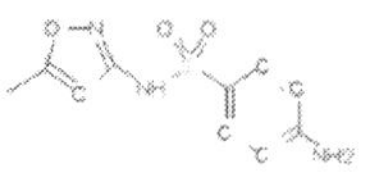

D.

a) Drug D
b) Drug C
c) Drug B
d) Drug A
e) None of the above

244. What is the following structure?

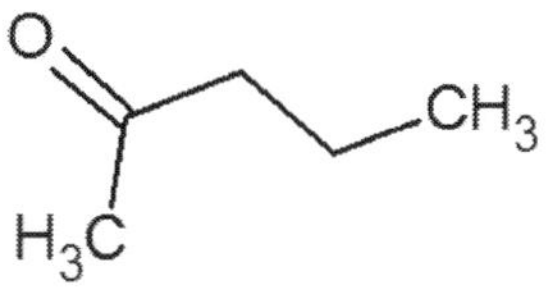

a) Carboxylic acid
b) Ester
c) Ether
d) Alcohol
e) Ketone

245. What is the following drug on the right?

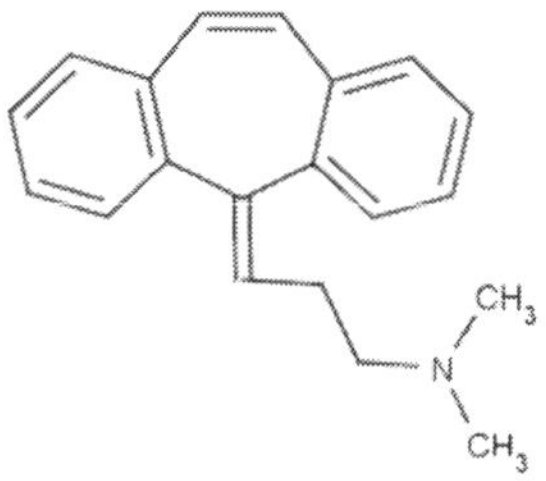

a) Cyclobenzaprine
b) Sildenafil
c) Tadalafil
d) Methotrexate
e) Isosorbide mononitrate

246. LM is an 20-year-old woman who is leaving for her first semester of college next month. She would like to know what vaccinations she needs before going to college. Her vaccination record shows the following: DTaP at 2, 4, 6, and 15 months, and 5 years; Hib (ActHIB) at 2, 4, and 6 months; PCV at 2, 4, 6, and 15 months; IPV at 2, 4, and 6 months, and 5 years; MMR at 15 months and 5 years; Varicella at 15 months and 5 years; Hep A at 12 and 18 months; Hep B at 11 years, 11 years 2 months, and 11 years 6 months; Tdap at 15 years. LM does not have any medical conditions and is not allergic to any medications or vaccines. What vaccines should LM receive today?

a) MPSV and HPV
b) Tdap and MCV
c) MCV and HPV
d) Tdap, MCV, and HPV
e) HPV, Varicella, MMR

247. Kaly, a 5-year-old girl, has an appointment today with her pediatrician to receive vaccines. Her vaccination record shows the following: Hep B at birth, 2 months, and 6 months; RV at 2, 4, and 6 months; DTaP at 2, 4, 6, and 15 months; Hib (ActHIB) at 2, 4, 6, and 15 months; PCV at 2, 4, 6, and 15 months; IPV at 2, 4, and 6 months; MMR at 15 months; Varicella at 15 months; and Hep A at 15 months. What vaccines should she receive today?

a) DTaP, IPV, MMR, Varicella, and Hep A
b) DT, PPSV, IPV, MMR, MCV, and Hep A
c) DTaP, PPSV, IPV, MMR, Varicella, and Hep A
d) Tdap, IPV, MMR, Varicella, and Hep A
e) DT, IPV, MMR, Hep A, HPV

248. TR is a 54-year-old man with HCV genotype 2 infection, he is treatment naïve. Which of the following would be the best treatment option for TR?

a) Peginterferon and ribavirin for 24 weeks
b) Sofosbuvir and ribavirin for 12 weeks
c) Sofosbuvir and daclatasvir for 12 weeks
d) Sofosbuvir and daclatasvir for 24 weeks
e) Sofosbuvir and velpatasvir for 12 weeks

249. Which of the following drugs has the highest incidence of hemolytic anemia?

a) Ribavirin
b) Peginterferon alpha 2a
c) Lamivudine
d) Tenofovir
e) Efavirenz

250. MJ is a 55-year-old African American man newly diagnosed with acute lymphoblastic leukemia (ALL). His physician has recommended part A hyper-CVAD regimen (cyclophosphamide, vincristine, doxorubicin, and dexamethasone)

Patient's specifics: Height 5'8", weight 180 lb
Notable laboratory test results: SrCr 1 mg/dL, total bilirubin 2.5 mg/dL
Dosing recommendations: CrCl <50 mL/min: No dosage adjustment necessary; serum bilirubin 1.2 to 3 mg/dL: Administer 50% of dose; serum bilirubin 3.1 to 5 mg/dL: Administer 25% of dose

Regimen
Cyclophosphamide 300 mg/m2 IV q12h days 1 to 3
Mesna 600 mg/m2 CIVI days 1 to 3
Vincristine 2 mg IV days 4 and 11
Doxorubicin 50 mg/m2 IV over 24 hours day 4
Dexamethasone 40 mg po days 1 to 4 and days 11 to 14

Why is MJ receiving mesna given continuously with cyclophosphamide on days 1 to 3?

a) Prevention of renal toxicity associated with cyclophosphamide
b) Neutropenic fever prophylaxis
c) Prevention of chemotherapy-induced nausea and vomiting
d) Reduction in incidence of cyclophosphamide-induced hemorrhagic cystitis
e) Prevention of hypocalcemia, hypouricemia, and hyperkalemia

Section 1 Calculations: Answers and Explanations

1. 1095

Ratio strengths are expressed in g/mL (or g/g) and are represented as 1:[value].
54 mg x 8 = 432 mg
432mg/1000 = 0.432 g

Recall that the conversion factor for a pint is 1 pt = 473 mL
0.432 g / 473 mL = 1 / x; x= 1095

2. 1069 mL

KCl volume = 18mEq x mL/2 mEq = 9mL
NaCl volume = 25 mEq x mL/4 mEq = 6.25 mL
Mg Sulfate volume = 10 mEq x mL/4.08 mEq = 2.45 mL
Calcium Gluconate volume= 15 mEq x mL/ 0.465 mEq = 32.26 mL
Potassium Phosphate volume = 17 mmol x mL/ 3 mmol = 5.67 mL

500 mL (AA) + 500 mL (Dextrose) + 6.25 mL (NaCl) + 9 mL (KCl) + 2.45 mL (Mg Sulfate) + 32.26 mL (CaGluconate) + 5.67 mL (Potassium Phosphate) + 10 mL (MVI) + 3 mL (TE) = 1068.63 mL

3. C. 2.82 kg

Molecular Weight (MW) = grams / 1 mole

Calculate the MW of calcium gluconate: 40(1) + 12(6) + 1(11) + 16(7) = 235 g/mole

Multiply by the number of moles present: 235 grams/mole x 12 moles = 2820 grams

Convert to kilograms: 2820 grams x 1 kg/1000 g = 2.82 kilograms

4. **B. 39 mL**

Specific gravity is a useful tool to convert between weight and volume. Remember the formula:

$$\text{Specific gravity} = \frac{\text{mass (in grams)}}{\text{Volume (in mL)}}$$

$$0.92 = \frac{36 \text{ g}}{X} \quad X = 39 \text{ mL}$$

5. **E. Give 0.8 mL by mouth every 6 to 8 hours**

Pharmacists are routinely expected to help parents evaluate appropriate doses of over the counter products for their children. In this case the following steps should be followed.
   a. Convert 15 pounds to kilograms. 1 kilogram is equal to 2.2 pounds. Divide 15 by 2.2=6.8kg is the child's weight in kg
   b. Multiply the child's weight by the dose range for acetaminophen. Multiply 6.8kg by 10mg/kg=68mg or 6.8kg by 15mg/kg=102mg. The dose range for the child for acetaminophen is from 68mg to 102mg.
   c. Finally convert the dose to a volume of medication. Multiply the dosage of medication by (0.8ml/80mg of acetaminophen). 68mgx(0.8/80mg)=0.7ml and 102mgx (0.8/80mg)=1ml. The infant's dose of acetaminophen should be between 0.7ml and 1ml.

An answer of 3.3ml or 5ml would be reached if the weight in pounds was multiplied by 2.2 instead of dividing appropriately. 1.5ml occurs if using 15 pounds without converting to kilograms. 0.8ml is a 2-fold error on the higher end of the dosing range.

6. **24**

Determine the molecular weight for calcium carbonate or $CaCO_3$

MW $CaCO_3$ = 40+12+16(3) MW = 100

Then, calculate mEq using the following formula: $mg = \frac{mEq \text{ (molecular weight)}}{\text{valence}}$

Valence = #ions x net charge

CaCO3¹ Ca⁺² + 1 [CO3]⁻² therefore valence = (1)(2) = 2

$$\frac{600 \text{ mg CaCO3}}{\text{dose}} \times \frac{2 \text{ doses}}{\text{day}} = 1200 \text{ mg/day}$$

$$1200 \text{ mg CaCO3} = \frac{x \text{ mEq}(100)}{2} \qquad x = 24 \text{ mEq}$$

7. **139 mg NaCl**

   Determine the weight, in mg, of Drug X and Drug Y:
   Drug X $\frac{0.004g}{100mL} = \frac{xg}{30mL}$ x = 0.0012g = 1.2mg
   Drug Y $\frac{1.2g}{100mL} = \frac{xg}{30mL}$ x = 0.36g = 360mg

   Determine the sodium chloride equivalents of Drug X and Y by multiplying weight by the E-value, and add them together:
   Drug X 1.2mg x 0.92 = 1.104mg
   Drug Y 360mg x 0.36 = 129.6mg
   1.104 + 129.6 = 130.7mg NaCl equivalents

   Determine how much sodium chloride would be necessary to make the solution isotonic, assuming no other compounds are present:

   $\frac{0.9g}{100mL} = \frac{xg}{30mL}$ x = 0.27g or 270mg

   Subtract the NaCl equivalents from the total NaCl needed to determine how much NaCl should be added: 270 - 130.7 = 139.3mg NaCl

8. **B. 5.91 grams**

   This calculation requires 3 steps:
   1) Calculate this patient's ideal body weight:
   IBW = 45.5 kg + 2.3kg(inches over 5')
   IBW = 45.5 kg + 2.3(7)
   IBW = 61.6 kg

   2) Calculate the maintenance dose:
   $\frac{2 \text{ mg}}{} = \frac{x \text{ mg}}{}$ x = 123.2 mg/hr

Kg IBW   61.6 kg

$\dfrac{123.2 \text{ mg}}{\text{Hr}} = \dfrac{x \text{ mg}}{48 \text{ hours}}$ x = 5913.6 mg

3) Convert the answer to grams: 5913.6 mg x (1 g/1000 mg) = 5.91 grams

9. B. 1.2 L

Determine the number of parts of high and low concentrations needed:
25   parts of high conc = 12-3 or 9 parts of 25%

   12

3   parts of low conc = 25-12 or 13 parts of 3%
                            22 parts total (12%)

Use the ratio to determine how much solution you can make with the 500 mL of high (25%) concentration solution:

High: $\dfrac{9 \text{ parts}}{22 \text{ parts}} = \dfrac{500 \text{ mL}}{x \text{ mL}}$ x = 1222 mL or 1.2 L

10. 54 mg

Determine the patient's body surface area:
BSA = $\dfrac{\sqrt{\text{height (cm) x weight (kg)}}}{3600} = \dfrac{\sqrt{180.34 \text{ cm x } 112 \text{ kg}}}{3600} = 2.37 \text{ m}^2$

Multiply the dose during the second phase by the BSA to obtain a daily dose:
45 mg/m2 x 2.37 m2 = 106.7mg or 107 mg

Divide the dose in half to determine the morning dose: 107 mg / 2 = 54 mg

11. B. 0.09 L

Density is the weight of a substance divided by volume, usually in grams/mL:
Density = $\dfrac{\text{weight}}{\text{Volume}}$

$\dfrac{0.62 \text{ g}}{1 \text{ mL}} = \dfrac{56 \text{ grams}}{x \text{ mL}}$ x = 90.3mL x 1 L/1000 mL = **0.09L**

12. B. 639 grams

The best way to solve this concentration problem is by setting up an alligation.

Available Strengths (%)	Desired Strength (%)	Parts
10.7		1.7 parts of 10.7%
	4.6	
2.9		6.1 parts of 2.9%
		= 7.8 total parts (of 4.6%)

If we know the final concentration is 4.6% and the total parts of the ointment are 7.8, we can use the ratio between parts of high/low concentration and total parts to determine how much ointment to prepare. Since we have a smaller amount of the 2.9% ointment, we can calculate the total amount prepared by assuming we will use all of it to prepare the 4.6% ointment.

$\dfrac{6.1 \text{ parts of 2.9\% ointment}}{7.8 \text{ parts of 4.6\% ointment}} = \dfrac{500 \text{g of 2.9\% ointment}}{x}$

x = 639 grams of 4.6% ointment

13. 14 bags

$\dfrac{50 \text{ mL}}{1 \text{ g}} \times 1.5 \text{ g} = \dfrac{75 \text{ mL}}{\text{dose}} \times \dfrac{3 \text{ doses}}{\text{day}} = \dfrac{225 \text{ mL}}{\text{day}} \times 3 \text{ days} = 675 \text{ mL};$ $675 \text{ mL} \times \dfrac{1 \text{ bag}}{50 \text{ mL}} = 13.5$ bags

14. E. 337 mg

To solve this problem, begin by converting the patient's weight to kg using the conversion factor of 2.2 lbs/kg: 145 lbs/ (2.2 lb/kg) = 66 kg

Multiply (1.7 mg/kg) x 66 kg = 112.2 mg for each dose. Each dose is given three times a day so the total daily dose is 112.2 mg x 3 = 336.6 or 337 mg

15. C. 31 mL

Specific gravity refers to the weight of a substance relative to the weight of an equal volume of water. At atmospheric pressure and room temperature this value is similar to the density of a substances, which is weight per volume:

SG @ $\dfrac{\text{weight}}{\text{volume}}$ $\dfrac{0.84 \text{ g}}{1 \text{ mL}} = \dfrac{26 \text{ g}}{\text{x mL}}$ x = 31 mL

16. 2.5%

Final dilution: Q1 (quantity) X C1 (concentration) = Q2 (quantity) X C2 (concentration)

(250 mL) X (20%) = (2000 mL) X (x %);   x = 2.5%

17. 774,000 mg

To solve equations involving moles, it is important to remember the formula below:
Molecular Weight = $\dfrac{\text{grams}}{1 \text{ mole}}$

Calculate the molecular weight of sodium citrate.
23(3) + 12(6) + 1(5) + 16(7) = 258 g/mole

Multiply by the number of moles present:
258 grams/mole x 3 moles = 774 grams

Convert to milligrams:
774 grams x 1000 mg/g = 774000 milligrams

18. B. 2.05 mg

Convert his weight in pounds to kg: $\dfrac{258 \text{ lb}}{\text{x kg}} = \dfrac{2.2 \text{ lb}}{1 \text{ kg}}$ x = 117.3 kg

Calculate the dose in mcg/kg: $\dfrac{17.5 \text{ mcg}}{\text{kg}} = \dfrac{\text{x mcg}}{117.3 \text{ kg}}$ x = 2052.75 mcg

Convert mcg to mg: 2052.75 mcg = 2.05 mg

19. 605 mL of Dextrose

W = 156 lb/2.2 lb x kg = 70.91 kg   H = 63 in x 2.54 cm/in = 160.02 cm   A = 31 years old

655 + (9.6 x 70.91 kg) + 1.8 x 160.02 cm) – (4.7 x 31 age) = 655 + 680.74 + 288.04 – 145.7 = 1478.08 kcal/day x 1.2 = 1773.69 kcal/day

Daily protein requirement (grams) = 0.75 g protein/kg x body weight (kg)/2.25 kg = 0.75 g protein x (156 lb x lb) = 51.18 gram protein

Daily protein requirement = 4 kcal/g = kcal from protein = 53.18 g x 4 kcal/g = 212.72 kcal from protein

53.18 kg x 100 mL/ 7g = 759.71 mL of amino acids

Total daily Calories x 30% = kcal of lipid/day = 1773.69 kcal/day x 0.3 = 532.11 kcal of lipids/day

Total Daily Calories – kcal protein – kcal lipids = kcal dextrose = 1773.69 kcal – 212.72 kcal – 532.11 kcal = 1028.86 kcal dextrose

1028.86 kcal dextrose x g/3.4 kcal = 3021.61 g dextrose x 100 mL/50 g = 605.22 mL Dextrose

20. E. 333 mL

Flow rate (mL/hr) = total volume (mL) = 1000 = 333.33 ml/hr
                    Infusion time (hr)   3

21. B. 24 mL

Percentage volume-in-volume indicates the number of parts by volume of the active ingredient contained in the total volume of the liquid preparation considered as 100 parts by volume. The answer to this problem can be found by multiplying the volume (in mL) by the percent (expressed as a decimal) to get the mL of active ingredient: 300 mL X 0.08 = 24 mL

2. D. 0.15 mg

50 mcg per ml would be equal to 150 mcg per 3 mL, which is the same as 0.15 mg in 3 mL

$\dfrac{50 \text{ mcg}}{1 \text{ mL}} \times 3 \text{ mL} = 150 \text{ mcg} \times \dfrac{1 \text{ mg}}{1000 \text{ mcg}} = 0.15 \text{ mg}$

3. C. 5.4 L

Convert tablespoons to mL:
$\dfrac{4 \text{ tbsp}}{x \text{ mL}} = \dfrac{1 \text{ tbsp}}{15 \text{ mL}}$ x = 60 mL per dose

Determine how many mL the patient would receive in a day:
$\dfrac{60 \text{ mL}}{\text{dose}} = \dfrac{x \text{ mL}}{3 \text{ doses}}$ x = 180 mL per day

Determine how many mL in a 30 day supply:
$\dfrac{180 \text{ mL}}{\text{day}} = \dfrac{x \text{ mL}}{30 \text{ days}}$ x = 5400 mL

Double check the question for the requested units. In this case, convert to liters: 5400 mL = 5.4 L

4. D. 34 grams

2 oz × $\dfrac{28.35 \text{ g}}{\text{oz}}$ = 56.7 g   Conversion factor: $\dfrac{56.7 \text{ g}}{1000 \text{ g}}$ = 0.0567 × 600 g = 34.02 g

5. 280 kcal

Calculate the number of grams of each component in 8 oz, or 240 ml (30 mL/fl.oz.), of liquid:

Protein
$\dfrac{6.9 \text{ g}}{100 \text{ ml}} = \dfrac{x}{240 \text{ ml}}$ x = 16.56 g

Fat
$\dfrac{3.2 \text{ g}}{100 \text{ ml}} = \dfrac{x}{240 \text{ ml}}$ x = 7.68 g

Carbohydrate
$\dfrac{15 \text{ g}}{100 \text{ ml}} = \dfrac{x}{240 \text{ ml}}$ x = 36 g

Calculate the number of calories. There are 9 calories/gram of fat and 4 calories/gram of carbohydrate and protein.

Protein
16.56 g x 4 cal/g = 66.24 kcal

Fat
7.68 g x 9 cal/g = 69.12 kcal

Carbohydrate
36 g x 4 cal/g = 144 kcal

Add the number of calories from each component to determine the total calorie intake.
66.24 kcal (protein) + 69.12 kcal (fat) + 144 kcal (carbohydrate) = 279 kcal

26. 35 drops

Determine how many mg of gentamicin solution will be added to the IV bag:
$$\frac{40 \text{ mg}}{\text{mL}} = \frac{127.5 \text{ mg}}{x \text{ mL}} \quad x = 3.2 \text{ mL}$$

Add the volume of the solution to the volume of gentamicin to obtain your total volume:
50 mL NS + 3.2 mL gentamicin solution = 53.2 mL total volume

Set up a chain of ratios to determine drops per minute:
$$\frac{(53.2 \text{ mL})}{30 \text{ min}} \quad \frac{(20 \text{ drops})}{\text{mL}} = 35.5 \text{ drops/min}$$

27. D. 1:25 (w/v)

$$\frac{40 \text{ mg}}{\text{mL}} \times \frac{1 \text{ g}}{1000 \text{ mg}} = \frac{40 \text{ g}}{1000 \text{ mL}} = \frac{0.04 \text{ g}}{\text{mL}} = \frac{1 \text{ mL}}{0.04 \text{ g}} = 25 \quad \text{thus} \quad 1:25 \text{ (w/v)}$$

28. A. 800 mg/day

At first, you may think the answer would be 40 mg/hr x 24 hr = 960 mg/day; however, aminophylline contains about 80% theophylline, which is the moiety measured in therapeutic drug monitoring. The appropriate conversion is 960 mg/day x 0.8 = 768 mg/day Theo-24 is available in 100 mg, 200 mg, 300 mg and 400 mg strength capsules. Round up to the appropriate unit dose available which would be 4 x 200 mg capsules/day or, more conveniently, 2 x 400 mg capsules/day

29. C. 1.316

Ratio strength is expressed as 1:x (g:mL for solid in liquid preparations). The easiest way to solve the problem is to set up an equation to solve for x:

$$\frac{0.380 \text{ g}}{120 \text{ ml}} = \frac{1}{x} \qquad x = 316 \text{ mL or } 1:316$$

The same concentration expressed as a percentage strength would be 0.32% (0.32 g/100 mL)

30. C. 26.25 ml/hr

For the 70kg patient - multiply 70 by 10 ug/kg/min= 700ug/min. Then multiply 700ug/min by 60 min/hr= 42,000ug/hr. Then multiply 42,000ug/hr by 250ml/400mg by 1000ug/mg=26.25ml/hr

31. 15.6

Determine the weight of the active ingredient in each product:

12.2% w/w $\quad \dfrac{12.2 \text{ g}}{100 \text{ g}} = \dfrac{x \text{ g}}{37.5 \text{ g}} \quad x = 4.575 \text{ g}$

17.6% w/w $\quad \dfrac{17.6 \text{ g}}{100 \text{ g}} = \dfrac{x \text{ g}}{62.5 \text{ g}} \quad x = 11 \text{ g}$

Add the weights together to determine the final weight: 4.575 g + 11 g = 15.575g
Divide the weight of the active ingredient by the final weight of the ointment to determine the final concentration:

$$\frac{15.75}{37.5\text{g} + 62.5\text{g}} = 15.575\% \text{ w/w}$$

32. 7

The formula to calculate mEq is: $\quad mg = \dfrac{mEq \text{ (molecular weight)}}{valence}$

Valence = # of ions x net charge; KCL =1 K+1 + 1 Cl-1; therefore, valence = (1)(1) = 1

500 mg KCl = $\dfrac{x \text{ mEq}(74.5)}{1}$ $\quad$ x = 6.7 or 7 mEq

33. 360

Calculate the molecular weight of potassium chloride (KCl) and sodium chloride (NaCl):
KCl = 1K+1 + 1Cl-1   MW = 39 + 35.5 = 74.5
Number of species formed = 2 (1 K + 1 Cl)

NaCl = 1 Na+1 + 1Cl-1   MW = 23 + 35.5 = 58.5
Number of species formed = 2 (1 Na + 1 Cl)

Determine mOsm, for each, using the formula: mOsm = $\frac{\text{weight (g)} \times 1000 \times \text{number of species}}{\text{MW}}$

KCl: mOsm = $\frac{0.5 \times 1000 \times 2}{74.5}$ = 13 mOsm in 250 mL

NaCl: mOsm = $\frac{2.25g \times 1000 \times 2}{58.5}$ = 77 mOsm in 250 mL

Normal saline is 0.9% w/v sodium chloride. Determine the weight of sodium chloride in 250 mL, you must set up a ratio using the 0.9% w/v and solve for the grams of sodium chloride:

$\frac{X \text{ mg}}{250 \text{ mL}} = \frac{0.9 \text{ g}}{100 \text{ mL}}$ X = 2.25 g

If there are 2 products, you need to figure out each one separately and add mOsm together:
13 mOsm KCl + 77 mOsm NaCl = 90 mOsm in 250 mL

Convert to liters, since osmolarity is reported as the number of millisomoles in 1 liter of solution:
$\frac{90 \text{ mOsm}}{250 \text{ mL}} = \frac{x \text{ mOsm}}{1000 \text{ mL}}$ x = 360 mOsm/L

34. 8.7 mmol

Molecular Weight = $\frac{\text{milligrams}}{1 \text{ millimole}}$

Calculate the total amount of potassium consumed: $\underline{680 \text{ mg}} \times 0.5 \text{ servings} = 340 \text{ mg}$ potassium
 serving

Use the formula to determine millimoles of potassium using the atomic weight of K (not Potassium Chloride):

$\dfrac{39 \text{ mg}}{\text{mmole}} = \dfrac{340}{\text{x mmol}} \qquad x = 8.7 \text{ mmol}$

35. A. 2.2 g/mL

Density is determined by dividing mass by volume. Density is usually reported in g/mL

$\text{Density} = \dfrac{\text{mass (g)}}{\text{Volume (mL)}} \qquad \text{Density of drug } z = \dfrac{55020 \text{ g}}{25000 \text{ ml}} = 2.2 \text{ g/mL}$

36. B. 1 gm in 10,000 mL

The abbreviation ppm stands for parts per million, or a concentration in grams per 1,000,000 mL of water. Therefore, 100 ppm would be equal to 100 grams in 1,000,000 mL of water, or 1 gram in 10,000 mL, or 1 gram in 10 L

37. C. 170 kcal

1 gram of dextrose provides 3.4 kilocalories (kcal). A 5% dextrose solution provides 5 gm/100 ml, or 50 gm in 1000 mL (1 L). The calories provided by the solution would be 50 gm x 3.4 kcal/gm = 170 kcal

38. 5.3 mg/gtt/day

$\text{Progesterone} = \dfrac{0.8 \text{ g}}{10 \text{ mL}} \times \dfrac{1 \text{ mL}}{15 \text{ gtt}} = \dfrac{0.00533 \text{ g}}{\text{gtt}} \times \dfrac{1000 \text{ mg}}{\text{g}} = 5.33 \text{ mg/gtt/day}$

39. A. 10 days

The patient is to receive 100 mL of a 500 mg/5 mL ciprofloxacin suspension. The directions are for the patient to take 1 teaspoon (5 mL) twice daily (Q12H and BID) till all is taken (tat):
2 teaspoons = 10 mL/day   100 mL/10 mL per day = 10 days

40. B. 30 mL

3 g x mL/0.5 g = 6 mL/bag x 5 bags = 30 mL

41. 1% (w/v)

10 mg/per ml would be equivalent to 1 gm/100 ml which is 1%

42. 0.08 mL

Insulins are dosed in terms of units of activity rather than milligrams or grams. "U-100" refers to a potency of 100 Units/mL of activity, while "U-500" refers to a potency of 500 Units/mL. The U-500 product is 5-times more concentrated. To convert dosing volumes the equation $C_1V_1 = C_2V_2$ is used:

(0.4 mL) (100 Units/mL) = (X) (500 Units/mL) where X (= 0.08 mL) is the volume of insulin

43. 11.6 mL

Specific gravity refers to the weight of a substance relative to the weight of an equal volume of water. At atmospheric pressure and room temperature this value is similar to the density of a substances, which is weight per volume:

SG @ weight/volume   0.43 g = 5 g   x = 11.6 mL
                          1 mL   x mL

44. D. 18.5 mmol

Millimoles formula:
Molecular Weight = milligrams / 1 millimole

Calculate the total amount of potassium consumed: 240mg x 3 servings = 720 mg potassium
Use the formula above to determine millimoles of potassium using the atomic weight of K (not Potassium Chloride):   39 mg = 720   x = 18.5 mmol
                                                                     1 mmole   x mmol

45. A. 1907 kcal

W = 198 lb x (kg / 2.2 lb) = 90 kg
H = 73 in x (2.54 cm / in) = 185.42 cm   A = 47 years old (yo)

66 + (13.7 x 90 kg) + (5 x 185.42 cm) - (6.8 x 47 yo) = 66 + 1233 + 927.1 - 319.60 = 1906.50

46. B. 0.37 kg

$$\text{Molecular Weight} = \frac{\text{grams}}{1 \text{ mole}}$$

Calculate the molecular weight of potassium chloride (KCl): 39 + 35.5 = 74.5 g/mole
Multiply by the number of moles present: 74.5 grams/mole x 5 moles = 372.5 grams
Convert to kilograms: 372.5 grams x 1 kg/1000 g = 0.37 kilograms

47. 30 gtt/min

$$\frac{50 \text{ g}}{\text{hr}} \times \frac{50 \text{ ml}}{1 \text{ g}} = 100 \text{ ml/hr} \times 18 \text{ gtt/ml} = \frac{1800 \text{ gtt}}{\text{hr}} \times \frac{\text{hr}}{60 \text{ min}} = 30 \text{ gtt/min}$$

48. A. 1.3 kg

$$\text{Molecular Weight (MW)} = \frac{\text{grams}}{1 \text{ mole}}$$

Calculate the MW of ferrous gluconate: 56(1) + 12(12) + 22(1) + 16(14) = 446 g/mole
Multiply by the number of moles present: 446 grams/mole x 3 moles = 1338 grams
Convert to kilograms: 1338 grams x 1 kg/1000 g = 1.3 kilograms

49. A. 119

$C_1Q_1 = C_2Q_2$ where Q = quantity and C = concentration

(2.7%)(x ml) = (10.7%)(30 mL);   X ml = 119 mL

50. 0.000154

It's important to know metric system: 1 gram = 1000 mg   1 mg = 1000 mcg   1 mcg = 1000 ng
To solve this problem: 154 ng / X = 1,000,000 ng / 1mg ; X = 0.000154 mg

Section 2 Calculations: Answers and Explanations

1. **C. 210 mg**

    The patient has been diagnosed with chronic kidney disease (CKD). Ferric citrate (Fe3+[C3O7]x ? y H2O (x = 0.7 – 0.87; y = 1.9 – 3.3) has an approximate average molecular weight of 265.93 g/mol; it is available as a 1 gram (1000 mg) oral tablet. Ferric chloride is used to treat hyperphosphatemia by formation of insoluble precipitates. According to the package insert, each gram of ferric citrate provides 210 milligrams of ferric iron:

    $$\frac{1000 \text{ mg ferric citrate}}{265.93 \text{ g/mol}} = \frac{X \text{ mg Fe3+}}{55.85 \text{ g/mol}} \quad X = 210 \text{ mg}$$

2. **1000**

    Mega (M) is 1000 times bigger than kilo. It's important to know the metric system.

3. **C. 32.36 mL**

    Calcium Gluconate volume = 15 mEq x mL/ 0.465 mEq = 32.26 mL

4. **0.4**

    Determine the weight, in g, of Drug Z and Drug X:
    Drug Z $\frac{0.05 \text{ g}}{100 \text{ mL}} = \frac{x \text{ g}}{60 \text{ mL}}$ x = 0.03 g   Drug X $\frac{2.7g}{100mL} = \frac{x \text{ g}}{60mL}$ x = 1.62 g

    Determine the sodium chloride equivalents of Drug Z and X and add them together:
    Drug Z 0.03 g x 0.82 = 0.0246 mg   Drug X 1.62 g x 0.07 = 0.1134 mg
    0.0246 + 0.1134= 0.138 g NaCl equivalents

    Determine how much sodium chloride would be necessary to make the solution isotonic, assuming no other compounds are present:
    $\frac{0.9 \text{ g}}{100mL} = \frac{x \text{ g}}{60mL}$ x = 0.54 g

Subtract the NaCl equivalents from the total NaCl needed to determine how much NaCl should be added: 0.540 – 0.138 = 0.402 g NaCl

5. **D. 2.7 L**

   Convert tablespoons to mL:
   $$\frac{2 \text{ tbsp}}{x \text{ mL}} = \frac{1 \text{ tbsp}}{15 \text{ mL}} \quad x = 30 \text{ mL per dose}$$

   Determine how many mL the patient would receive in a day:
   $$\frac{30 \text{ mL}}{\text{dose}} = \frac{x \text{ mL}}{3 \text{ doses}} \quad x = 90 \text{ mL per day}$$

   Determine how many mL in a 30 day supply:
   $$\frac{90 \text{ mL}}{\text{day}} = \frac{x \text{ mL}}{30 \text{ days}} \quad x = 2700 \text{ mL}$$

   Double check the question for the requested units. In this case, we need to convert to liters:
   $$2700 \text{ mL} \times \frac{1 \text{ L}}{1000 \text{ mL}} = 2.7 \text{ L}$$

6. **E. 9 mL**

   KCl volume = 18 mEq x mL/2 mEq = 9 mL

7. **18 mL**

   Specific gravity refers to the weight of a substance relative to the weight of an equal volume of water. At atmospheric pressure and room temperature this value is similar to the density of a substances, which is weight per volume:
   $$\text{SG @ } \frac{\text{weight}}{\text{volume}} \quad \frac{0.84 \text{ g}}{1 \text{ mL}} = \frac{15 \text{ g}}{x \text{ mL}} \quad x = 17.9 \text{ mL}$$

8. **B. 1:1,666 (w/v), 0.06%**

   $$30 \text{ mg} = 0.03 \text{ g}; \quad \frac{0.03 \text{ g}}{50 \text{ ml}} = \frac{x \text{ g}}{100 \text{ ml}}; \quad x = \frac{0.06 \text{ g}}{100 \text{ ml}} = 0.0006 = \frac{1 \text{ g}}{x \text{ ml}}; \quad x = 1,666$$

   ratio strength = 1: 1,666 (w/v)   Percent Strength= 0.06 g/100 ml x 100 = 0.06% (w/v)

9. **198 mg NaCl**

   Determine the weight, in mg, of Drug A and Drug B:
   Drug A $\underline{0.5 g} = \underline{x g}$ x = 0.9 g = 900 mg
               100 mL 180 mL
   Drug B $\underline{2 g} = \underline{x g}$ x = 3.6 g = 3600 mg
               100 mL 180 mL

   Determine the sodium chloride equivalents of Drug A and B and add them together:
   Drug A 900 mg x 0.54 = 486 mg   Drug B 3600 mg x 0.26 = 936 mg
   486 + 936 = 1422 mg NaCl equivalents

   Determine how much sodium chloride to make the solution isotonic (normal saline solution):
   $\underline{0.9 g} = \underline{x g}$ x = 1.62 g or 1620 mg
   100 mL 180 mL

   Subtract the NaCl equivalents from the total NaCl needed to determine how much NaCl should be added: 1620 - 1422 = 198 mg NaCl

10. **C. 180 mg/L**

    Valence of Mg is +2 and molecular weight is 24, 1 mEq equals 24 mg/2 = 12 mg so 1.5 mEq = 18 mg. For 18 mg in 100 mL, the corresponding strength in terms of mg/L will be 180 mg/L

11. **B. 2.45 mL**

    MgSulfate volume = 10 mEq x mL/ 4.08 mEq = 2.45 mL

12. **D. 588,000 mg**

    Molecular Weight (MW) = $\underline{\text{grams}}$
                                              1 mole
    Calculate the MW of sodium bicarbonate: 23(1) + 1(1) + 12(1) + 16(3) = 84 g/mole
    Multiply by the number of moles present: 84 grams/mole x 7 moles = 588 grams
    Convert to milligrams: 588 grams x 1000 mg/g = 588000 milligrams

13. **855 mL**

Determine the number of parts of high and low concentrations needed:
12.5   parts of high conc = (7 - 3) or 4 parts of 12.5%

3   parts of low conc = (12.5 - 7) or 5.5 parts of 7%
                              9.5 parts total (7%)

Use the ratio to determine how much solution you can make with the 360 mL of 12.5%:
High: $\frac{4 \text{ parts } 12.5\%}{9.5 \text{ parts } 7\%} = \frac{360 \text{ mL } 12.5\%}{x \text{ mL}}$ x = 855 mL of 7%

14. 1.7 mL

To maintain the buffer capacity of a buffer used in the compounding of ophthalmic products, it is recommended that approximately 1/3 of the final volume contains buffer. For this product, it requires a minimum of 5 mL/3, which is equal to 1.7 mL of Sorensen's Phosphate Buffer.

15. A. 50 drops/minute

The total volume (100 mL) will be infused over 30 minutes, a rate of 3.33 mL/minute. If the administration set delivers 15 drops/mL, set up a ratio to solve for drops per minute:

$\frac{15 \text{ drops}}{1 \text{ mL}} = \frac{x \text{ drops}}{3.33 \text{ mL/min}}$ x = 50 drops/minute

16. C. 28

BMI = weight (kg)/[height(m)]^2

Calculate the patient's weight in kg: 1 kg/2.2 lbs X 185 lbs = 84.1 kg

Calculate the patient's height in meters: 2.54 cm/1 in X 68 in X 1 m/100 cm = 1.72 m
1.72 m X 1.72 m = 2.96 m^2 84.1 kg/2.96 m2 = 28 kg/m^2

This patient's BMI indicates that he is overweight, and lifestyle modifications should be encouraged to help him reach a normal BMI (<25).

17. 75 tablets

30 mg daily/5 mg/tab = 6 tabs per day x 5 days = 30 tabs

25 mg daily/5 mg/tab = 5 tabs per day x 3 days =   15 tabs
20 mg daily/5 mg/tab = 4 tabs per day x 3 days =   12 tabs
15 mg daily/5 mg/tab = 3 tabs per day x 3 days =   9 tabs
10 mg daily/5 mg/tab = 2 tabs per day x 3 days =   6 tabs
5 mg daily/5 mg/tab = 1 tab per day x 3 days =   3 tabs
End of taper   75 tabs

18. A. 0.38 g

Convert her weight in pounds to kg: $\frac{140\ lb}{x\ kg} = \frac{2.2\ lb}{1\ kg}$ x = 63.6 kg

Calculate the dose in mg/kg: $\frac{6\ mg}{kg} = \frac{x\ mg}{63.6\ kg}$ x = 381.6 mg

Convert mg to g: 381.6 mg = 0.38 g

19. A. 1:10

Ratio strength is the expression of concentration of a pharmaceutical formulation by using a ratio. A 1% (w/v) percentage strength would indicate a ratio of 1 gram per 100 ml. The conversion from a 10% solution to x ratio strength would be 10 gm/100 ml = x part/100 parts where x = 10 and the ratio strength is 1:10.

20. 4628 kcal/day

Dextrose 500 ml x 70g/100 mL= 350 g x 3.4 kcal/g = 1190 kcal; 170 kcal + 1190 kcal=1360 kcal
KCl volume = 15mEq x mL/2 mEq = 7.5mL
NaCl volume = 20 mEq x mL/4 mEq = 5 mL
Mg Sulfate volume = 8 mEq x mL/4.08 mEq = 1.96 mL
Calcium Gluconate volume= 12 mEq x mL/ 0.465 mEq = 25.81 mL
Potassium Phosphate volume = 23 mmol x mL/ 3 mmol = 7.67 mL

500 mL (AA) + 500 mL (Dextrose) + 5 mL (NaCl) + 7.5 mL (KCl) + 1.96 mL (Mg Sulfate) + 25.81 mL (CaGluconate) + 7.67 mL (Potassium Phosphate) + 10 mL (MVI) = 1057.94 mL

1360 kcal/1058 mL x 150 mL/hr= 192.82 kcal/hr x 24 hr/day = 4,627.6 kcal/day

21. 390 mL

120 lbs/ 2.2 = 54.54 kg;   5g/kg x 54.54 kg = 272.73 g;   272.73 g x 100 mL/70g = 389.6 mL

22. E. 0.04 L

Specific gravity refers to the weight of a substance relative to the weight of an equal volume of water. At atmospheric pressure and room temperature this value is similar to the density of a substances, which is weight per volume: SG @ weight / volume

$\dfrac{0.62 \text{ g}}{1 \text{ mL}} = \dfrac{24 \text{ g}}{x \text{ mL}}$ x = 38.7 mL x $\dfrac{1 \text{ L}}{1000 \text{ mL}}$ = 0.04 L

23. 0.38 mL

A 0.025% mixture contains 0.25 mg of active ingredient per gram of total mixture (= 0.25 g AI /100 g oint x 1000 mg/g). The prescription for 60 grams requires 15 mg of triamcinolone acetonide (= 0.25 mg/1 g oint x 60 g oint). Since each vial contains 40 mg/mL, the prescription would require 15 mg/40 mg/mL = 0.375 mL. It is rounded up to 0.38 mL to accommodate the fact that 1 mL syringes are graduated only in 1/100 mL measurement.

24. C. Amoxicillin 250 mg/5 mL sig: 2 teaspoons PO Q12hr x 10 days

The patient weighs 33.3 kg. Dr. Santheimer wants him to receive 30 mg/kg per day, and he wants it divided into 2 doses. To calculate this multiply 33.3 kg by 30 mg/kg/day to get a total daily dose of 999 mg (approximately 1000 mg). Then, divide 1000 mg by 2 to get the dose for every 12 hours, and that equals 500 mg. To get approximately 500 mg in each dose, you would give 2 teaspoonfuls of Amoxicillin 250 mg/5ml q 12 hours for 10 days. An alternative is trying Amoxicillin 250 mg chewable tablets that the patient may also take, take 2 tablets by mouth twice daily for 10 days. The patient should be counseled on taking a probiotic after the antibiotic course to help replenish the gut flora and lessen concerns for GI upset.

25. 0.99 g/mL

Density is determined by dividing mass by volume. Density is usually reported in g/mL

Density = $\dfrac{\text{mass (g)}}{\text{Volume (mL)}}$ Density = $\dfrac{775 \text{ g}}{785 \text{ mL}}$ = 0.99 g/mL

26. A. 348 mOsm/L

Calculate the molecular weight of potassium chloride (KCl) and sodium chloride (NaCl):
KCl: MW = 39 + 35.5 = 74.5   NaCl: MW = 23 + 35.5 = 58.5
Determine mOsm, for each, using the formula below:

$$mOsm = \frac{weight\ (g)}{MW} \times 1000 \times number\ of\ species$$

KCl: mOsm = $\frac{0.75}{74.5}$ x 1000 x 2 = 20 mOsm in 500 mL

NaCl: mOsm = $\frac{4.5g}{58.5}$ x 1000 x 2 = 154 mOsm in 500 mL

If there are 2 products, you need to figure out each one separately and add mOsm together:
20 mOsm KCl + 154 mOsm NaCl = 174 mOsm in 500 mL

Convert to mOsm per liter:
$\frac{174\ mOsm}{500\ mL} = \frac{x\ mOsm}{1000\ mL}$ x = 348 mOsm/L

27. 25 days

Rx #889 is ProAir inhaler. With each fill, the patient receives 1 inhaler containing 200 puffs. The patient can use up to 2 puffs 4 times per day, which comes to a total of 8 puffs per day. 200 puffs total divided by 8 puffs per day equals 25 days; the patient's prescription will last of 25 days. If a patient is filling for ProAir every month then it is a sign their asthma is not well-controlled.

28. C. 5% dextrose in water

Dextrose at 5% concentration is isotonic and has the same osmotic pressure as blood. To determine the tonicity of the solution, convert the concentration of dextrose to an equivalent concentration of sodium chloride using the E-value ($E_{dextrose}$ = 0.18):

$\frac{5\ g\ dextrose}{100\ mL}$ x 0.18   = $\frac{0.9\ g\ NaCl}{100\ mL}$

29. 36 ml/min

To calculate CrCl, first calculate ideal body weight (IBW):

IBW = 45.5 kg + 2.3 kg (each inch >5 ft)

IBW = 45.5 kg + 2.3 kg (6) = 59.3 kg

Cockcroft-Gault equation for a <u>female</u>:
CrCl = (0.85) X [(140-age) X IBW (kg)]/(72 X Scr)
CrCl = (0.85) X [(140-41) X 59.3kg]/(72 X 1.8)
CrCl = (0.85) X (99 X 59.3)/136.8
CrCl = (0.85) X (45.29)
CrCl = 36.48, approximately 36.5 mL/min. Answer is rounded down to 36 ml/min

30. A. 100 drops/minute

The prescribed dose of Zantac is 50 mg and the drug is available as a 25 mg/mL solution. The volume of drug that should be injected into the 100 mL NSS bag is 50 mg x 1 mL/25 mg = 2 mL. The total volume of the infusion is therefore 100 mL + 2 mL = 102 mL. The physician has order the infusion to run for 20 minutes; the appropriate infusion rate would be 102 mL/20 min = 5.1 mL/min. Convert this value to drops/minute for the IV administration set: 5.1 mL/min x 20 drops/mL = 102 drops/min. Remember, the volume of Zantac being added to the IV bag is < 10% of the initial bag volume; it would be ignored in the calculation of the infusion rate: 100 mL/ 20 min = 5 mL/min x 20 drops/mL = 100 drops/min

31. D. 5 mL PO daily for 10 days

The patient weighs 39 lbs. Convert the weight from pounds to kilograms. There are 2.2 pounds per kilogram, so 39 lbs divided by 2.2 lbs/kg equals 17.73 kg. To calculate the daily dose, multiply the weight, 17.73kg, by 14 mg/kg to get 248.2 mg (approximately 250 mg) every 24 hours. You should then calculate the daily dose using the specified strength of 250 mg/5 ml. Multiply 250 mg by 5 ml and divide by 250 mg to get 5 ml.

32. 0.58 grams

Use the sodium chloride equivalent (E-value) method. First, determine the weight, in g, of Drug A and Drug B:

Drug A $\dfrac{0.75 \text{ g}}{100 \text{ mL}}$ = $\dfrac{X}{480 \text{ mL}}$ X = 3.6 g

Drug B $\dfrac{3 \text{ g}}{100 \text{ mL}}$ = $\dfrac{X}{480 \text{ mL}}$ X = 14.4 g

Determine the sodium chloride equivalents of Drug A and B and add them together:

Drug A 3.6 g x 0.52 = 1.872 g
Drug B 14.4 g x 0.13 = 1.872 g
1.872 + 1.872 = 3.744 g NaCl equivalents

Determine how much sodium chloride would be necessary to make the solution isotonic, assuming no other compounds are present (normal saline solution):

NSS $\dfrac{0.9 \text{ g}}{100 \text{ mL}} = \dfrac{X}{480 \text{ mL}}$ X = 4.32 g

Subtract the NaCl equivalents from the total NaCl needed to see how much NaCl to add:
4.320 – 3.744 = 0.576 g NaCl

33. 3 mL

Conversion Factor 45 mL/10 mL = 4.5
Amount of cherry flavor x conversion factor = 10 gtts x 4.5 = 45 gtts
Total drops x drop factor = 45 gtts x mL/15 gtts = 3 mL

34. 2 mL/min

$\dfrac{1 \text{ L}}{8.5 \text{ hr}} \times \dfrac{1000 \text{ mL}}{1 \text{ L}} = 117.64$ ml/hr x $\dfrac{\text{hr}}{60 \text{ min}} = 1.96$ ml/min = 2 ml/min

35. C. 26 mL

Calcium Gluconate volume = 12 mEq x mL/0.465 mEq = 25.81 mL = 26 mL

36. E. 39 Kcal

Calculate the number of grams of fat in 4 ounces, or 120 ml (30 mL/ fl.oz.), of liquid:
$\dfrac{3.6 \text{ g}}{100 \text{ ml}} = \dfrac{x}{120 \text{ ml}}$ x = 4.32 g
Calculate the number of calories from fat. There are 9 kcal/g of fat:
4.32 g x 9 kcal/g = 38.9 kcal

37. 1501 kcal/day

W = 136 lb/2.2 lb x kg = 61.82 kg   H = 65 in x 2.54 cm/in = 165.1 cm   A = 35 years old
655 + (9.6 x 61.82 kg) + 1.8 x 165.1 cm) – (4.7 x 35 age) = 655 + 593.5 + 166.9 – 164.5 = 1,250.9 kcal/day x 1.2 = 1501.08 kcal/day

38. C. 630 mL

Convert teaspoons to mL:
$\frac{3 \text{ tsp}}{x \text{ mL}} = \frac{1 \text{ tsp}}{5 \text{ mL}}$ x = 15 mL per dose

Determine how many mL the patient would receive in a day:
$\frac{15 \text{ mL}}{\text{dose}} = \frac{x \text{ mL}}{3 \text{ doses}}$ x = 45 mL per day

Determine how many mL in a 14 day supply:
$\frac{45 \text{ mL}}{\text{Day}} = \frac{x \text{ mL}}{14 \text{ days}}$ x = 630 mL

39. E. 100 mg TID

The patient should be given a gentamicin dose of 1.5 mg/kg IBW every 8-12 hours depending on renal function (CRCL). Ideal body weight (IBW) for adult males is calculated as 50 kg +(2.3)(Height), where height is given in inches over 5 feet. The patient is 5'7", calculate IBW = 50+ (2.3)(7) = 66.1 kg. Creatinine clearance (CRCL; mL/min) can be estimated using the
Cockcroft-Gault equation as follows: (140 – Age)(IBW) / (72)(SCr), where age is in years, IBW (ideal body weight) is in kilograms, and SCr (serum creatinine) is in mg/dL. CRCL = [(140 – 37)(66.1 kg) / (72)(0.8)] = 118.2 mL/min. Final dosing recommendation should be (1.5 mg/kg)(66.1 kg) = 99.15 mg every 8 hours = 100 mg every 8 hours (since CRCL > 60 mL/min).

40. A. 197

C1Q1 = C2Q2, where Q = quantity and C = concentration   1 pint = 473 mL

Determine the volume of a 0.12% solution needed to prepare 1 pint of a 0.07% solution:
0.12%(x mL) = 473 mL (0.07%)   X mL = 276 mL of 0.12% solution

Determine the amount of water to be added to the 0.12% solution by subtracting the volume of the 0.12% solution from the final volume: 473 mL – 276 mL = 197 mL

41. A. 1058 mL

KCl volume = 15 mEq x mL/2 mEq = 7.5 mL

NaCl volume = 20 mEq x mL/4 mEq = 5 mL
Mg Sulfate volume = 8 mEq x mL/4.08 mEq = 1.96 mL
Calcium Gluconate volume= 12 mEq x mL/ 0.465 mEq = 25.81 mL
Potassium Phosphate volume = 23 mmol x mL/ 3 mmol = 7.67 mL

500 mL (AA) + 500 mL (Dextrose) + 5 mL (NaCl) + 7.5 mL (KCl) + 1.96 mL (Mg Sulfate) + 25.81 mL (CaGluconate) + 7.67 mL (Potassium Phosphate) + 10 mL (MVI) = 1057.94 mL

42. 3.6 grams

Conversion Factor 45 mL/10 mL = 4.5
Amount of estrogen x conversion factor = 0.8 g x 4.5 = 3.6 g

43. B. 93.8 kg

Females: IBW = 45.5 kg + 2.3 kg for each inch over 5 feet
IBW = 45.5 kg + 2.3 (21) = 93.8

44. 760 mL

Daily protein requirement (grams) = 0.75 g protein/kg x body weight (kg)/2.25 kg = 0.75 g protein x (166 Ib x Ib) = 56.6 gram protein

Daily protein requirement (g) x 4 kcal/g = kcal from protein = 56.6 g x 4 kcal/g = 226.4 kcal from protein

56.6 kg x 100 mL/ 7g = 808.6 mL of amino acids

45. B. 2.54 mg/kg/dose

1) Divide the child's weight 13 lbs by 2.2 (1 lb=2.2 kg). The child weighs 5.91 kg
2) Divide the dose by the child's weight in kg – 15 mg/5.91 kg =2.54 mg/kg/dose
If the amount of mg/kg/day, rather than per dose, is calculated, then 5.1 mg/kg/dose is the result

46. 372 mg

BSA (m^2) = √ (Ht (in) x Wt (lb))/3131   BSA = √ (44 in x 70 lb)/3131   BSA = 0.99 m^2

Determine the dose:
$$\frac{375 \text{ mg}}{\text{m}^2} = \frac{x \text{ mg}}{0.99 \text{ m}^2} \quad = 372 \text{ mg}$$

7. 8.3 mL

Potassium phosphate volume = 25 mmol x ml/ 3 mmol = 8.3 mL

8. 0.06 mol

Molecular Weight = $\frac{\text{grams}}{1 \text{ mole}}$

Calculate the total amount of sodium consumed:
2(171 mg) x 3(192 mg) x 2(148 mg) x 4(27 mg) = 1322 mg sodium
1322 mg sodium x 1 g/1000 mg = 1.322 g sodium

Use the formula above to determine millimoles of sodium using the atomic weight of Na (not Sodium Chloride):

$$\frac{23 \text{ g Na}}{x \text{ mol}} = \frac{1.322}{} \quad x = 0.058 \text{ mol}$$

9. E. 360 mL

Convert tablespoons to mL: $\frac{4 \text{ tbsp}}{x \text{ mL}} = \frac{1 \text{ tbsp}}{15 \text{ mL}}$ $\quad x = 60$ mL per dose

Determine how many mL the patient would receive in a day:
$\frac{60 \text{ mL}}{\text{dose}} = \frac{x \text{ mL}}{3 \text{ doses}}$ $\quad x = 180$ mL per day

Determine how many mL in a 2-day supply: $\quad \frac{180 \text{ mL}}{\text{Day}} = \frac{x \text{ mL}}{2 \text{ days}} \quad x = 360$ mL

10. C. 250 ml/hr

Flow rate (ml/hr) = drug conc. (mg/ml) x infusion rate (mg/hr) = 500mg / hr x 200ml / 400mg = 250 ml/hr

Section 3 Calculations: Answers and Explanations

1. **0.23 mL**

   The prescription calls for 15 mL of a 0.35 % solution of cefazolin sodium: (0.35%)(15 mL) = 0.0525 g x 1000 mg/g = 52.5 mg of cefazolin. The vial contains 500 mg of cefazolin in a total reconstituted volume of 2.2 mL. Need total of: 2.2 mL/500 mg x 52.5 mg = 0.23 mL

2. **A. 80**

   Alligation alternate can be used to solve this problem. Determine the number of parts of high and low concentrations needed:

   ```
   25      parts of high conc = 15 - 10 or 5 parts of 25%
       15
   10      parts of low conc = 25-15 or 10 parts of 10%
                               15 parts total (15%)
   ```

   Use the ratio to determine the number of mL needed:
   High: 5 parts = x mL   x = 80 mL
         15 parts   240 mL

3. **C. 3 g**

   Conversion Factor: 10 g/1000g = 0.03   100 g x 0.03 = 3 g

4. **26 mOsm/L**

   Calculate the molecular weight of calcium chloride, or $CaCl_2$:
   MW = 40 + 35.5(2); MW = 111

   Determine the osmolarity (mOsm/L), using the formula below:
   mOsm/L = weight (g) x 1000 x number of species
              MW

   mOsm/L = 0.95 x 1000 x 3   mOsm/L = 25.68 or 26 mOsm/L
              111

5. **D. 4.9%**

    Determine the weight of the drug:
    $$\frac{x \text{ g}}{480 \text{ mL}} = \frac{15 \text{ g}}{100 \text{ mL}} \qquad x = 72 \text{ g}$$

    Determine the final volume: 480 mL + 1000 mL = 1480 mL

    Determine the concentration:
    $$\frac{72 \text{ g}}{1480 \text{ mL}} = \frac{x \text{ g}}{100 \text{ mL}} \qquad x = 4.9 \text{ g or } 4.9\%$$

    Strength of the diluted solution is calculated: C1V1 = C2V2: (15%)(480mL) = (C2)(1480 mL)
    C2 = 4.9%

6. **3**

    $$\text{BSA} = \sqrt{\frac{\text{height (cm)} \times \text{weight (kg)}}{3600}} = \sqrt{\frac{210.8 \text{ cm} \times 157.3 \text{ kg}}{3600}} = 3.03 \text{ m}^2$$

7. **B. 450 mL**

    According to the medication order, the patient is to receive 180 mmoles of sodium bicarbonate per liter of solution; 2.5 liters of solution is ordered. Sodium bicarbonate is available as a 8.4% solution (8.4 g/100 mL). First, using the molecular weight of the drug, convert the dose of sodium bicarbonate from mmoles to grams:

    $$\frac{180 \text{ mmoles}}{\text{L}} \times \frac{84 \text{ g}}{\text{mole}} \times \frac{1 \text{ mole}}{1000 \text{ mmole}} \times 2.5 \text{ L} = 37.8 \text{ g}$$

    Determine the volume of 8.4% sodium bicarbonate solution that will provide 37.8 g of the drug:
    $$\frac{8.4 \text{ g}}{100 \text{ mL}} = \frac{37.8 \text{ g}}{X} \qquad X = 450 \text{ mL}$$

8. **60 mL**

   Convert teaspoons to mL:
   $\dfrac{2\ tsp}{x\ mL} = \dfrac{1\ tsp}{5\ mL}\qquad x = 10\ mL\ per\ dose$

   Determine how many mL the patient would receive in a day:
   $\dfrac{10\ mL}{dose} = \dfrac{x\ mL}{3\ doses}\qquad x = 30\ mL\ per\ day$

   Determine how many mL in a 2-day supply:
   $\dfrac{30\ mL}{Day} = \dfrac{x\ mL}{2\ days}\qquad x = 60\ mL$

9. **D. 50 gtt/min**

   $\dfrac{0.5\ g}{hr} \times \dfrac{1000\ ml}{3\ g} = 166.67\ ml/hr \times 18\ gtt/ml = \dfrac{3{,}000\ gtt}{mL} \times \dfrac{hr}{60\ min} = 50\ gtt/min$

10. **A. 384 mL**

    17.5   parts of high conc = 15 - 5 or 10 parts of 17.5%
        15
    5   parts of low conc = 17.5 - 15 or 2.5 parts of 5%
                                            12.5 parts total (15%)

    Use the ratio to determine the number of mL needed:
    High: $\dfrac{10\ parts\ of\ 17.5\%}{12.5\ parts\ total\ (15\%)} = \dfrac{x\ mL}{480\ mL}\qquad x = 384\ mL$

11. **B. 15 mOsm**

    Calculate the molecular weight of calcium chloride ($CaCl_2$): $CaCl_2 = 1\ Ca^{2+} + 2\ Cl^-$
    MW = 40 + 35.5(2); MW = 111

    Number of species formed upon ionization = 3 (1 Ca^{2+} + 2 Cl^-)

    Determine mOsm, using the formula below: $mOsm = \dfrac{weight\ (g)}{MW} \times 1000 \times number\ of\ species$

    $mOsm = \dfrac{0.55}{111} \times 1000 \times 3;\qquad mOsm = 14.86\ or\ 15\ mOsm$

12. **C. 285 mg**

    Calculate this patient's ideal body weight:

    IBW = 45.5 kg + 2.3kg (inches over 5')
    IBW = 45.5 kg + 2.3(5)
    IBW = 57 kg

    Calculate the dose for the patient based on IBW:
    $$\frac{5 \text{ mg}}{\text{Kg IBW}} = \frac{x \text{ mg}}{57 \text{ kg}} \quad x = 285 \text{ mg}$$

13. **10 g**

    $$\frac{250 \text{ mg}}{5 \text{ mL}} = \frac{x \text{ mg}}{200 \text{ mL}} \quad x = \frac{250 + 200}{5} = 10{,}000 \text{ mg}$$

    $$\frac{250 \text{ mg}}{5 \text{ mL}} = \frac{50 \text{ mg} \times 200 \text{ mL}}{\text{mL}} = 10{,}000 \text{ mg} \times \frac{g}{1000 \text{ mL}} = 10 \text{ g}$$

14. **50 gtts/min**

    Flow rate (gtt/min) = 200 mL/hr × 15 gtts/mL × 1 hr/60 min = 50 gtts/min

15. **2.6 mL**

    The dose for Vincristine sulfate is 1.4mg/m^2. In order to calculate the dose for this patient, you need to calculate first the patient's body surface area (BSA): BSA = $\sqrt{((Ht \times Wt)/3600)}$, where height is in centimeters and weight is in kilograms. Therefore, BSA =$\sqrt{[(172.72 \text{ cm})(72.7)/3600]}$ = 1.87 m^2. The dose for this patient is then calculated as 1.4mg/m^2 × 1.87 m^2 = 2.61 mg. Vincristine is available as a 2 mg/2 mL solution for injection, the volume to inject into the infusion bag is (2.61 mg)/(2mg/2mL) = 2.61 mL, or 2.6 mL

16. **D. 213 kcal**

    Daily protein requirement (grams) = 0.75 g protein/kg × body weight (kg)/2.25 kg = 0.75 g protein × (156 lb × lb) = 51.18 gram protein

Daily protein requirement = 4 kcal/g = kcal from protein = 53.18 g x 4 kcal/g = 212.72 kcal from protein

17. A. 3.6 g

Conversion Factor 45 mL/10 mL = 4.5
Amount of progesterone x conversion factor = 0.8 g x 4.5 = 3.6 g

18. F

$$BSA = \frac{\sqrt{height\ (cm)\ x\ weight\ (kg)}}{3600} = \frac{\sqrt{180.34\ cm\ x\ 112\ kg}}{3600} = 2.37\ m^2$$

Determine the daily dose of prednisolone during every phase of the taper:
Phase 1 - 60 mg/m² x 2.37 m2 x 14 days = 1990.8 mg
Phase 2 - 45 mg/m² x 2.37 m2 x 14 days = 1493.1 mg
Phase 3 - 30 mg/m² x 2.37 m2 x 14 days = 995.4 mg
Phase 4 - 20 mg/m² x 2.37 m2 x 7 days (dose is every other day) = 331.8 mg
Total amount: 4811.1 mg

Set up a ratio to determine the volume needed:
$\frac{125\ mg}{5\ mL} = \frac{4811.1\ mg}{x\ mL}$ x = 192.4 mL

19. C. 1:605

Ratio strength is expressed as 1:x (g:mL for solid in liquid preparations).
$\frac{0.826\ g}{500\ ml} = \frac{1}{x}$ x = 605.33 mL or 1:605

20. 1445

W = 156 lb x (kg / 2.2 lb) = 70.9 kg
H = 63 in x (2.54 cm / in) = 160.02 cm   A = 38 years old (yo)

655 + (9.6 x 70.9 kg) + (1.8 x 160.02 cm) - (4.7 x 38 yo) = 655 + 680.64 + 288.04 – 178.6 = 1,445.08

21. E. 1.27 mL

The dose for fentanyl citrate sulfate is 100 mcg. Fentanyl citrate is available as a solution for injection containing 50 mcg/ mL of fentanyl base, the dose of fentanyl citrate needs to be converted to the equivalent dose of fentanyl base. This can be done using the molecular weights of the 2 drug forms:

Volume to inject into the infusion bag is:
$\dfrac{336.5 \text{ g/mole fentanyl base}}{528.6 \text{ g/mole fentanyl citrate}} \times 100 \text{ mcg fentanyl citrate} = 63.7 \text{ mcg fentanyl base}$

Volume of solution to be withdrawn from the vial to obtain the dose is:
$\dfrac{63.7 \text{ mcg fentanyl base}}{50 \text{ mcg/mL fentanyl base}} = 1.27 \text{ mL fentanyl citrate injection, USP}$

22. B. 9%

$\dfrac{x \text{ g}}{300 \text{ mL}} = \dfrac{15 \text{ g}}{100 \text{ mL}} \qquad x = 45 \text{ g}$

Determine the final volume prepared by combining the 15% solution and water:
200 mL + 300 mL = 500 mL

Determine the final concentration of solute:
$\dfrac{45 \text{ g}}{500 \text{ mL}} = \dfrac{x \text{ g}}{100 \text{ mL}} \qquad x = 9 \text{ g in 100 mL or 9\%}$

23. 7.2 L

$\dfrac{4 \text{ tbsp}}{x \text{ mL}} = \dfrac{1 \text{ tbsp}}{15 \text{ mL}} \qquad x = 60 \text{ mL per dose}$

Determine how many mL the patient would receive in a day:
$\dfrac{60 \text{ mL}}{\text{dose}} = \dfrac{x \text{ mL}}{4 \text{ doses}} \qquad x = 240 \text{ mL per day}$

Determine how many mL in a 30-day supply:
$\dfrac{240 \text{ mL}}{\text{Day}} = \dfrac{x \text{ mL}}{30 \text{ days}} \qquad x = 7200 \text{ mL}$

Double check the question for the requested units. Convert to liters: 7200 mL = 7.2 L

24. 75 drops/minute

The total volume (150 mL) will be infused over 60 minutes, a rate of 2.5 mL/minute. If the administration set delivers 30 drops/mL, set up a ratio to solve for drops per minute:

$$\frac{30 \text{ drops}}{1 \text{ mL}} = \frac{x \text{ drops}}{2.5 \text{ mL/min}} \qquad x = 75 \text{ drops/minute}$$

25. 225 tablets

The sig in the patient's profile calls for prednisone 60 mg daily for 3 days, then taper by 5 mg every 3 days to 10 mg daily. For the first 30 days:

60 mg/5 mg = 12 tablets daily for 3 days = 36 tablets
55 mg/5 mg = 11 tablets daily for 3 days = 33 tablets
50 mg/5 mg = 10 tablets daily for 3 days = 30 tablets
45 mg/5 mg = 9 tablets daily for 3 days = 27 tablets
40 mg/5 mg = 8 tablets daily for 3 days = 24 tablets
35 mg/5 mg = 7 tablets daily for 3 days = 21 tablets
30 mg/5 mg = 6 tablets daily for 3 days = 18 tablets
25 mg/5 mg = 5 tablets daily for 3 days = 15 tablets
20 mg/5 mg = 4 tablets daily for 3 days = 12 tablets
15 mg/5 mg = 3 tablets daily for 3 days = 9 tablets

Total number of tablets needed: 36+33+30+27+24+21+18+15+12+9=225 tablets

26. B. 25 days

This patient takes 5 mg per day which is the equivalent of 5 mg / (0.5 mg/mL) = 10 mL per day If a total volume of 250 mL; the total quantity of 250 ml divided by 10 ml per day equals 25 days

27. A. 1:625

Ratio strengths are expressed in g/mL for a solid dissolved in a liquid, such as the solution prepared in this problem, and are usually represented as 1:X.
100 mg x 4 = 400 mg = 0.4 g

$$\frac{0.4 \text{ g}}{250 \text{ ml}} = \frac{1}{x} = 625$$

28. D. 0.518 g

$$\frac{190 \text{ lb}}{x \text{ kg}} = \frac{2.2 \text{ lb}}{1 \text{ kg}} \qquad x = 86.4 \text{ kg}$$

Calculate the dose in mg/kg: $\frac{6 \text{ mg}}{\text{kg}} = \frac{x \text{ mg}}{86.4 \text{ kg}} \qquad x = 518.4 \text{ mg} = 0.518 \text{ g}$

29. 90 mL

According to the medication order, the patient is to receive 90 mmoles of sodium chloride per liter of solution; 2.5 liters of solution is ordered. Sodium chloride is available as a 14.6% solution (14.6 g/100 mL). Using the molecular weight of the drug, convert the dose of sodium chloride from mmoles to grams:

$$\frac{90 \text{ mmoles}}{\text{L}} \times \frac{58.5 \text{ g}}{\text{mole}} \times \frac{1 \text{ mole}}{1000 \text{ mmole}} \times 2.5 \text{ L} = 13.16 \text{ g}$$

Determine the volume of 14.6% sodium chloride solution that will provide 13.16 g of the drug:

$$\frac{14.6 \text{ g}}{100 \text{ mL}} = \frac{13.16 \text{ g}}{X} \qquad X = 90.1 \text{ mL}$$

30. 40 kg/m²

Body Mass Index (BMI) is calculated by dividing the patients weight in kg by the patient's height in meters squared. To accomplish this, first convert the weight from lbs to kg. There are 2.2 lbs per kg, so 250lbs divided by 2.2 lbs/kg equals 113.4 kg. Convert the height to meters. There are 12 inches per foot and this patient is 6 feet and 1 inch tall. So 5 feet multiplied by 12 inches/foot equals 60. Adding the 6 additional inches equals 66 in total. There are 39.37 inches per meter. So, divide 66 inches by 39.37 inches/meter, and this equals 1.68 m. To complete the calculation, divide 113.4 kg by (1.68 m x 1.68 m) to equal a BMI of 40.2 kg/m²

31. B. 74.5 mL

Conversion Factor = 240 ml / 5.8 parts = 41.38
1.8 part Nystatin x conversion factor = 1.8 x 41.38 = 74.5

32. C. 25

Determine how many mg of gentamicin solution will be added to the IV bag:

1.7 mg x 75 kg = 127.5 mg

Determine how many mL are needed to prepare each dose:
$$\frac{40 \text{ mg}}{\text{mL}} = \frac{127.5 \text{ mg}}{x \text{ mL}} \quad x = 3.2 \text{ mL}$$

Determine how many vials are needed per day:
3.2 mL x 3 doses = 9.6 mL/2 mL per vial

If 1 day requires 4.8 vials, and all doses for each day are made together, 5 vials are needed to prepare 1 day's worth of doses. Multiply the number of vials needed per day by the duration of therapy: 5 vials per day x 5 days = 25 vials

The order in which this calculation is solved is very important. If you calculate the total amount (in mg) needed and divide by 5, your number is 23.9 or 24 vials. This is not correct because the vials are single use; partial vials cannot be carried over to the next day.

33. B. Volume of Distribution

The volume of distribution of a drug multiplied by the desirable target concentration (or desirable change in concentration) will provide the numerical value of the amount of drug required for administration as a single dose. Clearance is useful for calculating the maintenance dose to be administered chronically. The protein binding of a drug can affect the distribution space but will not be useful in determining the dose required. The elimination half-life refers to the time interval for 50% of the dose to be eliminated. The oral bioavailability refers to the percent of an orally administered drug that reaches the systemic circulation.

34. E. 7 mL every 12 hours for 7 days

Find the patient's weight in kilograms:
56 lbs X 1 kg/2.2 lbs = 25.5 kg
The sig for this cefdinir prescription requires 7 mg/kg every 12 hours for 7 days:
25.5 kg X 7 mg/kg = 178.2 mg cefdinir q 12 hours
From a 125 mg/5 mL oral suspension of cefdinir:
178.2 mg X 5 mL/125 mg = 7.13 mL, or approximately 7 mL every 12 hours for 7 days

35. 47 mL/min

The Cockcroft Gault method estimates creatinine clearance rate by using the following equations: For males: CrCl = [(140 - the patient's age in years) X body weight in kg] / 72 X Serum creatinine in mg/dL. For females: CrCl = 0.85 X CrCl equation used for males

The body weight used in the Cockcroft Gault equation is either the ideal body weight (IBW) of the patient (in kg) or the actual body weight (in kg) of the patient, whichever is less. For obese patients, an adjusted body weight is conventionally used. The equation for calculating IBW is:

For males: IBW = 50 kg + 2.3 kg for each inch of patient's height over 5 feet
For females: IBW = 45.5 kg + 2.3 kg for each inch of patient's height over 5 feet
Adjusted Body Weight = IBW + 0.4[actual weight – IBW]

To solve the question for this patient, start by determining the patient's ideal body weight:
Height = 162 cm   162 cm X 1 inch/2.54 cm = 64 inches
64in - 60in = 4 inches above 5 feet

IBW = 45.5 kg + (2.3 X 4)
IBW = 45.5 kg + 9.2
IBW = 54.7 kg

Actual body weight is 79 kg, which is significantly higher than the ideal body weight. We can determine if this patient can be categorized as obese by calculating this patient's BMI:
BMI = Wt in kg = 79 kg = 30.1 kg/m^2
[Ht in meters]^2 [1.62m]^2

According to BMI categorization, this patient is considered to be obese. Actual body weight is 44% greater than ideal body weight), so an adjusted body weight should be used:
Adjusted Body Weight = 54.7 kg +0.4[79 kg – 54.7 kg]
Adjusted Body Weight = 54.7 kg +0.4(24.3 kg)
Adjusted Body Weight = 64.4 kg

CrCl = 0.85 X [(140-76) X 64.4 kg] / 72 X 1.03 = 47.2 mL/min

36. C. 1,203 mL

150 lbs x 1kg / 2.2 lbs. = 68.2 kg
1.5 g/kg x 68.2 kg = 102.3 grams needed

102.3 g × 100 mL/8.5 g = 1,203.5 mL

37. 41.38

Conversion Factor = 240 ml / 5.8 parts = 41.38
1 part viscous lidocaine × conversion factor = 1 × 41.38 = 41.38

38. 82.8

Conversion Factor = 240 ml / 5.8 parts = 41.38
2 parts Maalox × conversion factor = 2 × 41.38 = 82.8

39. 11.25

NaCl volume = 45 mEq × mL/4 mEq = 11.25 mL

40. 3.33

$$\text{Estrogen} = \frac{0.5 \text{ g}}{10 \text{ mL}} \times \frac{1 \text{ mL}}{15 \text{ gtt}} = \frac{0.00333 \text{ g}}{\text{gtt}} \times \frac{1000 \text{ mg}}{\text{g}} = 3.33 \text{ mg/gtt/day}$$

41. 17

Solve for K_e first using the equation: $\frac{Cl}{Vd} = \frac{\ln(C_1/C_2)}{(t_2 - t_1)} = \frac{\ln C_1 - \ln C_2}{(t_2 - t_1)} = \frac{\ln(28/24.7)}{3} = 0.042$

$T_{1/2} = \frac{0.693 \times V_d}{CL} = \frac{\ln(2)}{K_e} = \frac{0.693}{K_e} = \frac{0.693}{0.042} = 16.5 = 17$

42. B. 6

$T_{1/2} = \frac{0.693 \times V_d}{CL} = \frac{0.693 \times 80 \text{ L}}{9.37 \text{ L/hr}} = 5.92 = 6$

43. C. 100%

Bioavailability (F%) = 100 × $\frac{\text{AUC extravascular}}{\text{AUC intravenous}}$ × $\frac{\text{Dose intravenous}}{\text{Dose extravascular}}$

As the dosing for IV and PO are the same, 675 mg, it is safe to assume 100% bioavailability. The IV route provides 100% bioavailability as the drug is injected directly into the bloodstream.

44. 408

$$C_o = \frac{D}{V_d}; \quad \frac{8 \text{ mg}}{L} = \frac{x}{51 \text{ L}} \quad x = 408 \text{ mg dose left in body}$$

45. 2.16 ml/hr

$$Cl = \frac{\text{Dose} \times F}{\text{AUC}} = \frac{225 \text{ mg} \times 0.5}{52 \text{ mg*hr/mL}} = 2.16 \text{ mL/hr}$$

46. 1.8

$$T_{1/2} = \frac{0.693 \times V_d}{CL} = \frac{\ln(2)}{K_e} = \frac{0.693}{K_e} = \frac{0.693}{0.38 \text{ hr}^{-1}} = 1.82 = 1.8$$

47. 10

$$T_{1/2} = \frac{0.693 \times V_d}{CL} = \frac{\ln(2)}{K_e} = \frac{0.693}{K_e} = \frac{0.693 \times 65 \text{ L}}{4.5 \text{ L/hr}} = 10.01 = 10$$

48. 11

Convert the 38 mcg*hr/mL to L: $38 \text{ mcg*hr/mL} \times \frac{1000 \text{ mL}}{1 \text{ L}} \times \frac{1 \text{ mg}}{1000 \text{ mcg}} = 38 \text{ mg*hr/L}$

$$Cl = \frac{\text{Dose} \times F}{\text{AUC}} = \frac{400 \text{ mg} \times 100\%}{38 \text{ mg*hr/L}} = 11 \text{ L/hr}$$

49. 42

$$V_d = \frac{\text{Dose}}{K_e \times \text{AUC}} = \frac{400 \text{ mg}}{0.38 \text{ hr}^{-1} \times 25.18 \text{ mg*hr/L}} = 42 \text{ L}$$

50. D. 4.13

$pH = pK_a + \log[\text{salt/acid}] \quad pH = 3.13 + \log[0.5 \text{ M}/0.05 \text{ M}]$
$pH = 3.13 + \log[10] = 3.13 + 1 = 4.13$

Section 1 Pharmacotherapy and Case Questions: Answers and Explanations

1. **B. Etanercept**

   Etanercept is a dimeric fusion protein consisting of the extracellular ligand-binding portion of the human 75 kilodalton tumor necrosis factor receptor (TNFR) linked to the Fc portion of human IgGl. Etanercept is supplied in a single-use prefilled 1 mL syringe as a sterile, preservative-free solution for subcutaneous injection. Etanercept binds specifically to tumor necrosis factor (TNF) and blocks its interaction with cell surface TNF receptors. TNF is a naturally occurring cytokine that is involved in normal inflammatory and immune responses. It plays an important role in the inflammatory processes of rheumatoid arthritis (RA), polyarticular-course juvenile rheumatoid arthritis (JRA), and ankylosing spondylitis and the resulting joint pathology. It is indicated for use in various forms of arthritis, ankylosing spondylitis, and plaque psoriasis.

2. **A. Caffeine (i.e. Coffee), calcium carbonate**

   Hangover can be effectively treated with systemic analgesics (relieving headache and minor aches and pains), antacids (relieving gastric distress), and caffeine (potentially relieving fatigue and drowsiness). Caffeine is allowed in internal analgesics mainly because it boosts the potency of aspirin. However, it is irrational to choose therapy consisting only of caffeine combined with an antacid, because caffeine is a proven stimulator of gastric acid secretion.

3. **D. Take a sip of water with capsule, flex the head forward, and swallow**

   The easiest way to swallow a capsule is to sip some water, let a capsule float to the top when flexing the head forward, and swallow that way. Remember that a capsule is lighter than water and will therefore float. Although many capsules will dissolve in apple juice, the drugs may be incompatible with each other, and others have not been studied in that way. Extending the head when swallowing is ok with tables, but it increases difficulty in swallowing capsules.

4. **A. Nitrofurantoin**

   Nitrofurantoin is an antibacterial agent specific for urinary tract infections. Nitrofurantoin is bactericidal in urine at therapeutic doses. The mechanism of the antimicrobial action of nitrofurantoin is unusual among antibacterials. Nitrofurantoin is reduced by bacterial flavoproteins to reactive intermediates, which inactivate or alter bacterial ribosomal proteins and other macromolecules. As a result of such inactivations, the vital biochemical processes of protein synthesis, aerobic energy metabolism, DNA synthesis, RNA synthesis, and cell wall synthesis are inhibited. Macrobid is indicated only for the treatment of acute uncomplicated urinary tract infections (acute cystitis) caused by susceptible strains of *Escherichia coli* or *Staphylococcus saprophyticus*.

5. **E. Albuterol/Ipratropium**
   Ipratropium bromide is an anticholinergic bronchodilator; while albuterol is a relatively selective beta2 adrenergic agonist. Combivent Inhalation Aerosol contains a microcrystalline suspension of ipratropium bromide and albuterol sulfate in a pressurized metered-dose aerosol unit for oral inhalation administration. Albuterol/Ipratropium (Combivent) is indicated for use in patients with COPD who require a second bronchodilator to control bronchospasm

6. **C. Sulfamethoxazole/Trimethoprim**

   Bactrim is an antibacterial combination product indicated for various infections including urinary tract infections and exacerbations of chronic bronchitis. It is contraindicated in infants less than 2 months of age

7. **E. Powders for Inhalation**

   Patients can purchase Primatene Inhalers (epinephrine), aspirin, or acetaminophen suppositories, enteric-coated aspirin and enteric-coated bisacodyl tablets, and insulin injections, all on a nonprescription basis. However, powders for inhalation such as Foradil Capsules (formoterol fumarate) have never been available on a nonprescription basis.

8. **A. Tablet Lubricant**

   Magnesium stearate is used as a tablet lubricant in tablet formulation. Other common lubricants include calcium stearate, mineral oil, and zinc stearate. These substances reduce friction during tablet compression.

Tablet disintegrants are used to promote the breaking apart of solid dosage forms into smaller particles that can be more readily dispersed. Examples of tablet disintegrants are alginic acid, carboxymethylcellulose calcium, and microcrystalline cellulose.

Tablet glidants (e.g., cornstarch and talc) are used to improve the flow properties of powder mixtures.

Tablet opaquants are used to decrease the transparency of tablet coatings and may be used in combination with colorants. Titanium dioxide is an example of a tablet opaquant.

Tablet polishing agents (e.g., white wax and carnauba wax) are used to give coated tablets a pharmaceutically elegant sheen.

9. B. Gallstone formation

Estrogen/progesterone contraceptives cause several different beneficial and harmful side effects. Estrogens promote formation of bones thus decrease risk of osteoporosis, decrease vaginal dryness, slightly increase risk of stroke, decrease serum cholesterol levels (progesterone may increase), and promotes gallstone formation is susceptible women.

10. D. Nonprescription insomnia products are contraindicated with prostate enlargement

FDA-approved nonprescription products for insomnia are all antihistamines, and are contraindicated in patients with difficulty breathing, chronic lung disease, shortness of breath, emphysema, glaucoma, or trouble urinating because of an enlarged prostate gland. His insomnia is short-term, and should cease when the CPA exam is completed.

11. A. Bisacodyl

Bisacodyl (Dulcolax) and glycerin are the 2 most common rectal formulations for constipation.
Lubiprostone is a chloride channel activator taken by mouth, 24 mcg BID.
Methylcellulose is available as oral tablets or powder.
Docusate sodium is available orally as a liquid or capsule.
Sorbitol is an oral hyperosmolar agent for the treatment of constipation.

12. B. Viral

This patient has a cold sore, which is usually caused by herpes simplex 1, Herpes Simplex Labialis. The virus lies dormant between outbreaks, which are triggered by stress, sunlight (e.g., spring break), or hormones. It can occur on any mucosal surface, but usually the lips. Prodromal symptoms are burning, pruritus, and swelling. Vesicles are clustered on an erythematous base, which evolves into a crusted erosion.

13. D. 31G, 5/16 inch

Insulin syringes for home use are available with pre-attached 30 or 31 gauge needles. The lengths are 0.5 or 5/16 inch. The smaller 30 and 31 gauge needles cause less discomfort than a 25 gauge would. In any case, 25 and 33 gauges' needles are not available on insulin syringes. The shorter 5/16-inch needle is more likely to deliver an appropriate subcutaneous injection than the ½ inch needles that are also available. 1-inch needles are not available on insulin syringes.

14. C. Oxymetazoline Nasal Spray

When recommending a non prescription product, pharmacists must consider all aspects of a patient's current medical situation including active disease states, current medical therapy, and symptoms.
In this case the patient needs relief of acute nasal congestion related to a cold. The most appropriate treatment from this list of choices would be the oxymetazoline nasal spray. Topical nasal decongestants can be used for a limited time frame (2-3 days) to alleviate symptoms effectively.
In this patient, diphenhydramine may improve symptoms but may cause daytime somnolence and increases risks of falls in the elderly. Pseudoephedrine may also improve symptoms but should be used only cautiously in patients with a history of hypertension. Nasal saline is less effective for moderate to severe nasal congestion. Loratadine is a poor choice because it does not treat nasal congestion.

15. E. Mild Nausea and Vomiting after a single pill use

Patient presents with vaginal candidiasis infection, which is treated with fluconazole single pill or vaginal creams. Most frequent adverse effect after single fluconazole dose in the treatment of vaginal yeast infections is mild nausea and vomiting.
Teeth discoloration may occur with doxycycline, anaphylaxis and cross reactivity may occur with cephalosporins, and disulfiram-like reaction occurs with metronidazole.

16. B. Benzocaine 20%

The patient's symptoms indicate fever blisters.
Benzocaine 20% topical is used as a topical anesthetic for pain. Benzocaine is a common ingredient, used as a local anesthetic, found in Oragel Max, Anbesol, and Orabase.

Carbamide peroxide acts as a debriding agent or oral wound cleanser in the treatment of canker sores, not cold sores. Carbamide peroxide is also used as an agent to remove ear wax, as found in Murine Ear Wax Removal.
Camphor is a topical anesthetic agent found in Anbesol and CamphoPhenique. However, a concentration of 20% is excessive; 3-10.8% is more commonly used.
Capasacin is a counterirritant and is not indicated for treatment of fever blisters.
Oxybenzone is a common sunscreen agent and is not used for treatment of any condition.

17. D. Ultraviolet Radiation

This patient has a cold sore, which is usually caused by herpes simplex 1, Herpes Simplex Labialis. The virus lies dormant between outbreaks, which are triggered by stress, sunlight (e.g., spring break), or hormones. It can occur on any mucosal surface, but it is usually on the lips. Prodromal symptoms are burning, pruritus, and swelling. Vesicles are clustered on an erythematous base, which evolves into a crusted erosion.
Avobenzone is a sunscreen.
Shingles is a reactivation of chicken pox and does not trigger fever blister formation.
Chicken pox is a childhood condition and is not associated with fever blister formation.

18. D. 48 hours at controlled room temperature

According to USP <797> Low-risk level products must contain not more than 3 commercially manufactured products and not more than 2 entries into any 1 sterile container. The process involves only transfer, measuring, and mixing manipulations, and it occurs under ISO Class 5 conditions. Therefore, the fentanyl citrate product meets all criteria to be considered a low-risk product. Low-risk product beyond-use dating is designated as 48 hours under controlled room temperature, 14 days under cold temperatures, or 45 days in a solid frozen state. According to the label for Fentanyl Citrate Injection, USP, the product should be stored at controlled room temperature (20 - 25oC). The appropriate storage conditions and dating would therefore be 48 hours at controlled room temperature.

19. A. The dose needs to be decreased by 8%

Although there is no difference in bioavailability between the 2 formulations, there is a difference in the amount of active drug. The suspension contains phenytoin as a free acid. On the other hand, phenytoin capsule contains phenytoin as a sodium salt, which is equivalent to 92% of the free phenytoin acid. Even though the difference in active drug amount between the 2 formulations is relatively small, phenytoin has a narrow therapeutic index and its concentration needs to be within a range of 10 to 20 mcg/ml for optimal efficacy and minimal toxicity. In addition, its kinetic profile is non-linear, which means that any small difference in dose can result in a disproportional change in drug concentration. Therefore, the most prudent step is to reduce the dose in small increments based on the available strength of the suspension, especially if the patient's phenytoin concentration is close to the upper end of the therapeutic range.

20. C. Take a multivitamin once daily at bedtime

The patient using alli must take a once-daily multivitamin, as alli can cause a loss of oil-soluble vitamins. Pharmacists should also counsel the patient that alli works best when combined with a program of physical activity to maximize weight loss results.

21. A. Monitor your blood pressure for additional decreases

Terazosin, an alpha adrenergic antagonist, is used for the treatment of benign prostatic hyperplasia and hypertension. This patient is already taking anti-hypertensives, and the addition of terazosin may provide additional blood pressure-lowering effects. Patients should be counseled to check their blood pressure and rise or sit up slowly while their body adjusts to this medication. Women of childbearing age should be counseled to avoid handling 5-alpha reductase inhibitors, another class of medications used in the treatment of benign prostatic hyperplasia. Terazosin does not lower PSA levels; however, 5-alpha reductase inhibitors do. Patients may experience common side effects upon initiation of terazosin; however, the effects are transient, mild, and do not require as much attention as blood pressure lowering.

22. C. 17%

Nonprescription salicylic acid is available in 17% and 40% concentrations. A concentration of 17% is recommended for common warts, especially in a child. A concentration of 40% is recommended for the treatment of plantar warts.

23. B. High Risk, 3 days refrigerated

Because this product is prepared using at least 1 non-sterile ingredient (thimerosal) requiring terminal sterilization by the compounder, the product must be considered a high risk product by USP <797> standards. The general beyond-use dating requirement for high risk products is 3 days at cold temperature (refrigerated), 24 hours at room temperature, or 45 days if frozen solid, unless sterility and endotoxin testing is performed. In the presence of a preservative such as thimerosal, the beyond-use date may be extended; in the case of this formulation, the USP official monograph suggests a beyond-use date of not more than 5 days refrigerated.

4. C. Doxycycline
This patient presents with signs and symptoms consistent with nongonococcal urethritis (NGU). *C. trachomatis* is the organism associated with NGU. The treatments of choice for NGU are doxycycline and azithromycin. Since this patient has an allergy to clarithromycin, doxycycline is the most appropriate treatment option.

5. A. Cool

The best option provided for storage of Latisse is a cool place. To ensure the stability of a pharmaceutical preparation for the period of its intended shelf life, the product must be stored under proper conditions. The labeling of approved pharmaceutical products includes the desired conditions of storage specifically for that product. Latisse's labeling indicates the proper storage for the solution is 2° to 25°C (36°-77°F). The USP defines storage conditions as follows:

Cold - Less than 8°C; a refrigerator is a cold place in which the temperature is maintained between 2° and 8°C. A freezer is a cold place in which the temperature is maintained between -20° and -10°C.

Cool - Any temperature between 8° and 15°C; a product for which storage in a cool place is directed may be stored in a refrigerator unless otherwise specified.

Room Temperature - The temperature prevailing in a working area, usually between 20° and 25°C, but also allows for temperature variations between 15° and 30°C.

Warm - Any temperature between 30° and 40°C.

Excessive Heat - Any temperature above 40°C.

The criteria for frozen, cold, and warm conditions do not meet the specifications for storage of Latisse. This product could be stored at cooler room temperatures, but the maximum temperature it should be exposed to is 25°C. Therefore, the best option of those listed for a pharmacist to recommend is a cool place.

6. C. Escitalopram
Among the SSRIs listed, the only one that is developed and marketed as a pure isomer is escitalopram

27. A. Compound W Freeze Off

Salicylic acid is available as an OTC agent in 17% or 40% concentrations to treat warts. Salicylic acid is available as paint-on liquid, gel, disc pads, and in an adhesive pad. Compound W Freeze Off in a canister that contains dimethyl ether, propane, and isobutene.

28. B. Viscous vehicle

Insoluble steroids must be formulated as a suspension dosage form. Frequently, polymers are used as vehicles to enhance the viscosity of the formulation, thus decreasing the settling rate of the drug particles while also increasing residence time of administered drops on the eye.

29. C. Vancomycin

Both metronidazole and vancomycin are effective and useful for treatment of *C. difficile* infection. However, only vancomycin is approved by the FDA for this therapeutic indication. Metronidazole is likely to be less expensive, but vancomycin can achieve much higher concentration within the colon.

30. A. 10%

In general, a pharmaceutical product is considered to be not usable if more than 10% of its active ingredient, as determined by appropriate assay, is lost.

31. B. Phenytoin

Gingival hyperplasia, an overgrowth of gum tissue inside the oral cavity, predisposes a patient to loss of tooth integrity and oral infection. It is a known side effect of phenytoin and patient receiving this anticonvulsant should be advised to have good oral hygiene.

32. E. Nortriptyline 25 mg twice daily

Nortriptyline is the best option for this patient because it will assist with quitting smoking and treat signs/symptoms of depression. Although it may cause weight gain, it can also cause nausea, vomiting, and weight loss, so the patient would need to try the medication before the medication's side effects (for him specifically) could be discerned.
Bupropion is not an acceptable option for this patient because of his history of seizures. Nicotine gum is not an acceptable option for this patient because he is a chronic gum chewer. In order for nicotine gum to be effective, the patient must not chew the gum constantly.

The nicotine 21 mg patch is not indicated for patients smoking fewer than 10 cigarettes per day (only the 7 mg patch).
Clonidine is not as effective as the other options for treatment of smoking cessation. If the nortriptyline does not work for this patient, clonidine therapy may be initiated.

33. D. Spatula and electronic balance

Crude coal tar is a highly viscous liquid that cannot be poured into a measuring device, making **liquid graduates** inappropriate. It is too viscous to be drawn into either an **oral** or **injectable syringe**. Rather, the pharmacist must use a spatula to place a specific amount in a weighing boat on the pan of a tarred electronic balance. The spatula is used to continue placing the coal tar in the weighing boat or to return excess to the mother container until the measurement is proper. The coal tar and polysorbate 80 are levigated on an ointment slab and then incorporated into the zinc oxide by spatulation and geometric dilution until the mixture is uniform. The mixture is placed in a 1 ounce ointment tube.

34. A. Henderson-Hasselbalch

The **Henderson-Hasselbalch** equation takes into account the relationship between the ionized and the unionized form of a weak electrolyte, e.g. solution of a weakly acidic compound. With all other factors being equal, it is the unionized form of the drug that will be primarily transported across the biological cell membrane. The Arrhenius equation is useful for predicting drug product stability and shelf life. The Cockcroft Gault equation is used to estimate a patient's creatinine clearance. The Michaelis-Menton equation is used to calculate non-linear kinetic reactions such as enzyme kinetics or non-linear drug absorption, distribution, and elimination kinetics. Pharamcokinetic equations are used to predict drug plasma concentrations.

35. A, B, C, E

All are appropriate except intramuscular administration of heparin is painful and can cause hematomas. Heparin flush via a heparin lock is used for maintaining fluid flow through an intravenous line.

36. C. 2PAM and atropine

The presentation of a patient with organophosphate exposure shows all cholinergic symptoms: diarrhea, flushing, urination, miosis, bradycardia, emesis, lacrimation, lethargy, and salivation. Atropine and 2 PAM are used to treat organophosphate overdose. N-acetylcysteine is used in acetaminophen overdose per nomogram. Naloxone is used to reverse opioid intoxication. Physostigmine is used in anticholinergic overdose. Activated charcoal may be useful in someone who ingested a toxin orally. It is unlikely to be beneficial in this case.

37. B. DHS Tar Shampoo (Coal Tar Extract)

The only nonprescription ingredients proven safe and effective for psoriasis are coal tar, hydrocortisone, and salicylic acid, in appropriate concentrations.

38. E. 2 to 8° C

Biological agents are readily susceptible to degradation by heat, light, or other processes such as protein aggregation, storage conditions are highly specific. Most biologicals are stored in a refrigerator at 2 to 8° C.

39. D. The formulations have same bioavailability as immediate-release formulations

Controlled-release formulations use different matrix materials to surround the active drug. The matrix slowly dissolves in the stomach and the small intestine, resulting in a sustained-release of the active drug. The pharmacokinetic profiles of these formulations result in slower rate of absorption (longer Tmax) and therefore lower Cmax. However, the bioavailability is usually the same as that of immediate-release formulations, as the systemic exposure is sustained over a longer time period after drug administration. The primary site of drug absorption is usually in the small intestine as a result of its much greater absorptive surface area compared to other sites within the gastrointestinal tract.

40. E. Seborrheic dermatitis

The manifestations are those of seborrheic dermatitis. Further, the locations affected are those classically associated with seborrheic dermatitis.

41. A. Ointment Tile

To prepare this product, the pharmacist would weigh out 60 grams of Velvachol and place it on an ointment tile. Next, the pharmacist should agitate the vials of triamcinolone suspension and measure out the appropriate amount of triamcinolone using a sterile syringe. The suspension should be squirted gently onto the Velvachol. Using a spatula, the pharmacist should levigate the mixture until the suspension is fully and evenly incorporated into the Velvachol. The mixture is then transferred into an ointment jar with use of the spatula. Since the triamcinolone is measured with a syringe, there is no need for a graduated cylinder or conical graduate. A stirring rod would not be appropriate for mixing the suspension and cream. Placing the Velvachol in a mortar for mixing is possible, but doing so would be a poor choice, as it would be more difficult to remove the cream with a spatula after mixing.

42. D. Exact dose of the drug prescribed for the patient

A unit dose package contains the exact amount of a drug (single dose) to be given to the patient per the physician's order. This packaging is in contrast to bulk packaging in which multiple doses are included in the same package, to be measured out at the time of administration.

43. E. Is more easily penetrated by lipophilic molecules

The blood brain barrier consists of a lipid-bilayer that is more easily penetrated by lipophilic molecules, which include most of the CNS-acting drugs.

44. A. Exhale. Place inhaler in mouth. Begin inhaling slowly. Activate inhaler while continuing to inhale then hold breath for 10 seconds and exhale

The recommended technique for the proper use of a metered-dose inhaler includes: Exhale. Hold inhaler upright and place lips around mouthpiece or spacer. Inhale slowly and activate inhaler while continuing to inhale. Inhale completely and hold breath for 10 seconds or as long as possible. Repeat treatment if more than one inhalation is prescribed allowing 1 to 2 minutes between inhalations. Rinse mouth with water and expel contents when steroidal inhaler is used.

45. C. Phase III

A New Drug Application (NDA) is filed after completion of Phase III clinical testing. An Investigational New Drug Application (IND) is submitted after preclinical animal investigations have been performed. The testing then proceeds to Phases I, II, and III of human clinical trials to determine safety and efficacy. If the results of these trials are promising, the drug's sponsor may then submit an NDA to the FDA. An NDA may be over 100,000 pages in length. The FDA has 180 days to act on an NDA according to law; however, significant delays are common. An NDA is required to provide proof of safety and efficacy of any of the following before the new drug may be marketed:

1) A new molecular entity
2) A new salt of a previously approved drug

3) A new formulation of a previously approved drug
4) A new combination of 2 or more drugs
5) Duplication of an already approved drug product - i.e. new manufacturer
6) A new indication for a previously marketed drug
7) A drug product already marketed that has no previously approved NDA.

The drug is also assigned a letter to designate its review priority: S for standard review or P for priority review, indicating the new drug represents significant advances over existing treatments. If the FDA approves the NDA, the new drug then becomes available for physicians to prescribe. The FDA requires additional studies (Phase IV) on some drugs to evaluate long-term effects.

46. A. Trichomoniasis

STI	Men	Women
Gonorrhea	Mucopurulent urethral discharge. Can lead to prostatitis, epididymitis, and urethral stricture.	Often asymptomatic. Abnormal vaginal discharge or bleeding, urinary tract complaints. Can lead to pelvic inflammatory disease, infertility, chronic pelvic pain, and tubal pregnancy.
Trichomoniasis	Asymptomatic	Up to 50% asymptomatic. Greenish, malodorous vaginal discharge, itching, painful intercourse, postcoital bleeding.
HPV	Many asymptomatic. If symptomatic – lesions may be present on genitalia, anus, rectum, or mouth	Many asymptomatic. If symptomatic - lesions on external genitalia, anus, rectum, mouth, vagina, urethra, cervix
HSV	Many asymptomatic. Vesicular or ulcerative lesions on genitalia, thighs, buttocks.	Many asymptomatic. Vesicular or ulcerative lesions on genitalia, thighs, buttocks. Symptoms more severe in women.
Syphilis	Painless, temporary, and localized chancre Secondary – rash, generalized	Painless, temporary, and localized chancre Secondary – rash, generalized lymphadenopathy, hepatosplenomegaly, alopecia, oral mucous patches

| | lymphadenopathy, hepatosplenomegaly, alopecia, oral mucous patches | |

47. E. Stomach ulcers

Nicorette gum is contraindicated in patients with heart disease, recent heart attack, irregular heartbeat, stomach ulcers, and diabetes requiring insulin. The product can delay healing of stomach ulcers.

48. A. Healthy eating habits

Drug therapy should be considered in patients with a body mass index greater than 30 kg/m2 or greater than 27 kg/m2 with risk factors of hypertension, dyslipidemia, coronary heart disease, type 2 diabetes, or sleep apnea. Sibutramine and phentermine are effective weight loss agents. If this patient qualified for treatment based on BMI, these agents would not be appropriate because the patient has hypertension. Orlistat 60 mg daily is helpful only if the patient is consuming a diet containing moderate to high amounts of fat. Since this patient is following a low fat eating regimen already, orlistat would not be as effective in this patient.
Asking the patient to make a drastic change in her exercise habits is unlikely to result in long term adherence to the regimen. Instead, the patient should be encouraged to gradually increase exercise as tolerated.
Based on the options, encouraging the patient to follow healthy eating habits is the most appropriate treatment at this time. The combination of health eating and increased physical activity should result in a gradual (1-2 lb/week) weight loss.

49. B. Activated Charcoal

Syrup of ipecac is contraindicated in this situation because rapid neurologic or hemodynamic deterioration may occur. Gastric lavage will not be effective in this situation because at least 2 hours have elapsed. Gastric lavage would be beneficial if initiated within 1 hour of ingestion. There is limited evidence to suggest that hemodialysis is effective in tricyclic antidepressant overdose. Administration of activated charcoal is the most appropriate treatment approach in this patient. The charcoal will adsorb the amitriptyline in the gut and prevent further absorption.

50. C. Akathisia

The newer atypical antipsychotics such as clozapine and olanzapine are less likely than the typical antipsychotic drugs to cause extrapyramidal side effects including akathisia and dystonia. On the other hand, they have been reported to cause other side effects more often, including sedation, weight gain, and agranulocytosis. Orthostatic hypotension is a common side effect of the low potency typical antipsychotic agents such as chlorpromazine.

51. A. Binder

Binders hold the ingredients in a tablet together. Binders ensure that tablets and granules can be formed with required mechanical strength, and give volume to low active dose tablets. Examples of common binders include starch, lactose, sucrose, sorbitol, or cellulose.

52. A, B, C, D

CGMP refers to the Current Good Manufacturing Practice regulations enforced by the US Food and Drug Administration (FDA). CGMPs provide for systems that assure proper design, monitoring, and control of manufacturing processes and facilities. Adherence to the CGMP regulations assures the identity, strength, quality, and purity of drug products by requiring that manufacturers of medications adequately control manufacturing operations. This includes establishing strong quality management systems, obtaining appropriate quality raw materials, establishing robust operating procedures, detecting and investigating product quality deviations, and maintaining reliable testing laboratories. This formal system of controls at a pharmaceutical company, if adequately put into practice, helps to prevent instances of contamination, mix-ups, deviations, failures, and errors. This assures that drug products meet their quality standards

53. D. Generally large stainless steel spatula blades are used, except plastic spatulas are used for chemicals (e.g. iodine) that can react with stainless steel blades

For answer choice a. it is the opposite, porcelain usually has a smoother surface and Wedgewood has a harsher surface. Choice b. is not true, glass is usually used for oily staining chemicals. Choice c. is not true as the ointment or cream will seep into the bond paper. Choice e. is not true as glass mortars are the smoothest of surfaces

54. A. A liquid preparation of soluble chemicals dissolved in solvents such as water, alcohol, or propylene glycol

For answer choice b. this represents a suppository, answer choice c. is referring to an external application of a cream, ointment, or other type of liquid preparation. Choice d. is referring to a emulsion, and choice e. is a suspension

55. A, B, C

Sorbitol is used for these multiple uses in compounding. It's important to note Sorbitol may cause GI distress, should be avoided in patients with IBS and Crohn's disease.

56. A, B

Compounded medications has been a hot topic in the news due to the catastrophes and deaths it has caused. There is speculation of the FDA regulating compounding; however, if a compounding pharmacy does exceed making compounded batches from it's usual and customary amount then it may require FDA registration and regulation.

57. A. Creams have a higher percentage of oil than lotions

Lotions, creams, and ointments are oil in water preparations. Lotions have the most water, creams, and then ointments have the most oil.

58. B, C, D

Tween is a hydrophilic, non-ionic surfactant that is used for oil in water emulsions. Surfactants decrease the surface tension of a liquid or between a liquid and a solid.

59. B. Aquaphor, Aquabase, Eucerin, petrolatum

The other agents listed in the other answer choices represent other compounding agents that are used to help bind, sweeten, and be used as a surfactant.

60. B. Etanercept

Etanercept or Enbrel by it's brand name, is commonly used for rheumatoid arthritis among many other conditions it's indicated by the FDA. Humira, Simponi, Rasuvo are others that are used in this class. These medications are quite expensive and often require a prior authorization to get coverage for the patient after trying and failing common gold standards such as methotrexate.

61. E. The total billing for CMS is < 5% total of the pharmacy's total sales for the previous three years

Either the total billing for CMS needs to be less than 5% of the total pharmacy sales for the previous 3 years or the pharmacy has been a DMEPOD provider for 5 years or more. This is because many pharmacies and providers have created false claims to get extra pay incentives from CMS fraudulently.

62. A, B, C

Applying creams or other lubricants can loosen the adhesive of the patch from the skin. Shaving and using other chemicals to remove hair may irritate the skin. It's best to counsel the patient to trim or place the patch on a non-hairy area.

63. A, D, E

The FDA and DEA have created a list to help patients and healthcare providers know which patches are safe to flush. It's important to also educate the patient on drug take back days that are offered in the community on certain days throughout the year.

64. C. The nebulizer, glucose meter and strips are all billed under Part B

CMS does provide a short, often outdated, list of Part B versus Part D drugs. It's very important to understand the difference as insurance companies will reject the medication being filled and ensure it is billed appropriately to the patient and the insurance health plan

65. A, B, D, E

If your female patient has had cancer in any reproductive tract including breast, vaginal, and uterine then estrogens may be contraindicated as it increases the risk of these cancers to reform

66. A, C, D, E

CR is controlled release, XL is extended release, ER is extended release, and LA is long-acting. These formulations should not be crushed or chewed as they contain a special lining formulation to slowly release. IR is immediate release so it doesn't matter as you quickly want the drug.

67. A, C, E

If adherence is a concern, longer acting formulations are available. Haldol decanoate is administered every 4 weeks, Abilify Maintena is every 4 weeks, Invega and Risperdal Consta is every 2 weeks

68. C. Fentanyl

Oxycodone comes in an immediate-release (IR) formulation but not sublingual. Buprenorphine/Naltrexone comes in a buccal film used more for addiction, and Morphine and Hydrocodone do not come in a sublingual film. Fentanyl is one of the stronger pain relieving medications

69. C. Imitrex STATdose

The ODT Maxalt-MLT formulation would help decrease nausea but due to vomiting and sudden onset, an injection is the preferred choice

70. A. Long lasting items used for a medical condition kept in the patient's home

DME is kept in the patient's home such as canes, walkers, etc.

71. D. Refills for supplies come only from the patient or the patient's caregiver

CMS frowns upon automatic refills of supplies as it may lead to wastefulness. The request for refills must come from a patient or patient designated caregiver. Delivery documents need to be kept for 7 years and refill orders must be written for "as-needed".

72. A, B, C, D

Other DME supplies include insulin pumps, canes, blood glucose meters, and walkers.

73. E. The patient will bring in an order for the DME, and the pharmacy will be paid by CMS under Part B

DME requires an order (prescription) from a provider to be covered under medical insurance Part B. Drugs taken in an outpatient setting are covered under Part D (D for drugs) except for vaccinations which are under Part B.

74. B. To treat constipation

Glycerin is the main ingredient used in bisacodyl to treat constipation

75. B. She would have less dry mouth if she used a longer-acting formulation or the patch formulation

Long-term formulations generally don't reach drug peak concentrations that cause side effects. Dosing less frequently and having a slow release formulation prevents the drug levels from increasing too high and rapidly

76. D. Instruct the child not to chew the capsule contents

Pancreatic enzyme medications may be opened and added with food with a low pH like applesauce, blended pears or bananas. These medications need to be taken with a meal or right before eating to help absorb food nutrients

77. A. Intermezzo

Edluar and Intermezzo are both zolpidem sublingual formulations. Intermezzo is used for insomnia with middle of night awakening

78. C. Remeron

Remeron is considered a safer medication to take and is an anti-depressant. Usually it's used in skilled nursing facilities, cancer patients, and children

79. A, C, D

A prescription does not require a new order if the supplier has changed for a drug, but CMS requires a new order if the supplier has changed the DME. If the item has been stolen and a new order is written the pharmacy should request a police report because DME may require it

80. D. Copaxone

There is a generic available for Copaxone

81. B. The drug is unlikely to have any significant adverse effects

The therapeutic index is a measurement of the margin of safety of the drug. The greater the difference between a therapeutic dose and a toxic dose, the greater will be the therapeutic index. Therefore, a drug with a high therapeutic index is one that likely has few significant side effects and does not need close monitoring of its concentration or amount in the body. The drug interaction potential for a drug is usually influenced by its metabolism as well as its effect on the drug metabolizing enzymes in the body

82. A. Noninferiority

Noninferiority trial is designed to show that a treatment is no less effective than an existing treatment. The treatment may be more effective or may have a similar effect
Superiority trial is designed to detect a difference between treatments and show that one treatment is more effective than the other
Equivalence trial is designed to show the absence of meaningful differences between treatments.
Cohort clinical trial is a longitudinal study that begins with the gathering of 2 groups of patients, 1 which receives the exposure of interest and 1 which does not, and then following the groups over time (prospective) to measure the development of different outcomes
Randomized clinical trial is a trial in which the participants are assigned randomly to different treatments

83. B. Martindale

A pharmacist should have access to various resources while taking care of patients. In this example, the key reference is Martindale; this reference includes information about medications available from other countries.
Facts & Comparisons is a comprehensive resource for prescription and nonprescription medications available in the Unites States and Canada.
USP contains information about the pharmacology, adverse effects, contraindications, and doses of prescriptions medications along with patient information.
Remington is a reference for isotonicity, sterilization, and theoretical science.
Micromedex is a a comprehensive resource for prescription and nonprescription medications available in the Unites States.

84. C. Mode

The most common value in data distribution is described by the mode. The mean, also known as the average, is the sum of all values divided by the total number of values. The mean is most commonly used to measure central tendency. The median is the point at which half of the observations fall below and half lie above the value. Standard deviation applies only to data normally or near normally distributed. It uses a formula that sums the squares of the differences between each value from a sample and the mean of the sample

85. C. Phase 3 study is performed for evaluation of response in a large number of patients with the target disease

A Phase 1 study primarily determines the pharmacokinetic profile of a drug in a small number of healthy volunteers. Post-marketing surveillance studies are performed after approval. There is no official designation of a Phase 4 study

86. E. The Study is unethical

Any new medication, regardless how good it seems to be in small phase I or II trials, should be compared to the standard of care in phase III trials. Placebo is not the standard of care in the treatment of early stage breast cancer. Tamoxifen administration should not skew results in a well-organized trial. The patients will be randomly assigned to groups based on their ER/PR positivity status; therefore, both groups should have same number of ER/PR positive patients.
Most phase I and II trials are not designed to assess clinical response or efficacy; therefore, their data should be interpreted with caution

87. A. Remington

A pharmacist should have access to various resources while taking care of patients. In this example, the key reference is Martindale; this reference includes information about medications available from other countries.
Facts & Comparisons is a comprehensive resource for prescription and nonprescription medications available in the Unites States and Canada.
USP contains information about the pharmacology, adverse effects, contraindications, and doses of prescriptions medications along with patient information.
Remington is a reference for isotonicity, sterilization, and theoretical science.
Micromedex is a a comprehensive resource for prescription and nonprescription medications available in the Unites States.

88. B. No nonprescription product can minimize or prevent hangover

No nonprescription product can be marketed with the claim of minimizing or preventing hangover. Such products are not effective and might encourage patients to drive while under the influence.

89. E. Range

The mean, median, and mode are statistical terms used to describe the frequency distribution of the data. The prevalence usually refers to the total number of occurrence of an event (e.g. adverse reaction to a drug). The range is typically used for describing the variability for a small set of data.

90. E. Young adult Caucasian women

The WHO criteria for osteoporosis compares an individual's BMD to that of young adult Caucasian women. The T score is the number of standard deviations from the mean BMD of young Caucasian women. A T score of 0 would mean a patient's BMD is the same as the mean of young women, and a T score of -2.0 means the patient has a BMD at that site, and by that method, 2 standard deviations less than the mean. A T score of greater than -1.0 is considered normal; a T score between -1.0 and -2.5 is called osteopenia. A T score of less than -2.5 is osteoporosis

91. B. Reduce purine-rich foods

There are many lifestyle and dietary factors that contribute to a patient's increased risk of experiencing a gouty attack. Patients should be counseled to reduce intake of purine-containing foods, for example, meats (especially organ meats), seafood, and beer. Recent information also suggests an association between consumption of fructose-containing beverages and gout. Therefore, a patient with gout should also be counseled to reduce or avoid fructose-containing beverages. Based on this patient's cardiovascular risk factors, this patient should be counseled to increase his intake of fruits and vegetables and reduce fat, cholesterol, and sodium intake.

92. C. 11 to 12 g/dl

The target range for hemoglobin levels during treatment with erythropoiesis-stimulating agent is 11 to 12 g/dl. Although labeling information suggests maintaining hemoglobin levels between 10 to 12 g/dl, the National Kidney Foundation Kidney Disease Outcome

Quality Initiative recommends a target range of 11 to 12 g/dl in patients receiving erythropoiesis-stimulating agent for treatment of anemia.

93. C. Increase haemoglobin concentration from baseline

The therapeutic goal for using erythropoietic agent is an increase in hemoglobin concentration from the baseline, usually about 1 g/dl over 4 weeks, as well as a reduction in the frequency of blood transfusions

94. A. 2 weeks

This patient's INR is supratherapeutic. An INR range of 2.0 - 3.0 is recommended for patients receiving warfarin for atrial fibrillation. Knowing that this result is inconsistent with his recent values, his INR should be rechecked sooner than 1 month. The result does not require urgent attention; therefore, the 2-week time frame is the most reasonable option provided.
It is unnecessary to check the INR again tomorrow because sufficient time will not have elapsed to see a significant change in the result

95. C. Serum Uric Acid

Since allopurinol decreases the rate of synthesis of uric acid and is used in the treatment of gout, monitoring of serum uric acid level would be appropriate to assess its therapeutic effect

96. B. 2.0 – 3.0

According to the CHEST guidelines regarding antithrombotic therapy, post-MI patients at a high risk for left ventricular thrombosis should be maintained in a therapeutic range of 2.0 - 3.0

97. A. Azithromycin

Azithromycin, erythromycin, and metronidazole are all classified as B category for the FDA pregnancy category. However, there are some concerns regarding the use of metronidazole and the estolate salt of erythromycin, and they should be used with caution and best avoided as there are alternatives. Doxycycline and tetracycline are class D drugs and need to be avoided in pregnancy

98. B. 3.5

99% of the gastric acid would be neutralized when the intragastric pH is increased from 1.0 to 3.5. Increasing the gastric pH to higher values would provide no additional therapeutic benefit

99. A. Increased use of broad-spectrum antibiotics

Lower cost of antibiotics and increased use of broad-spectrum antibiotics are associated with higher likelihood of antimicrobial resistance, resulting in increased incidence of treatment failure

100. C. An HDL of <40; age (men >45 yrs, women >55 yrs)

An HDL of <40 is undesirable, and so is the age factor (>45 years for men and >55 years for women). This case illustrates the rationale of pharmacotherapy in the presence of 2 or more risk factors. The specific LDL lipid level should be identified to guide the initiation and goal of pharmacotherapy. Drug therapy for patients with 2+ risk factors should be started when the LDL is >130. The LDL goal is <130.
The NCEP/ATEP has set forth explicit risk factors, as well as specific lipid goals/classifications, that clearly address what parameters dictate the initiation or cessation of pharmacotherapy. This question illustrates that in patients with a major risk factor (e.g., CHD, diabetes), the goal of drug therapy is to keep the level of LDL lipids <100. Likewise, drug therapy should be started when the LDL is >130.
A patient with a TC of <200 is already in the desirable range and would not need drug therapy based on lipid classification alone. It should be noted that the TC is only a general marker; therefore, the individual lipid molecules need to be identified via a lipid panel/profile. The presence of 0 - 1 risk factors (HBP) mandates that drug therapy should be started when the LDL is >190; the goal of therapy is an LDL <160. Once the LDL level is identified, then the decision whether or not to initiate drug therapy can be discussed.
An HDL of >60 is very desirable; there is a direct correlation between the level of HDL and the absence of coronary plaque. It should be noted that the LDL level should still be identified in order to ascertain the true lipid picture. Cigarette smoking is only 1 risk factor; therefore, drug therapy should be initiated when the LDL is >190. The goal of therapy is an LDL level of <160. Once the LDL lipid level is identified, the option of drug therapy can be discussed.
The VLDL lipid molecule can be a separate risk factor and is usually elevated along with TG. The VLDL level becomes important (VLDL >200 - 300) when it is accompanied by elevated TG (200 - 499). As in the above explanations, the LDL lipid level should be identified due to the direct correlation between LDL and CHD. A major risk factor (e.g.,

diabetes) mandates that drug therapy be initiated when the LDL is >130. The LDL goal is <100. Once the LDL level is lowered to an acceptable range, the elevated VLDL and TG (especially if TG is >500) should be addressed by initiating either a combination of diet and exercise (which will lower VLDL) and/or drug therapy. The statins have a modest effect on VLDL/TG, whereas niacin and gemfibrozil have been shown to dramatically reduce these lipid levels.

101. A. Naprosyn EC is not indicated for treatment of an acute gouty attack

Naprosyn is a very effective agent in regard to relieving pain and inflammation during an acute gout attack. However, it is important to pay attention to the specific dosage form in order to insure it will be effective for the condition being treated. When acute pain relief is necessary, an immediate-release product is most appropriate. When the patient requires relief from chronic pain and the medication is scheduled around the clock, EC or enteric-coated products are appropriate to provide pain relief while preventing potential gastric complications.

102. D. Discontinue the medication in 1 year

Patients with generalized anxiety disorder who respond to medication therapy should stay on the medication for at least 1 year prior to discontinuation, assuming the patient does not relapse during that time. If the patient has experienced multiple episodes of anxiety, lifelong therapy may be considered. Of course, the pharmacist should urge the patient not to discontinue the medication without obtaining his physician's permission.

103. C. 2.5 - 3.5

According to the recent CHEST guidelines regarding antithrombotic therapy, the therapeutic range for patients with bileaflet mechanical valves in the mitral position is 2.5-3.5.

104. E. Noncompliance

Mycoplasma pneumonia infection commonly presents with nonproductive cough, headache, runny nose, and chest pain. Erythromycin is a good agent for atypical pneumonias, but it needs to be taken several times per day and also it is associated with bad side effects such as diarrhea. Many patients will not tolerate erythromycin due to its side effects. Noncompliance is a major issue with erythromycin prescription.

105. B. Ciprofloxacin

The best choice of those listed for treatment of this patient's acute sinusitis would be ciprofloxacin (Cipro). Although amoxicillin (Amoxil) is generally first-line therapy for acute sinusitis and does not interact with this patient's other medications, the patient is allergic to penicillin and therefore should not be given amoxicillin. Bactrim (trimethoprim/sulfamethoxazole) and telithromycin (Ketek), while appropriate alternative therapies for acute sinusitis in penicillin-allergic patients, would interact significantly with the patient's ketoconazole. Gentamicin (Gentak) is inappropriate therapy for acute sinusitis

106. D. 7%

The ADA recommends the use of HbA1C level for monitoring glycemic control in diabetic patients. The target used by ADA is <7%, whereas the target recommended by the American College of Endocrinology and American Association of Clinical Endocrinologists is <6.5%.

107. E. Captopril

The only drugs that have been shown to improve survival in patients with heart failure are ACE inhibitors, spironolactone, and certain beta blockers. Despite decades of use, digitalis has never been proven to have a beneficial effect on survival. Entresto (Sacubitril/Valsartan) is a newer heart failure medication that is a combination of an ACEI and ARB has shown positive results for patients.

108. D. 7 days

Patients with severe generalized anxiety disorder may initially be treated with a benzodiazepine and an SSRI. It is important to counsel the patient about when they will notice the therapeutic effects of each drug. The full effects of the benzodiazepine will be evident within 1 week. The full effects of the SSRI will be evident in 8-12 weeks.

109. A. Rasagline

Rasagiline (Azilect) is a selective MAO-B inhibitor with recommended dosing of 1 mg given once daily. Amantadine (Symmetrel), an antiviral medication serendipitously discovered to treat symptoms of Parkinson's disease, has a recommended dose of 100 mg given twice daily. Carbidopa/Levodopa (Sinemet) is dosed 3 or 4 times daily. Pramipexole (Mirapex) and ropinirole (Requip) are dosed 3 times daily.

Caution should be exercised when administering a MAOI concomitantly with some antidepressants. Severe CNS toxicity associated with hyperpyrexia and death has been reported with the combination of tricyclic antidepressants and non-selective MAOIs (e.g., phenelzine, tranylcypromine) or the selective MAO-B inhibitor selegiline (selegiline). These adverse events have included behavioral and mental status changes, diaphoresis, muscular rigidity, hypertension, syncope, and death. Serious, sometimes fatal reactions with signs and symptoms, including hyperthermia, rigidity, myoclonus, autonomic instability with rapid vital sign fluctuations, and mental status changes progressing to extreme agitation, delirium, and coma, have been reported in patients receiving a combination of selective serotonin reuptake inhibitors (SSRIs), including fluoxetine (Prozac), fluvoxamine (Luvox), sertraline (Zoloft), and paroxetine (Paxil), and non-selective MAOIs or the selective MAO-B inhibitor selegiline. Similar reactions have been reported with serotonin-norepinephrine reuptake inhibitors (SNRIs) and non-selective MAOIs or the selective MAO-B inhibitor selegiline.

Rasagiline (Azilect) clinical trials did not allow concomitant use of fluoxetine or fluvoxamine with rasagiline, but the following antidepressants and doses were allowed in the trials: amitriptyline $\leq$ 50 mg/daily, trazodone $\leq$ 100 mg/daily, citalopram $\leq$ 20 mg/daily, sertraline $\leq$ 100 mg/daily, and paroxetine $\leq$ 30 mg/daily. Although most rasagiline drug interactions are based on theoretical considerations rather than actual clinical data, the potential severity of many of the adverse outcomes dictates a conservative approach when giving rasagiline concomitantly with these drugs. Many of the potentially interacting drugs are not lifesaving and have alternatives. For other drugs that may be important for the patient, such as antidepressants, one should weigh the benefits versus the (usually small) risk of using them with rasagiline. This patient is currently taking 50 mg amitriptyline daily, which has not had any reported adverse outcomes when used with rasagiline, but theoretically may interact with rasagiline. A patient in this situation should be counseled about the possibility of adverse interactions if the physician chooses to continue antidepressant therapy.

110. D. Its teratogenic classification

While all of the mentioned characteristics should be considered (mechanism of action, smoking status, alcohol use, lactation), at this time, the most important first consideration for a pregnant woman would be the potential teratogenicity of the drug.

111. A. <140/$\leq$90 mm Hg

This patient is a diabetic patient; her blood pressure goal is <140/$\leq$90 according to the American Diabetes Association guidelines. Allowing the blood pressure to reach levels in excess of this target could have long-term adverse consequences (e.g., stroke or heart attack). Attempting to achieve lower levels could lead to hypotension, with dizziness or syncope upon standing.

112. B. Schedule I

Currently there is no medical reason for any practitioner to prescribe a Schedule I medication for management of patient.

113. C. <140/90 mmHg

The Eighth Report of the Joint National Committee on Prevention, Detection, Evaluation, and Treatment of High Blood Pressure (JNC 8) recommends blood pressure be treated to <140/90 mmHg in patients less than 60 years of age, even those with diabetes or chronic kidney disease.

114. E. Infliximab

Per the American College of Rheumatology Guidelines, patients with moderate disease activity and features of poor prognosis (many swollen joints, moderate disease activity, radiographic erosion) with disease duration greater than 24 months are candidates for the following oral therapies: leflunomide, methotrexate, sulfasalazine monotherapy, or methotrexate and hydroxychloroquine combination therapy. Sulfasalazine and leflunomide is not a recommended combination in the ACR guidelines. Since the patient failed methotrexate monotherapy she is also a candidate for biologic therapy, specifically, a TNF antagonist. The patient has no contraindications to TNF antagonists, therefore rituximab is not necessary at this time. In addition, the patient is rheumatoid factor negative so rituximab may not be the most effective option in this patient. Combination biologic therapy is not warranted due to increased adverse effects without added efficacy.

115. A. 2.0 – 3.0

According to the CHEST guidelines regarding antithrombotic therapy, the therapeutic range for treatment of deep vein thrombosis is 2.0 - 3.0.

116. B. Recommend against its use, as it is only for patients aged 12 and above

Caffeine products such as NoDoz and Vivarin are contraindicated for self-use in patients under the age of 12 years. For this reason, he should be advised against their use. Caffeine-containing beverages are not necessarily safe for children and should not be recommended. If his concern continues, he should be urged to consult the physician

117. C. Therapeutic Interchange Protocol

Usually when new drugs are released, they are added to the therapeutic interchange protocol to provide an opportunity to switch to the drug or since it is a newer medication it is likely to be more expensive and switched to an alternative that is more cost-effective.

118. D. What the drug does to the body

Pharmacodynamics refers to the relationship between drug concentration at the site of action and the resulting effect, including the time course and intensity of therapeutic and adverse effects. The effect of a drug present at the site of action is determined by that drug's binding with a receptor. Receptors may be present on neurons in the central nervous system (i.e., opiate receptors) to depress pain sensation, on cardiac muscle to affect the intensity of contraction, or even within bacteria to disrupt maintenance of the bacterial cell wall. For most drugs, the concentration at the site of the receptor determines the intensity of a drug's effect.

119. B. Phenytoin exhibits Michaelis-Menten Kinectics

Phenytoin follows Michaelis-Menten or saturable pharmacokinetics. This is the type of nonlinear pharmacokinetics that occurs when the number of drug molecules overwhelms or saturates the enzyme's ability to metabolize the drug. When this occurs, steady-state drug serum concentrations increase in a disproportionate manner after a dosage increase. The clinical implication of Michaelis-Menten pharmacokinetics is that the clearance of phenytoin is not a constant as it is with linear pharmacokinetics, but is concentration- or dose-dependent. As the dose or concentration of phenytoin increases, the clearance rate (Cl) decreases as the enzyme approaches saturable conditions. This is the reason concentrations increase disproportionately after a phenytoin dosage increase.

120. A, B, D, E

Phenytoin exhibits Michaelis-Menten kinectics, when it is overdosed the elimination goes from first to zero-order due to the enzymes from being oversaturated. The extra phenytoin doesn't go through first-pass metabolism in the liver and instead raises the serum concentration to produce side effects and toxicity.

121. A, C, D

Michaelis-Menten starts as first-order kinectics, then as it becomes saturable the metabolism changes to zero order resulting in toxicity.

122. C. Hydrolysis

Hydrolysis is when the compound is cleaved into two parts by the addition of a water molecule.

123. C. What the body does to the drug

Pharmacokinetics is currently defined as the study of the time course of drug absorption, distribution, metabolism, and excretion.

124. D. Metabolism

The liver and gut wall can change the drug's structure or metabolize the drug so it can be more readily excreted outside the body or increase its therapeutic effect if it's a pro-drug.

125. B. Increase the surface area of the tablet

Increasing the surface area or decreasing the size of the tablet will increase the gut dissolution.

126. B. Noyes-Whitney

Solubility is an endpoint representing dissolution capacity. Dissolution rate can be expressed using the Noyes–Whitney equation.

127. E. Charged compounds dissolve more easily in water than uncharged compounds

Water is a polar molecule, with one end positively charged, and the other negatively charged. These charges interact with ionic bonds in substances like table salt. The water molecules surround the charged particles in the salt with oppositely charged ends of the water molecules. This reduces the effective charges on the sodium and chlorine ions, so they no longer attract one another as much as they did before. The rest of the work of dissolving the salt is done by heat and by the motion of the water, both of which jostle the ions apart, so they can be surrounded by water molecules and isolated. The polar nature of water is also why non-polar molecules do not dissolve in water. Substances like oils, fats, and waxes have no charged parts to attract water molecules. The water molecules are attracted to one another by their charges, and they leave the non-polar molecules alone. This pulling together of all the water molecules acts to pull them away from uncharged molecules, so oil and water don't mix.

128. A, D, E

A time measurement, which starts when the drug reaches equilibrium ("equilibrium" = "fully absorbed" = when equal amounts of drug are in circulation and at point of administration).
½ life is how much time it takes for blood levels of drug to decrease to half of what it was at equilibrium and there are two kinds of ½ life. Distribution ½ life is when plasma levels fall to half what they were at equilibrium due to distribution to/storage in body's tissue reservoirs.
Elimination ½ life is when plasma levels fall to half what they were at equilibrium due to drug being metabolized and eliminated. While both half-lives contribute to the effects of the drug on behavior, it is usually the elimination half-life that is used to determine dosing schedules, to decide when it is safe to put patients on a new drug.

129. A. Absorption

As the drug is being injected IV, it bypasses absorption as it directly enters systemic circulation.

130. A. A linear relationship between dose and serum level

First-order process takes place at a constant proportion of the drug concentration available at that time so the process is depending on the initial concentration. Rate of process increases linearly with increase in drug concentration

131. C. Protein Binding

Changes in albumin (normal lab range of 3.5 to 5) will cause significant changes in the amount of drug bound if it is a highly protein bound drug

132. B. Approximately 5 half-lives

Generally, 5 times the elimination 1/2 life is the time at which the drug is completely (~97%) eliminated from the body assuming that the drug was given in a single original dose.

1x 1/2 life - 50% of the original drug removed
2x 1/2 life - 75%
3x 1/2 life - 87.5% 4x 1/2 life - 93.75%
5x 1/2 life - 96.875%

133. A. There is a 95% chance that the interval contains the true population value

A confidence interval gives an estimated range of values that is likely to contain the unknown population metric, and can be calculated from a data set

134. D. The null hypothesis is false, but is accepted in error

A Type II error means that the null hypothesis is false, yet it is accepted in error. The study authors conclude that there's no difference but in fact there is a difference

135. D. Cohort study

A study group (or cohort) is followed over time and outcomes are compared to a subset group who were not exposed to the intervention. This is a type of prospective study design

136. 3.8

Absolute Risk Reduction (ARR) = % risk in control - % risk in treatment
ARR = (826/4652) – (650/4645) = 0.0376 x 100 = 3.8

137. 0.79

The relative risk is the probability of the event occurring in the exposed group versus the non-exposed group. The risk of the primary outcome is 14% in the Ramipril group vs. 17.8% in the placebo group. 14%/17.8% gives a relative risk of 0.79.

138. B. The null hypothesis is true, but is rejected in error

A Type I error is when the null hypothesis is true but the study authors reject it in error. If the p-value is 0.05, it means less than 5% of the time the null hypothesis will be rejected in error, a type I error will have occurred

139. B. The null hypothesis

The null hypothesis usually states there is no difference between two study groups

140. A, E

A cohort study is a type of observational study. This study describes a retrospective cohort (the cohort is discharged patients). These patients are then evaluated to determine if they were receiving PPIs, and then the outcome of the nosocomial pneumonia assessed. To be a case control study, you would need to start out by identifying the outcome (the patients who developed pneumonia) which was not done at the onset of the study

141. B. Controlled clinical trial

A study group is compared to one or more control (comparison) groups in a controlled setting

142. A, B, C, E

Relative risk (RR) gives you a measure of the risk of an event in one group compared to the risk of that event in a comparison group. It does not give you an idea of how important (or large) the treatment effect really is in the population-at-large

143. B. The value in the middle of the list

Median is the middle of the set, mode is the most common value, and mean is average of the set

144. E. Meta Analysis

A subset of systematic reviews; a method for systematically combining pertinent qualitative and quantitative study data from several selected studies to develop a single conclusion that has greater statistical power. This conclusion is statistically stronger than the analysis of any single study, due to increased numbers of subjects, greater diversity among subjects, or accumulated effects and results.

Meta-analysis would be used for the following purposes:
- To establish statistical significance with studies that have conflicting results
- To develop a more correct estimate of effect magnitude
- To provide a more complex analysis of harms, safety data, and benefits
- To examine subgroups with individual numbers that are not statistically significant

Advantages
- Greater statistical power
- Confirmatory data analysis
- Greater ability to extrapolate to general population affected
- Considered an evidence-based resource

Disadvantages
- Difficult and time consuming to identify appropriate studies
- Not all studies provide adequate data for inclusion and analysis
- Requires advanced statistical techniques
- Heterogeneity of study populations

145. A. A bell-shaped curve

The bell curve is the most common type of distribution for a variable, and due to this fact, it is known as a normal distribution. The term "bell curve" comes from the fact that the graph used to depict a normal distribution consists of a bell-shaped line. The highest point on the curve, or the top of the bell, represents the most probable event in a series of data, while all other possible occurrences are equally distributed around the most probable event, creating a downward-sloping line on each side of the peak.

146. E. The clinical trial may not have enough power

The trial is small and may not have enough patients to truly test for a difference

147. A. A cost minimization analysis

Cost-minimization analysis (CMA) measures and compares input costs, and assumes outcomes to be equivalent. Thus, the types of interventions that can be evaluated with this method are limited. The strength of each CMA lies in the acceptability by the readers or evaluators that outcomes are indeed equivalent. A common example of a CMA is the comparison of generic equivalents of the same drug entity. For a generic medication to be approved for market, the manufacturer must demonstrate to the Food and Drug Administration (FDA) that its product is bioequivalent to the initially branded medication. Therefore, when comparing medications that are the same chemical entity, the same dose, and have the same pharmaceutical properties as each other (brand versus generic or generic made by one company compared with a generic made by another company), only the cost of the medication itself needs to be compared because outcomes should be the same

148. B. Nominal

Discrete date can be divided into four categories (gender, martial status, etc). This is called nominal discrete value

149. C. Continuous

Discrete data have finite values, or buckets. You can count them. Continuous data technically have an infinite number of steps, which form a continuum. The number of questions correct would be discrete--there are a finite and countable number of questions. Time to complete a task is continuous since it could take 178.8977687 seconds. Time forms an interval from 0 to infinity. You can usually tell the difference between discrete and continuous data because discrete usually can be preceded by "number of..."

Discrete:
- Number of children in a household
- Number of languages a person speaks
- Number of people sleeping in stats class

Continuous:
- Height of children
- Weight of cars
- Time to wake up in the morning
- Speed of the train

150. C. Case-control study

A case control study compares patients who have a disease or outcome of interest (cases) with patients who do not have the disease or outcome (controls), and looks back retrospectively to compare how frequently the exposure to a risk factor is present in each group to determine the relationship between the risk factor and the disease. Case control studies are observational because no intervention is attempted and no attempt is made to alter the course of the disease.

The goal is to retrospectively determine the exposure to the risk factor of interest from each of the two groups of individuals: cases and controls. These studies are designed to estimate odds.

Case control studies are also known as "retrospective studies" and "case-referent studies."

Advantages
- Good for studying rare conditions or diseases

- Less time needed to conduct the study because the condition or disease has already occurred
- Lets you simultaneously look at multiple risk factors
- Useful as initial studies to establish an association
- Can answer questions that could not be answered through other study designs

Disadvantages
- Retrospective studies have more problems with data quality because they rely on memory and people with a condition will be more motivated to recall risk factors (also called recall bias).
- Not good for evaluating diagnostic tests because it's already clear that the cases have the condition and the controls do not
- It can be difficult to find a suitable control group

151. B. A cost-minimization analysis

View answer for question 147.

152. C. Cost-Effectiveness analysis

Cost-effectiveness analysis seeks to identify and place dollars on the costs of a program. It then relates these costs to specific measures of program effectiveness. Analysts can obtain a program's cost-effectiveness (CE) ratio by dividing costs by what we term units of effectiveness:
Cost-Effectiveness Ratio = Total Cost/Units of Effectiveness

153. 0.94

Hazard ratio (HR) = hazard rate in the treatment group/hazard rate in the control group.
HR = 32.7%/34.7% = 0.94

154. A, E

The specificity of a clinical test refers to the ability of the test to correctly identify those patients without the disease. A test with 100% specificity correctly identifies all patients without the disease. A test with 80% specificity correctly reports 80% of patients without the disease as test negative (true negatives) but 20% patients without the disease are incorrectly identified as test positive (false positives)

155. D. Cost-Utility Analysis

Cost-utility analysis is used to determine cost in terms of utilities, especially quantity and quality of life. This type of analysis is controversial because it is difficult to put a value on health status or on an improvement in health status as perceived by different individuals or societies. Unlike cost-benefit analysis, cost-utility analysis is used to compare two different drugs or procedures whose benefits may be different. Cost-utility analysis expresses the value for money in terms of a single type of health outcome. The ICER in this case is usually expressed as the incremental cost to gain an extra quality-adjusted life-year (QALY). This approach incorporates both increases in survival time (extra life-years) and changes in quality of life (with or without increased survival) into one measure. An increased quality of life is expressed as a *utility* value on a scale of 0 (dead) to one (perfect quality of life). An increased duration of life of one year (without change in quality of life), or an increase in quality of life from 0.5 to 0.7 utility units for five years, would both result in a gain of one QALY.

156. A. Test will be positive 79% of the time in patients who have breast cancer marker

Sensitivity is if a person has a disease, how often will the test be positive (true positive rate). Put another way, if the test is highly sensitive and the test result is negative you can be nearly certain that they don't have disease. A Sensitive test helps rule out disease (when the result is negative)

Specificity is if a person does not have the disease how often will the test be negative (true negative rate). If the test result for a highly specific test is positive you can be nearly certain that they actually have the disease. A very specific test rules in disease with a high degree of confidence

157. E. The patient should not receive clopidogrel

Clopidogrel is a pro-drug that needs to be converted by liver enzymes. If the patient lacks the enzyme, they should be switched to Brillinta.

158. A, B, D

Trastuzumab or Herceptin as the brand name requires pharmacogenomic testing to ensure patients are HER2 positive.

159. B. The patient cannot be dispensed Ziagen

If a patient is positive for HLA-B*5701 then they cannot receive Ziagen or abacavir either by itself or in combination due to a highly hypersensitive reaction causing mutli-organ syndromes

160. A, C

As the child is a rapid metabolizer of CYP 2D6, this means that the codeine in Tylenol #3 will rapidly convert into morphine leading to an overdose causing respiratory distress, depression, and possibly death in the child

161. A, B, E

A person with less expression of CYP 2C9 enzyme will be a higher risk of bleeding since less of the warfarin is metabolized to be excreted so higher levels remain in the blood. If a patient produces less VKORC1 they need a lower dose of warfarin for similar reasons

162. C. Fentanyl

Fentanyl, meperidine, and methadone do not cross react with opioids of the morphine-type; however, they do not always represent appropriate use

163. B, C

Clevidipine, propofol, and progesterone in Prometrium must be avoided in patients with a peanut allergy

164. B, D, E

A "true allergy" is a reaction triggered by the immune system, however there are a vast number of symptoms or conditions caused by sensitivities that may or may not involve the immune system. Mild rashes and other minor tendencies are intolerances as Benadryl and other antihistamine medications are applied to patients that have minor intolerances to certain medications needed in hospital settings.

165. A, B, C, D

A "sulfa" allergy is most likely due to the sulfamethaxazole component in Bactrim. If there is a reaction to this drug then sulfasalazine and sulfisoxazole. It's rare for a reaction with zonisamide or celecoxib but they are contraindicated with a sulfa allergy and should be avoided. Sulfate is not the same as sulfa and morphine sulfate may be used.

166. A, D, E

If a patient has anaphylactic reaction, they will need to go to the ER or call 911 immediately receiving an epinephrine injection and may also receive diphenhydramine. Patients who are at risk should always carry an epinephrine pen. In Florida, pharmacists are allowed to administer epinephrine pens in emergency situations and administer to patients.

167. B. Acetaminophen

Aspirin has a similar structure to the NSAID class; thus, patients with aspirin sensitivities may also have sensitivities in NSAIDs that should be avoided.

168. A, B, C, D

All except azithromycin are beta-lactam antibiotics. If you see an allergy to penicillin or other beta-lactam, assume on the exam that the patient will cross-react so do not choose any others in the same class. The cross-reactivity is very low; however, the exam is safety-focused so do not pick an agent that has the potential to cross-react.

169. E. After the shot, press the needle against a hard surface to bend the needle back. Put the injector back in its case, needle first

The EpiPen is designed to go through clothing. All of the following are correct except E as this poses a needle stick risk.

170. C. MedWatch

Use the MedWatch form to report adverse events that you observe or suspect for human medical products, including serious drug side effects, product use errors, product quality problems, and therapeutic failures for: Prescription or over-the-counter medicines, as well as medicines administered to hospital patients or at outpatient infusion centers, Biologics (including blood components, blood and plasma derivatives, allergenic, human cells, tissues, and cellular and tissue-based products (HCT/Ps)), Medical devices (including in vitro diagnostic products), Combination products, Special nutritional products (dietary supplements, infant formulas, and medical foods), Cosmetics, and Foods/beverages (including reports of serious allergic reactions)

171. B, C, D, E

A patient knows their body best and is ultimately the one in charge of their health. Thus, it's best to educate the patient. The majority of errors are found and resolved during counseling.

172. B. The Joint Commission

The Joint Commission is a United States-based nonprofit tax-exempt 501 organization that accredits more than 21,000 health care organizations and programs in the United States

173. A, C, D, E

The provider only provided the route and amount of the medication, but left out many other necessary pieces of information such as frequency, child's weight and height, indication, writing for one teaspoonful instead of 5 mL, and no age

174. C, D, E

You should always wear and use a mask that covers the nose and mouth. Placing items behind each other prevents the air to also hit that object

175. B. Placing the medications in high-risk bins, with notations on the front of the bins regarding name-mix-ups and other relevant alerts

A high alert drug such as insulin should be placed in a brightly colored bin with warning on front to avoid medication errors. A medication guide and syringes or other items to be dispensed can be placed in the bin. Warning on the front should include alerts for drug name mix ups, etc

176. B. PCAs require an educated, coordinated health care team

PCA devices contain narcotics and/or anesthetics for synergy usually in hospice, post-op, and cancer settings. They require coordinated health care teams to ensure all healthcare providers such as nurses and other assistants are aware how to use. PCAs help patients administer pain medication to themselves to help lower doses required and are cost-effective

177. E. UTIs, due to indwelling catheters

Indwelling catheters are the most common cause of UTIs and are sometimes due to patient non-compliance in removing and replacing catheters. Usually when the catheter is removed the infection most likely resolves

178. A, B, C

Use of single vial doses are preferred since multi-dose vials should be assigned to patients and labeled. The needle/syringe should be changed after each patient use if used for multiple different patients

179. C. Potassium chloride injection and hypertonic saline

These are high-alert medications per ISMP due to the high risk of potential death these may cause. Potassium fast push may stop the heart and hypertonic saline can cause pain and necrosis of the injection site if injected wrongly

180. C. Medication Reconciliation

Patients admitted to a hospital commonly receive new medications or have changes to previous medications. The new medication regimen prescribed at the time of discharge may be omitted or the patient may not understand to take the medication. Medication reconciliation is a crucial process to avoid many healthcare problems by reviewing medications

181. A. To ensure that the benefits of dangerous drugs outweigh the risks

The FDA requires high-risk drugs to have a Risk Evaluation and Mitigation Strategy (REMS) from the manufacturer to ensure benefits outweigh the risks. REMS drugs require specific restrictions, patient registries, and other regulations to ensure safety. An example is the iPLEDGE program for isotretinoin common among college students

182. A, B, D, E

In ADCs (automatic dispensing cabinets such as pyxis) kept off-site from a hospital the filling should be done at the pharmacy and the pockets/drawers should be transported securely. It's not advisable to have other healthcare professionals other than pharmacists or pharmacy technicians stock the pyxis. Over-rides are sometimes made and they are monitored usually by pharmacists to ensure appropriate stock and preventing theft

183. A. To determine safety, efficacy and dose-response relationships in the population

Please ensure to know the different phases of drug studies

184. D. AB

The publication Approved Drug Products with Therapeutic Equivalence Evaluations (commonly known as the Orange Book) identifies drug products approved on the basis of safety and effectiveness by the Food and Drug Administration (FDA) under the Federal Food, Drug, and Cosmetic Act (the Act) and related patent and exclusivity information. AA stands for no bioequivalence problems in conventional dosage forms, AB stands for meeting necessary bioequivalence requirements

185. E. Phase IV

The pharmacist should be making a report to FDA's MEDWATCH program

186. C. To determine efficacy

Phase II studies examine the effectiveness of a compound

187. E. The Food and Drug Administration's (FDA) Center for Drug Evaluation and Research (CDER)

The Center for Drug Evaluation and Research (CDER) performs an essential public health task by making sure that safe and effective drugs are available to improve the health of people in the United States. As part of the U.S. Food and Drug Administration (FDA), CDER regulates over-the-counter and prescription drugs, including biological therapeutics and generic drugs. This work covers more than just medicines. For example, fluoride toothpaste, antiperspirants, dandruff shampoos and sunscreens are all considered "drugs"

188. B, C, E

Kava is used for anxiety but it's not recommended due to hepatotoxicity

189. E. Vitamin B6

Pyridoxine (Vitamin B6) 25-50mg by mouth daily is used to reduce the risk of INH-induced peripheral neuropathy

190. A, C, E

It's important to know the names of vitamins

191. B. To reduce the risk of serious birth defects in children born to women with low folic acid intake

Any woman of child-bearing age who is planning to conceive should take a folic acid supplement of 400 mcg or more per day to help prevent birth defects such as to the brain and spinal cord. Folic acid needs to be taken months before pregnancy

192. B. If you take the antibiotic in the morning and at night, take the probiotic in the middle of the day

Probiotics are beneficial to take but it's important to separate out by at least a few hours from the antibiotic as the antibiotic will destroy the probiotic. Lycopene is used for prostate cancer prevention, saw palmetto prostate enlargement, and comfrey should not be recommended as hepatotoxic. Probiotics should be continued weeks after the antibiotic has stopped to prevent a rare but serious C. Diff. infection

193. A, C, D, E

Fat-soluble vitamins should be supplemented in patients on Orlistat

194. A, D, E

Feverfew, willow bark, butterbur, guarana (due to caffeine), fish oils, magnesium, CoQ10, and riboflavin may help prevent migraines

195. C. Oscal

Oscal is oyster-shell calcium and is a more expensive form of calcium carbonate. It may be best to advise the patient to take other calcium supplements that do not require an acidic environment to help with adherence

196. A. Homeopathic products may not be homeopathic but labeled as such to sound pleasing to the patient

Homeopathy is based on how very small amounts of an illness will protect and/or provide a cure to a patient. The amount of the active component is usually not detectable if it's truly homeopathic. This term is used on many products to appeal to customers

197. C. Take one with breakfast and the other with dinner

Calcium has a saturable absorption, the more taken the less absorbed. It's best to take two tablets divided. Calcium carbonate is taken with food and divided into two doses with meals

198. C. Vitamin D

Vitamin D is essential in helping the body absorb and use calcium; in fact, the body cannot absorb calcium at all without some vitamin D. Vitamin D comes from two sources. It is made in the skin through direct exposure to sunlight, and it comes from the diet

199. E. DHEA

DHEA may help with erectile dysfunction and is a precursor to testosterone. DHEA is safe at usual doses but higher doses can cause acne, hirsutism, and increase risk for hypertension or liver damage

200. E. Cholecalciferol is vitamin D3 and is the preferred source

Vitamin D2 is used for renal insufficiency or short-term in adults with deficiency to replenish stores. Vitamin D3 is the preferred source and is a prodrug. If the patient has severe renal impairment, they will need to use the active Vitamin D3 (Calcitriol) or newer D3 analogs (doxercalciferol, paricacitol)

201. C. This condition can lead to permanent cognitive deterioration, and cause psychosis

Wernicke's encephalopathy is caused by a deficiency of Vitamin B1 (thiamine). Korsakoff's can develop after leading to permanent neurological damage. B1 deficiency is most common due to alcoholism but may be due to malabsorption such as Crohn's disease

202. D, E

Estrogen contains black cohosh and soy. Phytoestrogens (plant estrogens) such as soy and red clover may provide mild benefit in some woman. Black cohosh is generally safe but lacks efficacy data. Some reports of liver toxicity have been noted. Willow bark is a salicylate-containing product used for mild pain, not menopausal symptoms

203. C. Pharmacists have easily accessible sources to check for drug interactions and safety concerns with natural products

Manufacturing may not follow good manufacturing practices (GMP); help customers choose a reputable product. A dietary supplement manufacturer doesn't have to prove a product's safety and effectiveness before it is marketed. Pharmacists use the Natural Medicines Database to look up dietary and natural supplement information

204. B, D, E

Plant stanols/sterols, statins such as atorvastatin and rosuvastatin, and red yeast rice which contains low doses of lovastatin can reduce cholesterol

205. D. Vitamin B12

Metformin can cause deficient levels of Vitamin B12. It's important for patients to take a vitamin B supplement especially if they present symptoms of fatigue

206. A, D

Breastfed infants or babies drinking less than 1 liter of baby formula need 400 IU of vitamin D daily such as Poly-Vi-Sol and 1 mg/kg/day of iron from 4-6 months old and until consuming iron rich foods such as spinach. The common iron supplements for babies are Fer-in-Sol Iron supplementation drops

207. B. Citracal

Calcium carbonate is acid-dependent absorption so it needs to be taken with food. Calcium citrate (Citracal) is absorbed well with food or without so it's acid-independent. Most dietary calcium is carbonate and is absorbed best with an acidic gut medium; long-term use of strong acid-suppressing agents lowers calcium intake and contributes to poor bone growth. Patients on pantoprazole and other acid-reducing agents should be cautioned about over use

208. B. Concurrent use of birth control pills and St. John's wort

St. John's Wort is a potent inducer of hepatic enzymes. It can't be used with oral contraceptives, transplant drugs, warfarin, and other CYP450 3A4 drugs as it induces this pathway leading to rapid metabolism

209. A, B, C, D

An SSRI plus sumatriptan has a risk of serotonin syndrome. The patient is also taking meperidine which is not effective for chronic pain and a serotogenic agent as well. Any combination of serotonergic agents has risks and are compounded when used in combination or newer medications in same class added to regimen

210. A. Drug A levels would stay the same, Drug B levels increase, Drug C levels increase

Drug C inhibits 2D6 and increases drug levels of B as it's a substrate. Drug A inhibits 3A4 and increases levels of Drug C as it's a substrate for 3A4. Neither Drug B or C inhibits or induces 2C9 so Drug A levels remain the same as it's a substrate for 2C9

211. B, C, D

NSAIDs do raise blood pressure including celecoxib and should be noted in patients with hypertension. Safer options for mild pain is Tylenol or acetaminophen use

212. B, C, E

Inducers increase the metabolism of drugs that are substrates of the affected enzyme so if a compound is a P-gp pump inducer, it can cause the levels of P-gp substrates to decrease as it has a higher level of metabolism. Inhibitors are the opposite as the block the enzyme. Tacrolimus, cyclosporine, dabigatran and rivaroxaban are examples of substrates of P-gp efflux pumps

213. C. Ziprasidone

Ziprasidone can cause additive QT prolongation and must be used with caution in patients with any arrhythmia risk

214. B, C, D, E

Potassium is renally cleared; severe renal disease causes hyperkalemia by itself, and potassium is cleared by dialysis. Additive potassium accumulation may be due to potassium retaining agents

215. A, B, D

Grapefruit knocks out the enzymes. This is not a gut interaction problem and the effects of grapefruit last a few hours. It is best to avoid grapefruit

216. C. Cyclosporine

Quinidine, verapamil, erythromycin, clarithromycin, itraconazole, cyclosporine, propafenone, spironolactone, and others can increase digoxin levels

217. C. Increased risk of bleeding and increased risk of arrhythmia

Fluoxetine and paroxetine inhibit the metabolism of warfarin. Drug inhibition results in increased drug levels and elevated INR/bleeding risk. SSRIs and SNRIs increase bleeding risk even if the INR is therapeutic (mostly 2-3 depending on what conditions). Citalopram is a QT-risk agent especially at higher doses and should not be used in this patient and two SSRIs should not be used concurrently

218. D, E

Lithium is 100% renally cleared and has drug interactions with renally cleared medications. Salt intake is inversely related to lithium: the kidneys do not distinguish between lithium and sodium so if the salt intake increases, the lithium excretion increases and lithium levels decrease. Patients on lithium should maintain a constant salt intake

219. B, E

Niacin and statins have an increased risk of muscle toxicity. Niaspan can be used with lower doses of simvastatin and lovastatin

220. A, B, E

A small percentage of Digoxin is metabolized hepatically (via liver). Quinidine, warfarin, and digoxin must have their doses reduced by 30-50% when starting amiodarone and grapefruit should be avoided with amiodarone

221. D. Lopid

HMG-CoA reductase inhibitors plus niacin, gemfibrozil (Lopid) and other major inhibitors if statin metabolism (erythromycin, itraconazole, etc) are high-risk to use in combo with statins (may use pitavastatin or pravastatin)

222. B. The "RIPE" regimen for treating active tuberculosis

Rifampin is one of four drugs used in combo in the "RIPE" regimen to treat tuberculosis (TB). The treatment for active TB is not short duration and would require a different method of contraception such as IUD, condoms, etc

223. C, D, E

Absorption of tetracycline and doxycycline is impaired by aluminum, magnesium, calcium and iron containing preparations. Sucralfate (Carafate) is an aluminum complex. It must be separated from other drugs and from the aluminum content it may cause constipation

224. B. Pravastatin

Pravastatin is not metabolized by CYP enzymes. When statin levels are increased due to statin enzyme inhibition, there is higher risk of muscle toxicity presenting symptoms like muscle aches, soreness, or rhabdomyolysis which may cause acute renal failure

225. A, B, D

Triptans cannot be used with MAO inhibitors

226. A, B, E

Quinolones such as levofloxacin are QT-prolonging agents similar to macrolides like azithromycin. The patient is not taking a usual dose of amitriptyline for neuropathy

227. A, B, C, D

With a CrCl of less than 50 ml/min, only one dose of voriconazole can be given IV; oral voriconazole can be used for additional dosing since it accumulates in the IV SBECD

228. D. Acute drop in blood pressure

Nitrates used with the PDE5 inhibitors is contraindicated because it also vasodilates the body. Caution should be used with alpha blockers such as doxazosin as it may cause more dizziness or hypotensive orthostasis due to the drop in blood pressure. Lower doses and titrating slowly up is advised when starting on these agents

229. A, B, C, D

The monoclonal antibodies ("mabs") can cause adverse effects but ototoxicity is not one of them

230. A. Bupropion

SSRIs and SNRIs increase bleeding risk. The combination is dangerous as even though the INR may not increase, the bleeding risk does increase. Wellbutrin (bupropion) is an atypical antidepressant that blocks dopamine/NE reuptake inhibitor. Effexor (Venlafaxine) is an SNRI, Pristiq (desvenlafaxine) is an SNRI, Lexapro (cscitalopram) an SSRI, Cymbalta (duloxetine) is an SNRI

231. A, B, D

Lamotrigine (Lamictal) has a severe rash risk and needs slow dose titration to reduce this risk. Inhibitors like valproate will increase the risk of the rash

232. C, E

A patient using a monoamine oxidase inhibitor can't take ephedrine and it's analogs like pseudoephedrine, buspirone, levodopa, linezolid, lithium, meperidine, SSRIs, TCAs, tramadol, mirtazapine, dextromethorphan, cyclobenzaprine along with other skeletal muscle relaxants, levodopa, St. John's Wort, some triptans, and others. Ensure to also read the question as it states which drug will NOT cause concern

233. A, B, E

CNS side effects caused by lipophilic drugs entering that system and cause sedation, dizziness, confusion, and altered consciousness. Flexeril (cyclobenzaprine) is a skeletal muscle relaxant, Restoril (temazepam) is a benzodiazepine, Remeron (mirtazapine) is an alpha-2 antagonist antidepressant, and Nuvigil (armodafinil) is a CNS stimulant known to be used for narcolepsy

234. C. CBC

The CBC or CBC with differential will include the blood cell lines and is used to monitor for myelosuppression. CBC with differential can help to calculate the ANC (absolute neutrophil count) which should be ordered for this case

235. A. A value that can be life-threatening if corrective action is not taken quickly

Critical values such as lab values and diagnostic tests must be reported to providers immediately and acted quickly within a set time frame

236. C. The patient will be at risk for serious internal bleeding

G6PD-deficiency condition causing red blood cells to break down in response to certain medications, infections, or other stressors. Patients with G6PD-defiency need to know drugs that put them at risk of hemolysis

237. D. aPTT, 44 seconds

The Anti-Xa or aPTT can be used to monitor heparin

238. E. Anti-Xa

Anti-Xa Level is very important to get for the pediatric population to repeat every 4 hrs after next dose depending on level

239. D. The most likely drug contributing to the decrease in folate is methotrexate

Methotrexate is a folate antagonist and patients should be taking folic acid in conjunction with the medication. This patient could have received a rescue agent after his high dose treatment

240. D. The platelets

HIT is indicated by more than a 50% drop from baseline for patients. Usually, hospital pharmacists run a report to monitor patient levels and advanced hospitals have programs developed that would alert clinicians if platelet counts dropped significantly

241. A. Low pH, low serum bicarbonate

Causes of metabolic acidosis are diabetic ketoacidosis, decreased renal excretion, severe diarrhea, and other conditions. It's important to quickly correct these conditions as well so for example in diabetic ketoacidosis administer insulin drips

242. C. BiDil

BilDil or isorbide dinitrate and hydrazaline may cause drug-induced lupus mainly from the hydrazaline portion of the drug

243. C. MCV

The volume (and size) will be lower (low mean corpuscular volume) in a small cell (microcytic) anemia, and larger in a large cell (macrocytic) anemia

244. A. Respiratory acidosis

The patient is unable to breathe out the CO2 that he produces through respiration. Carbon dioxide, when dissolved in the blood, is an acid and causes acidosis. This is due to a problem with respiration as the patient cannot breathe out and may develop respiratory acidosis

245. B, C, D

Severe renal insufficiency is a creatinine clearance less than 30 ml/min. CKD stage 3 is 30-59 ml/min, stage 4 is 15-29 ml/min and stage 5 is less than 15 ml/min or dialysis-dependent

246. D. Calcium Chloride

When serum potassium is high enough to effect cardiac conduction, calcium either as chloride or gluconate should immediately be administered IV

247. B. Higher calcium levels

PhosLo is calcium acetate. It binds to dietary phosphate which is excreted in the feces. Calcium salts are widely used but can cause hypercalcemia

248. B. Hyperphosphatemia causes an increase in the release of parathyroid hormone

Bone metabolism abnormalities are caused by a rise in phosphorous. The kidneys clear the excess phosphorous but cannot clear adequately if they are impaired. The rise in phosphorous causes the parathyroid gland to increase the release of parathyroid hormone (PTH). PTH elevation leads to bone disease so it's important to control phosphorous levels. Treating secondary hyperparathyroidism is aimed at restricting phosphorous levels

249. B. This drug is a cation exchange resin that binds potassium in the gut

Sodium polystyrene sulfonate (Kayexalate) powder comes as a premixed oral or rectal liquid or powder as mixing. This is a cation exchange resin that is taken orally and binds potassium in the gut, causing a reduction in serum potassium. Do not mix this with sorbitol. Common side effects of Kayexalate are loss of appetite, nausea, vomiting, or constipation

250. A, C, E

Propylthiouracil is used in the first trimester and if trying to conceive. It is preferred to treat and resolve the hyperthyroidism first as both medications are teratogenic. The medications also cause nausea and are liver-toxic

2017 NAPLEX Practice Exam Answers

1. **D, E**

Lithium is 100% renally cleared (excreted), but has important drug interactions with drugs that affect renal clearance. Salt intake is inversely related to lithium; the kidneys do not distinguish between lithium and sodium so if salt intake increases, lithium excretion increases and lithium levels decrease. Patients need to maintain a constant salt intake

2. **A, B, E**

Although digoxin is largely renally cleared, a percentage of the drug is metabolized hepatically. All these agents must doses decreased 30-50% when beginning amiodarone while avoiding grapefruit juice or products with amiodarone

3. **A. Atorvastatin and amiodarone**

Grapefruit is a CYP3A4 inhibitor so it needs to be avoided with these medications

4. **B. The physician should also order the magnesium level; this is not included in the BMP**

The BMP includes glucose, calcium, sodium, potassium, bicarbonate, chloride, blood urea nitrogen and creatinine

5. **A, D**

Using the acronym ACLS TIN (Amiodarone, Carmustine, Lorazepam, Sufentanil, Thiopental, Insulin, and Nitroglycerin) are the medications that have sorption issues

6. **A, B, C**

He is at risk for QT prolongation due to the history of atrial fibrillation and use of amiodarone and moxifloxacin. He is also at risk for blood sugar alterations due to diabetes and the use of moxifloxacin

7. **C. USP Chapter 797**

This chapter contains information for Sterile Compounding standards

8. **B. USP Chapter 795**

This chapter contains information for Non-Sterile Compounding standards

9. **A. Zyprexa**

10. **C. Verapamil; Calcium Channel Blocker**

11. **A; Linagliptin; DPP-4 inhibitor**

12. **B. Saxagliptin; DPP-4 inhibitor**

13. **C. Sitagliptin; DPP-4 inhibitor**

14. **E. This medication should be refrigerated**

E.E.S., Augmentin, ceftriaxone, zostavax (diluent is in freezer), cephalexin, Vovotif Berna capsules, and isoniazid need to be kept refrigerated. E.E.S. is a macrolide antibiotic and is not effective for treating infections like influenza. The drug should be taken with food to minimize stomach upset and should be stored under refrigeration. Erythromycin is a major inhibitor of CYP3A4. As a macrolide antibiotic and not a penicillin, this may be an option if a penicillin allergy was present in the patient

15. **E. Biaxin**

Biaxin does not need to be refrigerated. Refrigeration can cause thickening and the product may crystallize

16. **C, D, E**

Cetriaxone and Cefazolin need to be refrigerated

17. **A, B, D**

Sulfamethoxazole/Trimethoprim is compatible with D5W only (not saline). Phenytoin is compatible with saline only (not dextrose)

18. A, D, E

Linezolid is part of the oxazolidinone class of antibiotics and doesn't need to be dose adjusted in renal impairment. The oral suspension should be stored at room temperature

19. E. Isosorbide dinitrate decreases preload, hydralazine decreases afterload

Isosorbide dinitrate reduces preload as a result of venous dilation. Hydralazine reduces afterload via arterial dilation. The combination, when administered orally, has the same pharmacological effect as intravenous nitroprusside

20. E. Carbamazepine

Carbamazepine is very effective in relieving and preventing the pain associated with trigeminal neuralgia and remains the drug of choice for this disorder. Phenytoin has also been reported to be helpful in some patients

21. C. Emtricitabine

Emtricitabine is a new nucleoside reverse transcriptase inhibitor approved as part of a combination therapy regimen for HIV-1 infected patients older than 3 months old

22. E. Methacholine

Methacholine (Provocholine) is commonly used as a provocative agent in the testing of airway responsiveness. The powdered drug is reconstituted with 0.9% NaCl and delivered to the airways via nebulizer in precisely controlled concentrations to produce cholinergic stimulation of airway smooth muscle. Methacholine produces nearly pure muscarinic stimulation with virtually no nicotinic action. It is metabolized by acetylcholinesterase (more slowly than acetylcholine), but is resistant to hydrolysis by pseudocholinesterase. Neither acetylcholine nor plasma cholinesterase are employed as therapeutic or diagnostic agents. Bethanechol is a choline ester with predominantly muscarinic actions. Carbachol is a potent choline ester with both muscarinic and nicotinic actions and is used in the treatment of glaucoma. Bethanechol and carbachol, through their muscarinic actions, can produce profound bronchoconstriction, but their resistance to cholinesterases (acetyl and plasma) makes their duration of action unsuitable for diagnostic airway challenge testing

23. B. The patient cannot be dispensed *Ziagen*

If a patient is positive for this allele they cannot receive Ziagen or abacavir by itself or in combination as they are at high risk for severe hypersensitivity reactions like multi-organ syndromes

24. A, B, E

Epivir HBV (lamivudine for hepatitis B) tablets and oral solution are not interchangeable with Epivir used for HIV; the dose is lower when used for Hep B treatment. Muscle weakness with stomach upset and nausea along with mental confusion/dizziness, are symptoms of lactic acidosis. NRTIs may rarely cause lactic acidosis; it can be fatal. Entecavir must be taken on an empty stomach and these drugs are mainly used for hepatitis B

25. A, C, D, E

Epivir HBV uses a lower dose of drug for HBV than when used for HIV. This drug may cause HIV resistance if HIV is not recognized or undertreated

26. A, D, E

ACIP recommends woman wait 4 weeks post yellow fever vaccination before attempting to become pregnant. Any hypersensitivity to eggs, chickens, or gelatin will prohibit vaccination. Receiving strong chemotherapy agents, immunocomprised conditions such as HIV, and receiving immune-suppressing agents such as liver transplant patients

27. B. Atazanavir; protease inhibitor

28. C. Rilpivirine/emtricitabine/tenofovir DF

Genvoya has the same components as Stribild (elvitegravir/cobicistat/emtricitabine/tenofovir disoproxil fumarate), but substitutes tenofovir alafenamide, or TAF, for Stribild's tenofovir disoproxil fumarate, or TDF. TAF has been shown to be less toxic to bones and kidneys than TDF. Because TAF enters cells more efficiently than TDF, a lower dose is required and 91 percent less of the tenofovir winds up in the bloodstream, where it may lead to toxicities

29. C. Bactrim 240 mg IV Q6H

An alternative is Bactrim DS 2 tablets PO Q8H. Opportunistic Infection Prophylaxis is important and there are three main infections to be concerned about: Pneumocystis jirovecii pneumonia (PCP), Toxoplasma gondii encephalitis, and Mycobacterium avium complex (MAC). Ensure to remember the CD4 counts associated with these opportunistic infections: For PCP, we begin prophylaxis when the CD4 count dips below 200. For toxoplasma gondii encepalitis, the count is 100. And for MAC, the CD4 count is 50. Conveniently, sulfamethoxazole-trimethoprim (SMZ/TMP) covers both PCP and toxoplasma. MAC is covered with either azithromycin (preferred) or clarithromycin. To summarize:
- CD4 < 200 = PCP (SMZ/TMP)
- CD4 < 100 = Toxo (also SMZ/TMP)
- CD4 < 50 = MAC (azithromycin or clarithromycin)

Drug Interactions: Protease Inhibitors- almost all of them are metabolized by CYP3A4 and ritonavir should be monitored. It's not used for viral efficacy but more used as a booster (or a "pharmacokinetic enhancer") because it's a powerful CYP inhibitor. Always scan the med profile for potential drug interactions when you see ritonavir. A common scenario to watch out for is statin use with protease inhibitors. There are specifics for each agent, but the general rule is to completely avoid simvastatin and lovastatin in any patient using a protease inhibitor.

Another common interaction is with acid-suppressing agents. There are two HIV drugs to be watchful for here: atazanavir (a protease inhibitor) and rilpivirine (an NNRTI). Both of them are contraindicated with Proton Pump Inhibitors. Increasing the pH of the stomach lowers the bioavailability of the drugs significantly enough to cause treatment failures and resistance.

Atazanavir and rilpivirine can be used with H2 antagonists, but must be separated from the dose by 10 to 12 hours

30. B, C, D

A few main points to remember about renal adjustment for HIV medications:
- All NRTIs need a renal adjustment (EXCEPT abacavir)
- Combination products with cobicistat are not given below a CrCl of 70 ml/min
- All other combination products are not given below a CrCl of 50 ml/min

These are general points that should apply for most cases. In this specific case Genvoya is not recommended for patients below a CrCl of 30 ml/min despite having cobicistat as it contains tenofovir alafenamide which is easier on the kidneys instead of tenofovir disoproxil used in Strilbild. This is also true for Truvada, Atripla, and the majority of other HIV regimens. This patient needs to be recommended for a kidney transplant depending on how well-controlled his HIV infection is controlled

31. B. Maraviroc; CCR5 on Human CD4 cells

This drug is notable because it's the only HIV medication that has a human (not viral) target. It specifically targets a binding protein on your CD4 cells, which prevents HIV from entering. But unfortunately, it only targets one binding protein: the CCR5 receptor. Some patients only have the CCR5 receptor. If that's the case, maraviroc will work. However, if the patient's CD4 cells have a CCR4 or a CXCR4 receptor, maraviroc will not work. To prevent error in treatment, a profile test is completed if you have the appropriate binding receptor on your CD4 cells

32. A, B, E

Blockage of GLUT4 insulin-regulated transporters keeps glucose from entering fat and muscle cells causing insulin resistance and potential type II diabetes. At low doses, ritonavir can enhance protease inhibitors

33. D. Emtricitabine, efavirenz, tenofovir

34. A, C

Pre-exposure prophylaxis, or PrEP, is a way for people who do not have HIV but who are at substantial risk of getting it to prevent HIV infection by taking a pill every day. The pill (brand name Truvada) contains two medicines (tenofovir and emtricitabine) that are used in combination with other medicines to treat HIV. When someone is exposed to HIV through sex or injection drug use, these medicines can work to keep the virus from establishing a permanent infection

35. A, C, D

Fuzeon may have the powder stored at room temperature but once mixed needs to be kept in the refrigerator and used within 24 hours. Aptivus + norvir should be kept refrigerated before opening; once opened it may be kept at room temperature for up to two months. Norvir capsules can be stored up to 30 days at room temperature

36. E. Patients are more easily arousable and alert when stimulated, compared to propofol

Dexmedetomidine, sold under the trade names **Precedex** among others, is an anxiolytic, sedative, and analgesic medication. Similar to clonidine, it is an agonist of α_2-adrenergic receptors in certain parts of the brain. Dexmedetomidine is notable for its ability to provide sedation without risk of respiratory depression (unlike other commonly used sedatives such as propofol, fentanyl, and midazolam) and can provide cooperative or semi-arousable sedation

37. A. Oil-in-water emulsion

Propofol was originally developed using a form solubilised in cremophor EL. However, due to anaphylactic reactions to cremophor, this formulation was withdrawn from the market and subsequently reformulated as an emulsion of a soya oil/propofol mixture in water. The emulsified formulation was relaunched in 1986 by ICI (now AstraZeneca) under the brand name Diprivan. Propofol emulsion is a highly opaque white fluid due to the scattering of light from the tiny (about 150-nm) oil droplets it contains. A water-soluble prodrug form, fospropofol, has recently been developed and tested with positive results. Fospropofol is rapidly broken down by the enzyme alkaline phosphatase to form propofol. Marketed as Lusedra, this new formulation may not produce the pain at injection site that often occurs with the traditional form of the drug

38. D. If particles are present, the pharmacist should shake well to dissolve the particles prior to the infusion

IBW should be used to calculate the dose of IVIG. IVIG should not be shaken since this will inactivate the antibodies

39. 24.6 mL

At a concentration of 500 mg per ml, and 5 grams of drug, there would be a total volume of 10 ml. But only 9.6 ml of diluent was added, so the powder contributed 0.4 ml to the final volume. At 250 mg/ml, there would be 20 ml of volume and at 100 mg/ml there would be 50 ml of volume. In each case the amount of diluent added was 0.4 ml less than the final volume. The powder will contribute 0.4 ml to the volume.

- grams = 5000 mg 5000 mg (div by) 200 mg/ml = 25 ml of total volume
  25 ml (minus) 0.4 ml (the powder volume) = 24.6 ml of diluent to add to make 200 mg/ml

40. 5.6

0.89 PPM = 0.89 mg/L

0.89 mg/L = 5 mg/ x L

x= 5.62 Liters

41. E. Vitamin B6

Pyridoxine (Vitamin B6) 25-50mg PO daily is used to reduce the risk of INH-induced peripheral neuropathy

42. C. Pernicious anemia

Pernicious anemia is defined as a type of vitamin B12 deficiency that results from impaired uptake of vitamin B-12 due to the lack of a substance known as intrinsic factor (IF) produced by the stomach lining. Pernicious anemia is a condition caused by too little vitamin B12 in the body. It is one form of vitamin B12 deficiency anemia

43. A. Preservative

Preservation is the prevention or inhibition of microbial growth. In pharmacy, this is commonly accomplished by the addition of a preservative to a product, with the primary purpose of minimizing microbial growth (as in oral liquids, topicals, etc.), or for preventing microbial growth (as in sterile preparations such as parenterals)

44. On the exam, you will need to click and select these areas:

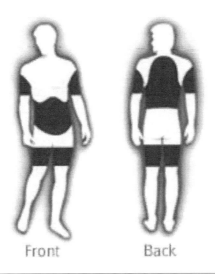

Front   Back

45. A, B, D, E

If a female had cancer in any reproductive tract part including breast, estrogen is contraindicated in any formulation

46. C. AndroGel

Androderm is a patch for the skin, think "derm=skin"

47. A. Administer 4900 units IV bolus, then 1100 units/hour continuous infusion

DVT & PE Prophylaxis
5000 units SC q8-12hr OR 7500 units SC q12hr
Treatment
80 units/kg IV bolus, THEN continuous infusion of 18 units/kg/hr, OR 5000 units IV bolus, THEN continuous infusion of 1300 units/hr, OR 250 units/kg (alternatively, 17,500 units) SC, THEN 250 units/kg q12hr

Weight based dosing is best to go by so choice a is the best answer to choose from

48. A, B, C

The sprinkle contents can be placed on a teaspoon of applesauce, pudding, or soft food and swallowed without chewing. If this is not able to be done, then the liquid can be used. The drug may cause serious birth defects but since this patient is so young this is not needed. This medication can't be used by a female patient with migraine headache prophylaxis due to pregnancy issues and concerns

49. A, B, D

Lamotrigine (Lamictal) has a risk of severe rash and needs a slow dose titration to reduce the risk. Inhibitors like valproate will increase the risk of rash

50. A, B

Many inhibitors increase the theophylline level and many inducers decrease the theophylline level. Theophylline has a narrow therapeutic index so it is easy to create subtherapeutic or toxic levels so the drug needs monitoring. Smoking (this includes marijuana) causes induction and can lower the efficacy of some substrates like theophylline or clozapine

51. A, B, D

Sulfamethoxazole/Trimethoprim is compatible with D5W only (not saline). Phenytoin is compatible with saline only (not dextrose)

52. A, B, D

Phenytoin may cause all of these side effects

53. C. Emtricitabine

About 86% of a dose of emtricitabine is eliminated unchanged by the kidneys, and dosage adjustment is necessary in patients with renal impairment

54. D. Quinidine

Even though quinidine, paroxetine, and fluoxetine can all inhibit CYP2D6, the effect of quinidine is the most potent. A small 50 mg dose of quinidine, which is much less than usual antiarrhythmic dose of 200 to 300 mg, can potently inhibit CYP2D6 and metabolically convert an EM into a PM. Fluvoxamine is not an inhibitor of CYP2D6

55. B. UGT1A1

Even though raltegravir is neither a substrate, inhibitor, nor inducer of the CYP family of isoenzymes, it is unique in that it is a substrate of UGT1A1, and therefore is susceptible to drug interactions with inhibitor or inducer of UGT1A1

56. E. Linezolid

Although vancomycin has been traditionally used for treatment of Gram-positive infection when other antibiotics fail, the emergence of vancomycin resistant bacteria has diminished its role, and other agents such as linezolid has been increasingly reserved for the treatment of serious Gram-positive infection that has failed or resistant to other antibiotics

57. B. Naloxone

Naloxone is an opioid antagonist that can be used to reverse the serious adverse effects of opiates in an overdose situation. Ketorolac is an NSAID. Pentazocine is a narcotic agonist-antagonist analgesic, whereas both codeine and methadone are narcotic analgesics

58. C. Lamotrigine 150 to 400 mg per day

The dosage regimens are too high for lithium, risperidone, and topiramate, and too low for valproic acid

59. A. Trimethoprim/Sulfamethazole and famcyclovir

Patients treated with alemtuzumab are susceptible to similar infections as patients with HIV, especially *P. jiroveci* and herpes viruses reactivation; thus, they require trimethoprim/sulfamethoxazole and famcyclovir prophylaxis. Gancyclovir is used for CMV with major side effect of myelosuppression. Due to this side effect, it is rarely if ever used for prophylaxis. Fluconazole is used for candida prophylaxis in bone marrow transplant recipients. Acyclovir and levofloxacin are other antibiotics used in many institutions following bone marrow transplant. Acyclovir has to be dosed 5 times per day, thus non-adherence plays a big role for this medication

60. D. HPV vaccine

Human papillomavirus vaccine (HPV) vaccine is currently recommended for 11 to 12-year-old females. It covers most common viruses associated with cervical cancer (HPV strains 16, 18) and genital warts (HPV strains 6, 8). It is given in a 3-dose schedule with the second and third doses administered 2 and 6 months after the first dose

61. B. Time > MIC is an appropriate measure for beta-lactams

Beta-lactams and macrolides exhibit concentration-independent bactericidal effect against susceptible bacteria. Therefore, the time or duration of concentration above the MIC is most predictive of efficacy for these antibiotics

62. A. Magnesium 2 g IV bolus

Magnesium is the drug of choice in the setting of torsades de pointes

63. D. Oral metronidazole 500 mg 3 times daily

Even though vancomycin can be administered orally for treatment of infection caused by *Clostridium difficile*, oral metronidazole is the drug of choice because of lower cost, comparable efficacy, and the possibility of emergence of vancomycin-resistant organisms. Vancomycin administered intravenously will not achieve high enough concentration within the gut. Antidiarrheal drugs would extend the toxin-related damage and worsen the course of pseudomembranous colitis caused by *Clostridium difficile*

64. B. Vitamin D

Orlistat decreases the oral absorption of vitamin D. Aspirin, lidocaine, and digoxin have not been reported to interact with vitamin D

65. C. Flurazepam

The optimal drug therapy for this patient would treat anxiety and decrease sleep latency period. Flurazepam is a benzodiazepine that is rapidly absorbed; the parent drug has a relatively long half-life and is converted to an active metabolite. The rapid onset of flurazepam is useful for sleep induction and the long half-life and active metabolite will alleviate anxiety symptoms during the day after a single bedtime dose. Although triazolam has a rapid onset, it is quickly converted to inactive metabolites, thus would not alleviate anxiety symptoms during the day after a single dose. Zolpidem, ramelteon, and diphenhydramine all have hypnotic effect, but do not alleviate the symptoms of anxiety

66. A. Increase cyclosporine levels

Even though ketoconazole is well known for its potent inhibitory effect on the cytochrome P-450 enzyme, specifically CYP3A4, it is occasionally combined with cyclosporine, which is metabolized by CYP3A4, to achieve the same therapeutic effect but with a lower cyclosporine dose and drug cost

67. B. Leucovorin should not be administered at a rate >160 mg/min

Leucovorin or folinic acid can prevent the side effects of a cancer medication called methotrexate. It can treat anemia caused by a lack of folic acid. It is also used in supportive care of patients with colon cancer and to treat overdoses of certain medicines. It should not be administered at a rate greater than 160 mg/min due to calcium content of the solution

68. C. Ampicillin and gentamicin

Ampicillin provides appropriate empiric coverage for *Listeria monocytogenes* and *Streptococcus agalactiae* (may cover some aerobic gram-negative bacilli as well). Gentamicin provides appropriate empiric coverage against aerobic gram-negative bacilli (and some synergy with ampicillin against gram-positives, like *L. monocytogenes*). Ampicillin and cefotaxime would also be an appropriate regimen. While gentamicin is appropriate, this regimen is missing first-line empiric coverage for *L. monocytogenes* (ie, ampicillin). Also, ceftriaxone is not a first-line agent for bacterial meningitis in neonates (≤28 days) due to risk of adverse events, for example, biliary sludging, kernicterus, and potentially life-threatening precipitation with calcium-containing products. While cefotaxime is appropriate, this regimen is missing empiric coverage for *L. monocytogenes* (ie, ampicillin). Also, vancomycin is broader empiric Gram-positive coverage than is generally needed for neonates. While ampicillin is appropriate, cefotaxime is the preferred third-generation cephalosporin in neonates. Ceftriaxone is not a first-line agent for bacterial meningitis in neonates (≤28 days) due to risk of adverse events, for example, biliary sludging, kernicterus, and precipitation potentially life-threatening with calcium-containing products

69. C. Water retention and osteoporosis

Water retention and osteoporosis both are adverse effects specific to corticosteroids. Water retention leads to weight gain and hypertension. It is important to ensure adequate calcium intake and screening for bone mineral density in patients taking corticosteroids chronically

70. A. Attempt immediate IV line placement and administer antibiotics IV for the duration of therapy

IV therapy is the preferred route for antimicrobial treatment of CNS infections in order to ensure optimal CNS penetration (including allowing for administration of high-dose regimens)

71. B. Diphenhydramine, dexamethasone, ranitidine

Paclitaxel is associated with severe hypersensitivity reactions. If a hypersensitivity reaction occurs stop the infusion and do not re-challenge if the patient experienced hypotension requiring treatment or angioedema. Premedication with dexamethasone, diphenhydramine, and ranitidine is recommended

72. B, E

Efavirenz and nevirapine are NNRTIs. Dual NNRTI therapy is contraindicated. Truvada and Atripla are complete HIV regimens, dual therapy is also contraindicated here

73. C. Procarbazine

Procarbazine may have a disulfiram reaction when a patient consumes alcohol. Procarbazine has a lot of unique drug/food interaction. Procarbazine possesses monoamine oxidase inhibitor activity and has the potential for severe food and drug interactions (eg, tyramine containing foods leading to hypertensive crisis)

74. A, E

Atazanavir requires an acidic environment for optimal absorption. In treatment experienced patients, combination therapy with proton pump inhibitors is contraindicated. In treatment naïve patients, doses of omeprazole 20 mg equivalence or less, may be used *with caution*. The risk versus benefit should be weighed when combining these agents

75. B. Cytarabine + idarubicin

The most active agents in AML are anthracyclines and the antimetabolite cytarabine. Cytarabine in combination with idarubicin is often referred to as "7+3" regimen (cytarabine 100 mg/m2 days 1-7, idarubicin 12 mg/m2 days 1-3). Accounting for age, other comorbidities, and patient's ejection fraction, this combination should be recommended for initial induction therapy

76. B. Toxoplasmosis

Diagnosis of Toxoplasmosis can be made by seropositivity for IgG, diagnosis of candidiasis can be made by evaluation of risk factors and isolating a Candida species from a culture, diagnosis of MAC can be made by a positive acid fast bacilli (AFB) culture from a blood specimen, diagnosis of PCP can be made by polymerase chain reaction (PCR) procedures

77. A. Azithromycin

Azithromycin may be utilized as MAC primary prophylaxis. Clarithromycin may be utilized as MAC primary prophylaxis; however, clarithromycin should not be administered to a patient receiving simvastatin because of a drug interaction and increased risk of rhabdomyolysis

78. C. To provide coverage against resistant *Streptococcus pneumoniae*

While third-generation cephalosporins, for example, ceftriaxone, provide adequate coverage against most isolates of *S. pneumoniae*, some resistance has been reported. Vancomycin is added to provide empiric coverage against these resistant strains of *S. pneumonia*

79. A. Bacterial meningitis

Elevated WBC (1000-10,000 cells/mm3), predominance of neutrophils (80%-90%), and elevated CSF protein (>100 mg/dL) as well as low CSF glucose (<40 mg/dL, and a likely CSF:serum glucose ratio of ≤0.4) are all consistent with bacterial meningitis

80. D. MCV4

MCV4 is the specific formulation of the meningococcal vaccine recommended as a routine vaccination for adolescents aged 11 to 12 years, with a booster dose at age 16 years. MCV4 is also recommended for children aged 2 months to 10 years, if risk factors for meningococcal disease are present, such as persistent complement deficiencies, anatomic or functional asplenia (eg, sickle cell disease), presence during an outbreak caused by a vaccine serogroup, or travel to the African meningitis belt or to the Hajj

81. C. Vancomycin, ceftriaxone, and ampicillin

Ceftriaxone provides appropriate empiric coverage for *N. meningitidis*, aerobic gram-negative bacilli, and most *S. pneumoniae*. Vancomycin provides additional empiric coverage for multidrug-resistant *S. pneumoniae*. Ampicillin provides additional empiric coverage for *L. monocytogenes*. Even though the patient has a penicillin allergy, he does not display any major life threatening symptoms and should be treated as meningitis is a life threatening disease

82. B. Combination hydralazine 25 mg and isosorbide dinitrate 10 mg TID

The combination of hydralazine and isosorbide dinitrate has demonstrated a significant mortality benefit in African Americans receiving optimal HF therapy with β-blockers and ACE inhibitors

83. B. Metoprolol succinate

Only three β-blockers have been demonstrated to reduce mortality in heart failure: carvedilol, metoprolol succinate, and bisoprolol. Metoprolol succinate is the correct answer because it has a proven mortality benefit in HFrEF and it is a cardioselective β-blocker. While metoprolol is β-1 selective, it is important to recognize that β-receptor selectivity may decrease as the dose is uptitrated

84. A, B, C, D

The brand name of Orlistat is Xenical not Xeniteel

85. B. Pulmonary Arterial Hypertension

ADCIRCA is a prescription medicine called a phosphodiesterase 5 inhibitor used to treat pulmonary arterial hypertension (PAH, high blood pressure in your lungs) to improve exercise ability

86. C. Medium-dose ICS and LABA

The patient is exhibiting severe persistent asthma which requires high-dose steps 4 to 6 combination therapy

87. B. Budesonide/Formoterol

Current 2016 list of inhaled asthma medication combinations containing both a corticosteroid and a bronchodilator:
- Fluticasone and salmeterol (Advair Diskus)
- Budesonide and formoterol (Symbicort)
- Mometasone and formoterol (Dulera)
- Fluticasone and vilanterol (Breo)

88. A, B, D

The medications used for the treatment of pinworm are either mebendazole, pyrantel pamoate, or albendazole. Any of these drugs are given in one dose initially, and then another single dose two weeks later. Pyrantel pamoate is available without prescription. The medication does not reliably kill pinworm eggs

89. A. Vitamin K1

Phytonadione or Vitamin K1 is used to reverse warfarin effects:

- INR 4.5-10, no bleeding: 2012 ACCP guidelines suggest against routine use; 2008 ACCP guidelines suggest considering vitamin K1 (phytonadione) 1-2.5 mg PO once
- INR >10, no bleeding: 2012 ACCP guidelines recommend vitamin K1 PO (dose not specified); 2008 ACCP guidelines suggest 2.5-5 mg PO once; INR reduction observed within 24-48 hr, monitor INR and give additional vitamin K if needed
- Minor bleeding, any elevated INR: Consider 2.5-5 mg PO once; may repeat if needed after 24 hr
- Major bleeding, any elevated INR: 2012 ACCP guidelines recommend prothrombin complex concentrate, human (PCC, Kcentra) plus vitamin K1 5-10 mg IV (dilute in 50 mL IV fluid and infuse over 20 min)

NOTE: High vitamin K doses (ie, 10 mg or more) may cause warfarin resistance for a week or more; consider using heparin, LMWH, or direct thrombin inhibitors to provide adequate thrombosis prophylaxis in clinical conditions requiring chronic anticoagulation therapy

90. C. H. Pylori

PYLERA capsules are used to treat H. Pylori infections and are a combination antimicrobial product containing bismuth subcitrate potassium, metronidazole, and tetracycline hydrochloride for oral administration. Each size 0 elongated capsule contains:
- Bismuth subcitrate potassium, 140 mg
- Metronidazole, 125 mg
- Smaller capsule (size 3) containing tetracycline hydrochloride, 125 mg

Tetracycline hydrochloride is encapsulated within a smaller capsule to create a barrier to avoid contact with bismuth subcitrate potassium

91. All of the above (A-E)

ESAs stimulate the bone marrow to make more red blood cells and are FDA approved for use in reducing the need for blood transfusions in patients with chronic kidney failure, cancer patients on chemotherapy, patients scheduled for major surgery (except heart surgery) and patients with HIV who are using AZT.

The following types of ESAs are available:
- Erythropoietin (Epo)
- Epoetin alfa (Procrit/Epogen)
- Epoetin beta (NeoRecormon)
- Darbepoetin alfa (Aranesp)
- Methoxy polyethylene glycol-epoetin beta (Mircera)

92. A, B, C

Alzheimer's disease (AD) is a progressive dementia with loss of neurons and the presence of two main microscopic neuropathological hallmarks: extracellular amyloid plaques and intracellular neurofibrillary tangles. This leads to interrupted neuron signaling and altered neurotransmitters

93. A, B, C, D

Short-intermediate acting benzodiazepine receptor agonist benzodiazepines (BzRA BZDs) are first-line therapy options for most patients and should be limited for 7-10 days for insomnia. A-D present short-intermediate acting benzodiazepines where as choice E. Alprazolam is a short-acting benzodiazepine that may lead to dependence

94. A. Every two weeks

RISPERDAL® CONSTA® is a long-acting injectable medication for Bipolar I Disorder and significantly delayed time to relapse, and is administered by a healthcare provider

95. B. Geodon, Zyprexa

Geodon is ziprasidone, and Zyprexa is olanzapine. Seroquel is quetiapine

96. A. Levonorgestrel 1.5 mg

Plan B One-Step is levonorgestrel 1.5 mg take 1 pill within 120 hours after unprotected sex. Ella is ulipristal acetate 30 mg take 1 pill within 120 hours after unprotected sex. Plan B is unrestricted so anyone can buy this medication

97. All of the above (A-E)

A thyroid panel is used to evaluate thyroid function and/or help diagnose hypothyroidism and hyperthyroidism due to various thyroid disorders. The panel typically includes tests for:
- Thyroid-stimulating hormone (TSH)
- Free thyroxine (free T4)
- Total or free triiodothyronine (total or free T3)

T4 and T3 are hormones produced by the thyroid gland. They help control the rate at which the body uses energy, and are regulated by a feedback system. TSH from the pituitary gland stimulates the production and release of T4 (primarily) and T3 by the thyroid. Most of the T4 and T3 circulate in the blood bound to protein. A small percentage is free (not bound) and is the biologically active form of the hormones.
The free T4 test is thought by many to be a more accurate reflection of thyroid hormone function and, in most cases, its use has replaced that of the total T4 test

98. A, C, D, E

Managing hypothyroidism requires getting a precise dose of medicine day after day. This precision is important because thyroid replacement therapy is a type of medication called a narrow therapeutic index (NTI) drug. With NTI drugs, if your dose is off even a little bit, you could experience symptoms of under-replacement (not enough medicine) or symptoms of over-replacement (too much medicine). Choice B is not correct as it allows for changes in the dose and drug levels. It's best to advise the patient to take Synthroid early in the morning 30-60 minutes before eating breakfast

99. B, C, E

Warfarin Table Identification

Tablet Strength	Tablet Color
1 mg	Pink
2 mg	Lavender (light purple)
2.5 mg	Green
3 mg	Tan
4 mg	Blue
5 mg	Peach (light orange)
6 mg	Teal (blue-green)
7.5 mg	Yellow
10 mg	White

100. A, C, D, E

Tricyclic antidepressants (TCAs) are used primarily as antidepressants. They are named after their chemical structure, which contains three rings of atoms. Tetracyclic antidepressants (TeCAs), which contain four rings of atoms

101. A, B, D, E

All of the following are correct except C. Ibandronate should not be taken with mineral water, only plain water due to potential absorption and interaction effects

102. A, B, D

Plavix or the generic name clopidogrel is a prodrug that is absorbed in the intestines along with Effient or the generic name prasugrel also metabolized in the intestine. Plavix is a second generation thienopyridine (Prodrug) whereas Effient is a third second generation thienopyridine (Prodrug)

103. A. CDC pink book, Trissels handbook

CDC yellow book is CDC's reference book on how devices and international travelers on health risk. Remington's provides compounding, manufacturing, and non-sterile compounding stability. Briggs drugs [in pregnancy and lactation] provides information on pregnancy and lactation. Stafford guide provides antimicrobial information, and the NLM provides a database of product package inserts

104. D. Dopamine agonist

Pramipexole is a non-ergot dopamine agonist with high relative *in vitro* specificity and full intrinsic activity at the D subfamily of dopamine receptors, binding with higher affinity to D3 than to D2 or D4 receptor subtypes

105. A, B, E

Amantadine and modafinil are used to treat fatigue in patients with MS. Pemoline is no longer used as it has severe liver toxicity. The rest are used in MS, brand name of Fingolimod is Gilenya

106. A. Montelukast 4 mg, leukotriene receptor antagonist, Singulair

The brand name of montelukast is Singulair and the mechanism of action is a leukotriene receptor antagonist to relieve symptoms of seasonal allergies. Accolate is another leukotriene receptor antagonist (generic is zafirlukast) and Zyflo (generic zileuton) inhibits the 5-lipoxygenase enzyme. 15 years and older: one 10-mg tablet. 6 to 14 years: one 5-mg chewable tablet. 6 to 23 months: one packet of 4-mg oral granules. Patients with both asthma and allergic rhinitis should take only one dose daily in the evening

107. C, D, E

Risperidone or Risperdal is indicated based off the PI:

- Treatment of schizophrenia
- As monotherapy or adjunctive therapy with lithium or valproate, for the treatment of acute manic or mixed episodes associated with Bipolar I Disorder
- Treatment of irritability associated with autistic disorder

108. A, B, C, D

Based off the 2016 CDC vaccine guidelines, A-D is recommended from the information you know about the patient. Since the patient has already received a Shingles vaccine (Zoster) he does not need to receive it again. The Zoster vaccine is only given once and recommended for adults 60 and older

109. A, C, D, E
Based off the 2016 CDC vaccine guidelines, the patient should avoid live vaccines especially with a CD4 count less than 200. However, she may get the Td/Tdap vaccine. If she had a CD4 count greater than 200 then she would be okay to receive all the vaccines

110. All the above (A-E)

All of above are recommended based off 2016 CDC vaccine guidelines

111. D. Fluzone Quadrivalent vaccine

There are no vaccines currently in the United States that contain peanut oils or other allergen oils. Table from CDC website:
http://www.cdc.gov/flu/pdf/protect/vaccine/rr6505-table-1.pdf

112. A, E

Sevelamer is a phosphate binding drug used to treat hyperphosphatemia in patients with chronic kidney disease. When taken with meals, it binds to dietary phosphate and prevents its absorption. The brand name of sevelamer is Renagel for sevelamer hydrochloride or Renvela for sevelamer carbonate. Cinacalcet is a drug that acts as a calcimimetic (i.e. it mimics the action of calcium on tissues) by allosteric activation of the calcium-sensing receptor that is expressed in various human organ tissues to treat secondary hyperparathyroidism in CKD patients on dialysis and severe hypercalcemia in patients with primary hyperparathyroidism. The brand name is Sensipar. Pamidronate and Fosamax are bisphosphates to help lower calcium serum levels in the body

113. B, D

On starting the infusion, there is no drug in the body and therefore, no elimination. The amount of drug in the body then rises, but as the drug concentration increases, so does the rate of elimination. Thus, the rate of elimination will keep rising until it matches the rate of infusion. The amount of drug in the body is then constant and is said to have reached a steady state or plateau. The factors affecting the steady state plasma drug concentration are:
- Infusion rate (Ro): The steady state drug concentration is proportional to the infusion rate. Thus, a higher infusion rate will result in a higher steady state plasma drug concentration
- Clearance: Higher clearance of the drug will result in lower plasma drug concentration at plateau

The time to reach the plateau is determined by the elimination half-life of the drug, which results from clearance and volume of distribution. Thus, the V_d does not influence the steady state concentration but merely the time required to approach the plateau. After 4 elimination half-lives the drug plasma concentration is 93,75% of the steady state plasma concentration. Likewise, when changing infusion rates, the time required to reach the new steady state also depends on the half-life of the drug

114. B, E

JR's dose of metformin can be doubled and switching from glyburide which is considered a high risk medication due to weight gain and higher rates of hypoglycemia vs. the second generations such as glimepiride and glipizide. The FDA in April 2016 has required labeling changes that replace serum creatinine (SCr) with estimated glomerular filtration rate (eGFR) as the parameter used to determine the appropriateness of treatment with the biguanide metformin (Glucophage, and others) in patients with renal impairment.

Metformin was previously contraindicated in women with a SCr level ≥1.4 mg/dL and in men with a SCr level ≥1.5 mg/dL, but use of SCr as a surrogate indicator tends to underestimate renal function in certain populations (e.g., younger patients, men, black patients, patients with greater muscle mass). The calculation of eGFR takes into account age, race, and sex, as well as SCr level, providing a more accurate assessment of kidney function. The eGFR should be calculated before patients begin treatment with metformin and at least annually thereafter. Metformin is now contraindicated in patients with an eGFR <30 mL/min/1.73 m2, and starting treatment with the drug in patients with an eGFR between 30 and 45 mL/min/1.73 m2 is not recommended. If the eGFR falls below 45 mL/min/1.73 m2 in a patient already taking metformin, the benefits and risks of continuing treatment should be assessed. Metformin should be not be administered for 48 hours after an iodinated contrast imaging procedure in patients with an eGFR <60 mL/min/1.73 m2 or a history of liver disease, alcoholism, or heart failure, or in those receiving intra-arterial contrast, and the eGFR should be re-evaluated before treatment is restarted

115. D. Oxacillin

Penicillins such as oxacillin and nafcillin as well as cefazolin which are used more to treat MSSA infections will not be effective for MRSA infections

116. B. Claritin

Fexofendaine (Allegra) is the least sedating even at higher doses but is considered a pregnancy category C. Claritin or loratidine is sedating at higher doses but it is less potent than Allegra and Zyrtec. Desloratadine or Clarinex is pregnancy category C, and Zyrtec or cetirizine may be sedating even at normally recommended doses due to the Hydroxyzine analog although it is more potent as well. Pregnancy category B agents are Zyrtec, Claritin, and Xyzal (levocetirizine). Chlorpheniramine is a first-generation antihistamine that causes a lot of sedative side effects

117. C, D

Only Lantus and Toujeo can be left outside of the refrigerator, at room temperature, up to 28 days. Novolin R or N and Levemir can be left out of the refrigerator for up to 42 days

118. A. Glargine

Only Lantus or glargine by generic name is a long-acting insulin that has a constant peak. Levemir has a peak at 6-8 hours, Novolin N 4-14 hours, Novolin R 2.5-5 hours, Apidra 30-60 minutes

119. A. Topiramate

Topiramate IR (immediate release) comes in sprinkle capsules as well as Depakote that comes in a sprinkle formulation (divalproex sprinkles)

120. A. Propranolol

Propranolol, metoprolol, timolol, and nebivolol all have high lipophilicity which means it's easier for these drugs to bypass the blood brain barrier and enter the brain. This may cause suicidal thoughts. Review the pharmacist letter PL Detail Document #281201

121. D. Daytrana

For JR, he is taking a methylphenidate long acting release medication, Concerta, and is failing treatment and also notes he does not like taking the oral version of the medication. It may be beneficial to recommend Daytrana which is also long-acting formulation of methylphenidate but comes in a patch version. Ritalin and Focalin are short-acting methylphenidate derivatives, and Adderall is an amphetamine short-acting derivative. Intuniv is a non-stimulant guanfacine

View: http://www.adhdmedicationguide.com/pdf/adhd_med_guide_081216.pdf

122. C. Restoring normal sinus rhythm control

Digoxin is a cardiac glycoside used in atrial fibrillation, heart failure, and atrial flutter. Digoxin is useful in controlling normal sinus rhythm response but has shown a lack of mortailtiy benefit and may increase the risk of death. Digoxin is no longer used first line for heart failure but is useful for symptomatic relief for patients who are already on an ACEI and diuretic

123. All of the above (A-E)

Medications in this class that do not cause QT prolongation are: Vraylar, Rexulti and Latuda (table below updated 6/2016 from Pharmacist Letter)

124. D. Kava Kava is not safe due to hepatotoxicity and should be avoided

Kava has been safely used in clinical trials, short-term. But there is concern that kava extracts might not be safe. Kava has been linked to over 100 reports of hepatotoxicity, including reports of liver transplantation and death. Hepatotoxicity has been report in some patients after as little as 3-4 weeks of use, even in normal doses. "Slow metabolizers" or those patients deficient in cytochrome P450 2D6 are theorized to be more susceptible. Due to these safety concerns, kava has been banned from the market in some countries

125. D. Feverfew

Feverfew (*Tanacetum parthenium*) is the most well-known natural medicine used to prevent migraine. Current theories are that feverfew inhibits platelet aggregation, serotonin release, leukotrienes, and prostaglandin synthesis. Most evidence suggests that feverfew can reduce the frequency of migraines, and when migraines do occur, they tend to have less severe symptoms of pain, nausea, vomiting, and sensitivity to light and noise. It might be more effective in patients who have more frequent migraine headaches.

126. C. There is no association between vaccines and autism

Between 1999 and 2001, thimerosal was removed or reduced to trace amounts in all childhood vaccines except for some flu vaccines. This was done as part of a broader national effort to reduce all types of mercury exposure in children before studies were conducted that determined that thimerosal was not harmful. It was done as a precaution. Currently, the only childhood vaccines that contain thimerosal are flu vaccines packaged in multidose vials. Thimerosal-free alternatives are also available for flu vaccine. A 2013 CDC study added to research showing that vaccines do not cause autism in children with the study population the first two years of life

127. B. Fentanyl should not be dispensed as Brock is opioid naïve and be at a high risk of respiratory depression and possibly death

Transdermal fentanyl "patches" should only be used in patients who are already receiving opioid therapy and who have demonstrated tolerance and who are not opioid naive. Giving potent, long-acting opioids like a fentanyl patch to opioid naive patients has resulted in deaths. Thus, fentanyl patches should NOT be used for acute pain

128. Click the following areas:

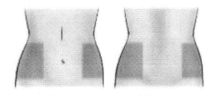

FIGURE 29-11. Sites for administration of enoxaparin

129. E. Olanzapine

First-generation antipsychotics have a high rate of extrapyramidal side effects, including rigidity, bradykinesia, dystonias, tremor, and akathisia. Tardive dyskinesia (TD)—that is, involuntary movements in the face and extremities—is another adverse effect that can occur with first-generation antipsychotics. Second-generation (novel or atypical) antipsychotics, with the exception of aripiprazole, are dopamine D2 antagonists, but are associated with lower rates of extrapyramidal adverse effects and TD than the first-generation antipsychotics. However, they have higher rates of metabolic adverse effects and weight gain

130. D. Normal Saline and hydrogen peroxide

The tracheostomy inner cannula tube should be cleaned two to three times per day or more as needed. Procedure:
1. Wash your hands.
2. Place 1/2 strength peroxide solution in one bowl and sterile salt water in second bowl.
3. Remove the inner cannula while holding the neck plate of the trach still.
4. Place inner cannula in peroxide solution and soak until crusts are softened or removed.
5. Use the brush or pipe cleaner to clean the inside, outside and creases of the tube.
6. Do not use scouring powder or Brillo pads.
7. Look inside the inner cannula to make sure it is clean and clear of mucus.
8. Rinse tube in saline or sterile salt water.

131. A. Diarrhea

Diarrhea is a common response to high doses of sorbitol. Sorbitol can also cause: Nausea, vomiting, gas, and stomach discomfort

132. D. Clopidogrel does interact with PPIs but it only applies to omeprazole

The U.S. Food and Drug Administration (FDA) is reminding the public that it continues to warn against the concomitant use of Plavix (clopidogrel) and omeprazole because the co-administration can result in significant reductions in clopidogrel's active metabolite levels and antiplatelet activity. This information was added to the drug label of Plavix in November 2009, and has been the source of continued discussion in the medical literature

133. 2.33

$$BSA = \sqrt{\frac{height\ (cm) \times weight\ (kg)}{3600}} = \sqrt{\frac{175.26\ cm \times 112\ kg}{3600}} = 2.33\ m^2$$

134. 1.72

$$BSA = \sqrt{\frac{height\ (cm) \times weight\ (kg)}{3600}} = \sqrt{\frac{160\ cm \times 66.4\ kg}{3600}} = 1.72\ m^2$$

135. C. FDA

A drug recall occurs when a prescription or over-the-counter medicine is removed from the market because it is found to be either defective or potentially harmful. Sometimes, the makers of the drug will discover a problem with their drug and voluntarily recall it. Recalls may be conducted on a firm's own initiative, by FDA request, or by FDA order under statutory authority. Class I recall: a situation in which there is a reasonable probability that the use of or exposure to a violative product will cause serious adverse health consequences or death. Class II Recall is a situation in which use of, or exposure to, a violative product may cause temporary or medically reversible adverse health consequences or where the probability of serious adverse health consequences is remote

136. A. Acute Sinusitis

The 2015 guidelines by the American Academy of Otolaryngology recommend either offer watchful waiting (without antibiotics) or prescribe initial antibiotic therapy for adults with uncomplicated acute bacterial rhinosinusitis or prescribe amoxicillin with or without clavulanate as first-line therapy for 5-10 days (if the decision is made to treat acute bacterial rhinosinusitis with an antibiotic). Nasal steroids such as fluticasone (Flonase) or beclomethasone (Beconase) may be added to help counter inflammation

137. C. Syphilis

Herpes is a virus and is treated by antivirals such as acyclovir. Chlamydia and Urethritis is usually treated with azithromycin or doxycycline. Syphilis can be treated similarly to gonorrhea in using Penicillin G. HIV is a virus as well that is treated with antivirals such as Genvoya

View CDC website: https://www.cdc.gov/std/tg2015/2015-wall-chart.pdf

138. B. Docusate

A surfactant is a compound that reduces the surface tension when dissolved in water and helps to increase the solubility of organic compounds. Docusate is an example of a surfactant. Psyllium is a bulk laxative used in the treatment of constipation. Senna and bisacodyl are stimulant laxatives, while milk of magnesia (magnesium hydroxide) acts as a laxative via promotion of electrolyte secretion in the gut

139. A. Lamivudine

Because emtricitabine (FTC), lamivudine (3TC), tenofovir disoproxil fumarate (TDF) and tenofovir alafenamide (TAF) have activity against both HIV and HBV, for patients co-infected with HIV and HBV, ART should be initiated with the fixed-dose combination of TDF/FTC or TAF/FTC, or the individual drug combinations of TDF plus 3TC as the nucleoside reverse transcriptase inhibitor (NRTI) backbone of a fully suppressive antiretroviral (ARV) regimen

140. D. Tenofovir alafenamide

Tenofovir disioproxil fumarate, tenofovir alafenamide, lamivuidine, emtricitabine, abacavir, and rilpivirine are examples of medications that may be used in combination to treat Hepatitis C infections.

Daclatasvir: The NS5A inhibitor daclatasvir is a substrate of CYP3A. When daclatasvir is given with a CYP3A inhibitor, the levels of daclatasvir can increase, particularly with strong inhibitors of CYP3A. The dose of daclatasvir should therefore be reduced to 30 mg when used with either ritonavir-boosted atazanavir or lopinavir. In contrast, when used with efavirenz, a CYP3A inducer, the dose of daclatasvir should be increased to 90 mg daily.

Ledipasvir-Sofosbuvir: The NS5A inhibitor ledipasvir is not metabolized by the cytochrome p450 system, but is a substrate of p-glycoprotein. Ledipasvir increases tenofovir levels by 1.3 to 2.6 fold when concomitantly given with either rilpivirine or efavirenz. Although ledipasvir administered concomitantly with tenofovir and an HIV protease inhibitor has not been studied, there is concern that tenofovir levels may increase substantially with this combination. Because of this concern and lack of data, the use of ledipasvir with ritonavir- boosted HIV protease inhibitors should, if possible, be avoided. For similar reasons, ledipasvir- sofosbuvir should not be used with cobicistat, elvitegravir, or tipranavir. Ledipasvir-sofosbuvir should not be used in HIV-infected patients on tenofovir if the baseline creatinine clearance is less than 60 ml/min.
Ombitasvir-Paritaprevir-Ritonavir: The major concern for drug interaction with this regimen is the significant p450 inhibition generated by ritonavir. This combination regimen should not be used with efavirenz, rilpivirine, darunavir, or lopinavir-ritonavir.
Ombitasvir-Paritaprevir-Ritonavir and Dasabuvir: The major concern for drug interaction with this regimen is the significant p450 inhibition generated by ritonavir. This combination regimen should not be used with efavirenz, rilpivirine, darunavir, or lopinavir-ritonavir.
Ribavirin: Significant and serious toxic drug-drug interactions and severe toxicities can occur with the simultaneous use of ribavirin and certain HIV nucleoside reverse transcriptase inhibitors. The use of ribavirin with didanosine is strictly contraindicated due to a marked increase in intracellular didanosine levels, which may cause hepatic failure, pancreatitis, and lactic acidosis. This can also occur with stavudine or zidovudine. Thus, simultaneous use of ribavirin with either didanosine, stavudine, or zidovudine should be avoided. Concurrent use of ribavirin and zidovudine should also be avoided because of additive hematologic toxicity and increased risk of severe anemia with this combination

141. A. SQ

Interferons such as peginterferon alfra-2a is administered SQ to the following injection sites-

142. D. Ethambutol

Ethambutol is not typically included in a child's regimen because of the potential inability to adequately assess visual acuity. Changes in visual acuity and color vision need to be assessed during ethambutol therapy due to the drug having potential to cause retrobulbar neuritis

143. A. Isoniazid 300 mg daily × 9 months

The patient does not have any symptoms or indications of active TB disease; so he needs treatment for latent TB infection. This is the correct first-line regimen for treatment of latent TB infection

144. A. They retain their stained color with acid-alcohol washes

Acid-fast bacteria keep their stain color despite acid-alcohol washes. *Mycobacterium tuberculosis* is acid fast

145. D. Immediately; do not wait for treatment

People with latent TB infection do not have symptoms, and they cannot spread TB bacteria to others. However, if TB bacteria become active in the body and multiply, the person will go from having latent TB infection to being sick with TB disease. For this reason, people with latent TB infection are often prescribed treatment to prevent them from developing TB disease. Treatment of latent TB infection is essential for controlling and eliminating TB in the United States.
Treatment of latent TB infection should be initiated after the possibility of TB disease has been excluded.
People with a positive IGRA result or a TST reaction of 5 or more millimeters
- HIV-infected persons
- Recent contacts of a TB case
- Persons with fibrotic changes on chest radiograph consistent with old TB
- Organ transplant recipients
- Persons who are immunosuppressed for other reasons (e.g., taking the equivalent of >15 mg/day of prednisone for 1 month or longer, taking TNF-α antagonists)

People with a positive IGRA result or a TST reaction of 10 or more millimeters
- Recent immigrants (< 5 years) from high-prevalence countries
- Injection drug users
- Residents and employees of high-risk congregate settings (e.g., correctional facilities, nursing homes, homeless shelters, hospitals, and other health care facilities)
- Mycobacteriology laboratory personnel
- Children under 4 years of age, or children and adolescents exposed to adults in high-risk categories

Persons with no known risk factors for TB may be considered for treatment of LTBI if they have either a positive IGRA result or if their reaction to the TST is 15 mm or larger

146. C. INR 2.5

Jamie's INR target is 2.5 with a range of 2.0 – 3.0 for DVT and PE treatment. Anticoagulant therapy is recommended for 3-12 months depending on site of thrombosis and on the ongoing presence of risk factors. If DVT recurs, if a chronic hypercoagulability is identified, or if PE is life threatening, lifetime anticoagulation therapy may be recommended. This treatment protocol has a cumulative risk of bleeding complications of less than 12%

147. A. Enoxaparin SQ 112 mg every 12 hours

Jamie is considered obese with a BMI of 43.6. Enoxaparin labeling indicates to use actual body weight when calculating for dosing, thus Jamie is 112 kg (246 lbs/2.2) and the dosing is 1 mg/kg/dose x 12 hours. Xarelto is prescribed as 15 mg twice daily with food for 21 days followed by 20 mg once daily with food for at least 3 months' duration. Pradaxa is given 150 mg twice daily after 5 to 10 days of parenteral anticoagulation

148. D. Direct stimulation of postsynaptic dopamine receptors

Dopamine agonists bypass the nigrostriatal neurons and provide direct receptor stimulation exerting effects like dopamine

149. E. Quetiapine

Quetiapine has a low likelihood to cause or exacerbate symptoms of Parkinson disease. The other antipyschotics are known to exacerbate movement disorders. Alprazolam is just a benzodiazepine and is not appropriate to treat pyschosis

150. A. Selegine

Selegiline has an amphetamine metabolite and has been associated with an increased incidence of insomnia. Doses should be given no later than early afternoon to help prevent this side effect in a patient for whom it is indicated. In a patient with uncontrolled insomnia, the drug is best avoided

151. C. Entacapone

Entacapone inhibits the action of catechol-*O*-methyltransferase in the periphery to avoid the breakdown of levodopa and dopamine before levodopa crosses the blood–brain barrier. It must be present with levodopa to achieve this outcome

152. A. Carbidopa/levodopa, rotigotine, rasagiline

For patients with moderate to severe symptoms, carbidopa/levodopa is the preferred agent to initiate therapy. The addition of a dopamine agonist is appropriate as second-line therapy. The addition of an MAO-B inhibitor will help prolong the effects of dopamine by minimizing its metabolism by monoamine oxidase

153. B. Sinemet is effective for many years and its loss of efficacy is due to the progression of the disease than with duration of treatment

It is a myth that Sinemet will lose its efficacy long-term. Levodopa is highly effective for many years, and its loss of efficacy has more to do with the progression of the disease than with the duration of treatment. Not all symptoms of PD respond to levodopa, and over time those symptoms become more prominent. As the disease progresses, people tend to develop more side-effects from levodopa

154. B, C

For bare metal stents, aspirin at a dose of 162 to 325 mg per day for one month should be taken then 75 to 162 mg per day indefinitely. Plavix or clopidogrel 75 mg daily should be taken up to one year

155. E, A, F, D, C, B

Garbing occurs in the ante area and should be sequenced from "dirtiest" to "cleanest":

1. Don shoe covers, hair and beard covers, and a mask.
2. Perform hand hygiene.
3. Don gown, fastened securely at the neck and wrists.
4. Sanitize hands using an ABHR and allow hands to dry.
5. Enter the buffer area (if facility layout dictates, this step may occur after the following two steps).
6. Don sterile powder-free gloves.
   Sanitize the gloves with application of 70% sterile IPA and allow gloves to dry.

156. D. Tylenol

As Sammie has poor renal function, it is not advisable to use NSAIDs and try Tylenol if that helps with his pain initially. Ibuprofen, naproxen, piroxicam, indomethacin, etodolac, sulindac and diclofenac are not recommended in patients with advanced renal disease (CrCl<30 ml/min)

157. B. Celebrex

For patients at risk for GI Ulceration and/or Bleeding, consider the following:

- All NSAIDs are associated with some level of increased risk for GI complications so it is best to use the lowest effective dose for the shortest duration of time
- Lowest risk for GI complications: Ibuprofen and celecoxib
- Relatively low risk for GI complications: Meloxicam, etodolac and nabumetone
- High (i.e. twice the risk associated with ibuprofen) for GI complications: Naproxen, indomethacin and diclofenac
- Highest risk for GI complications: Ketorolac and piroxicam

158. B. Use well-fitted walking shoes and inserts in addition to a pumice stone

Calluses occur more often and build up faster on the feet of people with diabetes. This is because there are high-pressure areas under the foot. Too much callus may mean that you will need therapeutic shoes and inserts. Calluses, if not trimmed, get very thick, break down, and turn into ulcers (open sores). Never try to cut calluses or corns yourself - this can lead to ulcers and infection. Let your health care provider cut your calluses. Also, do not try to remove calluses and corns with chemical agents. These products can burn your skin. Using a pumice stone every day will help keep calluses under control. It is best to use the pumice stone on wet skin. Put on lotion right after you use the pumice stone

159. A. Artificial Saliva

Treatment of dry mouth due to salivary gland hypofunction aims to alleviate symptoms and prevent complications such as dental caries, periodontal disease, halitosis, salivary gland calculi, dysphagia, and oral candidiasis. Various strategies are employed to compensate for the loss of normal salivary functions; these functions include lubricating the mucosa, helping to clear food residue that may lead to dental plaque and bacterial growth, buffering acids that favor demineralization of teeth, and providing antimicrobial effects. It's best to try artificial saliva and then if this is ineffective, move on to muscarinic agents such as pilocarpine and cevimeline. Chewing gum does help to produce saliva but in this member her salivary glands are not working. Tea and other acidic beverages due to acidity levels that affect dental enamel:

- Cola drinks – pH 2.6
- Coffee – pH 5.0
- Tea (herbal) – pH 3.2
- Tea (black) – pH 5.7 to 7.0
- Water from tap – pH 7.0 (but flavored waters are often acidic)
- Energy drinks – usually acidic

160. A. Tramadol

Cyproheptadine is an antidote to serotonin syndrome if benzodiazepines and supportive care fail to improve agitation and correct vital signs. Cyproheptadine is a histamine-1 receptor antagonist with nonspecific 5-HT1A and 5-HT2A antagonistic properties. It also has weak anticholinergic activity. Mirtazapine and bupropion have a very low risk of causing serotonin syndrome and Percocet does not have any activity on serotonin levels. Celebe is taking paroxetine- As with the other SSRIs, paroxetine is generally safe in overdose. Paroxetine ingestions had no symptoms, while common symptoms included vomiting, drowsiness, tremors, dizziness, and sinus tachycardia. Paroxetine has been associated rarely with brief, self-limited seizures and with an 18 percent incidence of developing serotonin syndrome in isolated ingestion, but rarely are cases severe. Among SSRIs, paroxetine has the highest rate of discontinuation syndrome because of its short half-life and lack of active metabolites. Symptoms are usually mild, lasting one to two weeks; they include nausea, dizziness, bad dreams, paresthesia, and a flu-like illness. Severe symptoms can occur and persist for prolonged periods, and may require restarting paroxetine

161. E. Dopamine receptor antagonist

Risperdal (risperidone as generic) and Invega are classified as prolactin-raising antipsychotics because their dopamine-blocking action can substantially increase levels of prolactin, a hormone released by the pituitary gland. In women, prolactin stimulates breast development and breast milk production. When high levels of prolactin are present in males, those excessive levels can prompt similar processes, resulting in gynecomastia, sometimes accompanied by galactorrhea (abnormal lactation). In severe cases, males have developed large, D-cup sized breasts. Risperdal is usually prescribed to treat bipolar disorder and autism spectrum disorders

162. C. Topical astringent and antiseptic

Aluminum acetate is produced when aluminum hydroxide reacts with acetic acid. The substance produced from this reaction is a salt that is white and water soluble. Utilized as a topical astringent and antiseptic in medicine, aluminum acetate may be prescribed by doctors for the treatment of many dermatologic conditions that can include poison ivy, rashes, athletes foot and insect bites. Because aluminum acetate is a drying agent, it is a medication that may be beneficial for ear infections, such as external otitis

163. A, E

HFA inhalers, more specifically their plastic actuators, need to be cleaned once weekly to ensure there is no debris or build up blocking the spray hole. CFC inhalers are no longer on the market due to ozone risk. Dry powder inhalers should not be washed and the canister should not be taken apart. Asthmanephrine is a handheld nebulizer device

164. E. Doxazosin, alpha 1 adrenergic receptor blocker

Doxazosin, under the brand names Cardura and Carduran, is an $α_1$-selective alpha blocker used to treat high blood pressure and urinary retention with benign prostatic hyperplasia (BPH)

165. C. Ginger

Ginger is known to help with nausea, motion sickness, and upset stomach. Emetrol is a OTC medication that is a phosphorated sugar solution that provides a direct local effect on the GI tract in reducing smooth muscle contractions and delaying gastric emptying

166. B. Indirect stimulation of alpha-adrenergic receptors

Cocaine causes indirect stimulation of the alpha-adrenergic receptors. Cocaine inhibits the cellular uptake of norepinephrine in the adrenergic neurons. Increased levels of norepinephrine result in enhanced sympathetic activity. Stimulation of the alpha-receptors on the coronary arteries produces vasoconstriction and myocardial ischemia

167. D. Serotonin receptors

Ondansetron is a 5-HT3 receptor antagonist. As such, it blocks serotonin receptors in the gastrointestinal tract and central nervous system, and is useful in the management of nausea and vomiting occurring either postoperatively or induced by chemotherapeutic agents

168. E. Hemorrhagic cystitis

Cyclophosphamide is metabolized to acrolein and this metabolite damages the bladder leading to hemorrhagic cystitis. Anthracyclines have cardiac toxicity, platinum agents have ototoxicity, and while antineoplastics cause myelosuppression the question asks about genitourinary effects

169. C. Amifostine

Amifostine reduces the cumulative renal toxicity associated with repeated administration of cisplatin and reduces the incidence of moderate to severe xerostomia in patients undergoing postoperative radiation treatment for head and neck cancer

170. B. Cisplatin

Cisplatin is associated with causing ototoxicity manifested by tinnitus or loss of high frequency hearing

171. D. Procarbazine

Procarbazine may have a disulfiram reaction when a patient consumes alcohol. Procarbazine has a lot of unique drug/food interaction. Procarbazine possesses monoamine oxidase inhibitor activity and has the potential for severe food and drug interactions (eg, tyramine containing foods leading to hypertensive crisis)

172. View rectangle below; maraviroc is a CCR5 receptor blocker

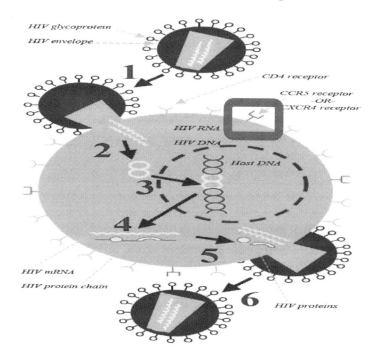

173. B. Urine may appear red, dark brown, or orange

This is a less common side effect of doxorubicin. Nail beds may turn darker, eyes watering, hair loss as chemotherapy agents destroy the fastest growing cells in body

174. View rectangle region below; efavirenz is an NNRTI

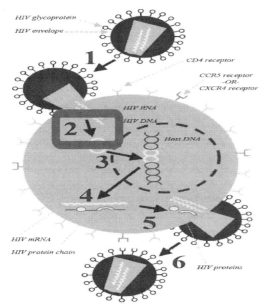

175. View rectangle below; raltegravir is an integrase inhibitor

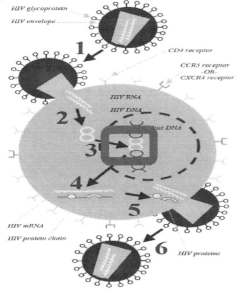

176. View rectangle below; clopidogrel irreversibly binds to P2Y$_{12}$, an adenosine diphosphate chemoreceptor on platelet cell membranes

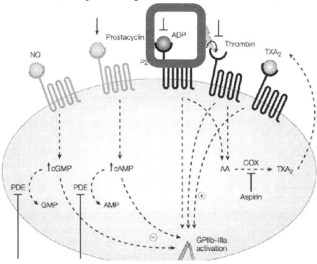

177. View rectangle below; Eptifibatide or Integrillin is an inhibitor of GPIIb/IIIa

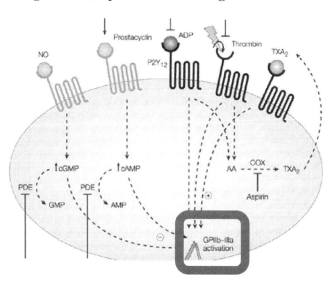

178. C. 16 mg

Tablets, capsules, and liquid:
Initial: 4 mg orally after the first loose stool, then
Maintenance: 2 mg after each loose stool, not to exceed 16 mg in any 24-hour period.
Clinical improvement is usually observed within 48 hours

179. A. Autohaler

Pulmicort is an example of a flexihaler, Spiriva as a handihaler, albuterol does come in a nebulizer vial solution, and inhaler is a generic term

180. A, B, C, D

Risperdal comes in all of these different types of formulations except an IV injection. Injections for Risperdal are administered IM

181. A

Boniva comes in an oral and injectable dosage form with a monthly dosage schedule. Reclast comes as an intravenous (IV) infusion given yearly, and Prolia an IV infusion given twice yearly

182. A, C, D

Also referred to as intrinsic sympathomimetic effect, this term is used particularly with beta blockers that can show both agonism and antagonism at a given beta receptor, depending on the concentration of the agent (beta blocker) and the concentration of the antagonized agent (usually an endogenous compound, such as norepinephrine). Some beta blockers (e.g. oxprenolol, pindolol, penbutolol, labetalol and acebutolol) exhibit intrinsic sympathomimetic activity (ISA). These agents are capable of exerting low-level agonist activity at the β-adrenergic receptor while simultaneously acting as a receptor site antagonist. These agents, therefore, may be useful in individuals exhibiting excessive bradycardia with sustained beta blocker therapy. Agents with ISA are not used after myocardial infarctions, as they have not been demonstrated to be beneficial

183. A, B, C

Tablet, Oral: Allegra Allergy: 60 mg, Allegra Allergy: 180 mg

Tablet, Oral, as hydrochloride: Allegra Allergy: 60 mg, 180 mg, Allegra Allergy Childrens: 30 mg, Allergy 24-HR: 180 mg, Mucinex Allergy: 180 mg

Generic: 60 mg, 180 mg

184. A, D

Patients susceptible to fat-soluble vitamin deficiencies: Use with caution in patients susceptible to fat-soluble vitamin deficiencies. Absorption of fat soluble vitamins A, D, E, and K may be decreased; patients should take vitamins ≥4 hours before colesevelam (Welchol). Medications should be separated out from Welchol by at least 4 hours due to chelation. Discontinue if triglyceride concentrations exceed 500 mg/dL or hypertriglyceridemia-induced pancreatitis occurs. The American College of Cardiology/American Heart Association recommends to avoid use in patients with baseline fasting triglyceride levels ≥300 mg/dL or type III hyperlipoproteinemia since severe triglyceride elevations may occur. Use bile acid sequestrants with caution in patients with triglyceride levels 250-299 mg/dL and evaluate a fasting lipid panel in 4-6 weeks after initiation; discontinue use if triglycerides are >400 mg/dL. A major side effect of Welchol is constipation not diarrhea

185. A, C, D

Allegra is a category C, Xanax is a category D drug. The others listed are category X

186. B, C, D

Trexall or methotrexate is a chemotherapy and immunosuppressant medication. It can also be used to treat rheumatoid arthritis and psoriasis. Alopecia (hair loss), thrombocytopenia, and stomatitis are side effects that may occur. Other side effects are anemia (not bleeding)

187. C, D, E

Colyte or PEG-3350 is used as a colon lavage to prepare for a colonoscopy. Start a clear liquid diet the day before the colonoscopy. Clear liquids are liquids that you can see through:
- Clear broth (chicken, beef, turkey, vegetable)
- Cranberry juice
- Water
- Sprite, 7-up, ginger ale
- Flavored waters

- Coffee/tea with sugar or honey
- White grape juice
- Gatorade, Kool-Aid, Jello (no red or blue)
- Apple juice
- Popsicles (no red or blue)

188. B. Commit 2 mg

IO's first cigarette is 95 minutes after waking in the morning, qualifying her to start with the 2-mg lozenge

189. A. Nicotine transdermal patch

Because the other three options for therapy were not appropriate given the woman's medical conditions and limitations, she could be tried on the nicotine patch. The first dose would be used for approximately 6 weeks and then she would begin to step down with her therapy. If she started with the 21-mg patch, then she would follow up with 2 weeks of the 14-mg patch and 2 weeks of the 7-mg patch. If she started with the 14-mg patch, she would only need to follow up with the 7-mg patch for 2 weeks

190. E. Varenicline

In this case, varenicline is the most appropriate choice because it would have the least negative impact on his other disease states and would increase his chances of quitting over quitting without pharmacologic assistance

191. E. Doxycycline 100 mg PO BID x 14 days

Treatment of Lyme disease*

Drug	Adult dosage	Pediatric dosage
Erythema migrans (early disease)		
Doxycycline	100 mg PO bid x 10 to 21 d	≥8 years: 2 mg/kg PO bid (maximum 100 mg per dose) x 10 to 21 d
or Amoxicillin	500 mg PO tid x 14 to 21 d	50 mg/kg/day divided tid PO (maximum 500 mg per dose) x 14 to 21 d
or Cefuroxime	500 mg PO bid x 14 to 21 d	30 mg/kg/day divided bid PO (maximum 500 mg per dose) x 14 to 21 d

Doxycycline is the preferred regimen unless in pregnant patients and children less than the age of 8 years old should be avoided

192. A. Vitamin B1

Thiamine or Vitamin B1 deficiency

193. E. Doxycycline 100 mg PO BID x 14 days

The drugs of choice for oral therapy are doxycycline, amoxicillin, and cefuroxime axetil, although doxycycline should **not** be used in children <8 years of age or in pregnant women

194. C. Ceftriaxone 2 grams IV once daily x 28 days

For patients with late Lyme neurologic disease, intravenous therapy with ceftriaxone, cefotaxime, or penicillin G is recommended

195. B. Flagyl 500 mg PO TID

Initial episode
Mild disease: metronidazole 500 mg orally three times daily or 250 mg four times daily for 10 to 14 days
Severe disease: vancomycin 125 mg orally four times daily for 10 to 14 days
First relapse
Confirm diagnosis (see text)
If symptoms are mild, conservative management may be appropriate
If antibiotics are needed, repeat treatment as in initial episode above. Alternative: fidaxomicin 200 mg orally twice daily for 10 days.
Second relapse
Confirm diagnosis
Tapering and pulsed oral vancomycin (below), with or without probiotics (for example, *Saccharomyces boulardii* 500 mg orally twice daily).
125 mg orally four times daily for 7 to 14 days
125 mg orally twice daily for 7 days
125 mg orally once daily for 7 days
125 mg orally every other day for 7 days
125 mg orally every 3 days for 14 days
Alternative: fidaxomicin 200 mg orally twice daily for 10 days

196. A, C, D

Cisplatin, high dose anthracycline, high dose alkylators, anthracycline and alkylator combination, and lomustine are examples of highly emetic drugs causing nausea and vomiting. Monoclonal antibodies, vinca alkaloids, bortezomib, and bleomycin are minimal emetic risk chemotherapy drugs

197. A-E (All of the above)

Adverse Reactions:
Central nervous system: Neurotoxicity (peripheral neuropathy is dose and duration dependent)
Gastrointestinal: Nausea and vomiting (76% to 100%)
Genitourinary: Nephrotoxicity
Hematologic & oncologic: Anemia (≤40%), leukopenia, thrombocytopenia
Otic: Ototoxicity

198. B, C, D, E

Monitoring Parameters: Blood pressure, heart rate (ECG) and rhythm throughout therapy; assess patient for signs of lethargy, edema of the hands or feet, weight loss, and pulmonary toxicity (baseline pulmonary function tests and chest X-ray; continue monitoring chest X-ray annually during therapy); liver function tests (semiannually); monitor serum electrolytes, especially potassium and magnesium. Assess thyroid function tests before initiation of treatment and then periodically thereafter (some experts suggest every 3-6 months). If signs or symptoms of thyroid disease or arrhythmia breakthrough/exacerbation occur then immediate re-evaluation is necessary. Amiodarone partially inhibits the peripheral conversion of thyroxine (T4) to triiodothyronine (T3); serum T4 and reverse triiodothyronine (rT3) concentrations may be increased and serum T3 may be decreased; most patients remain clinically euthyroid, however, clinical hypothyroidism or hyperthyroidism may occur. Ophthalmic exams should be performed

199. D. Simvastatin 20 mg/day, lovastatin 40 mg/day

Healthcare professionals, who prescribe simvastatin or simvastatin-containing medications (Simcor, Zocor, Vytorin), should be aware that patients taking amiodarone should not take more than 20 mg per day of simvastatin. Doses higher than 20 mg each day increase the risk of rhabdomyolysis, a rare condition of muscle injury. The dose of lovastatin should not exceed 40 mg daily in patients receiving concomitant medication with amiodarone. The combined use of lovastatin at doses higher than 40 mg daily with amiodarone should be avoided unless the clinical benefit is likely to outweigh the increased risk of myopathy. The risk of myopathy/rhabdomyolysis is increased when amiodarone is used concomitantly with higher doses of a closely related member of the HMG-CoA reductase inhibitor class

200. B. Stage B

The ACC/AHA staging system for heart failure is based on whether the patient has symptoms and structural heart disease. Stage A is reserved for patients with no symptoms and no structural heart disease. Stage B is for asymptomatic patients with structural heart disease. Stage C is for patients with symptoms as well as structural heart disease. Stage D is for patients with refractory heart failure. There is no Stage E

201. C. Nadir

In patients receiving chemotherapy, the term nadir usually refers to the time duration it takes for the chemotherapeutic agent to produce the stage of maximum bone marrow depression characterized by low WBC and ANC, with increased susceptibility to infection

202. A. Elevated; decreased

Cushing syndrome has elevated cortisol levels, while Addison's disease has decreased levels of cortisol. Both conditions have elevated ACTH levels, which normally increases production of cortisol. In Cushing's disease, the elevated cortisol is often due to elevated levels of ACTH as the primary cause. In Addison's disease, there is often atrophy and dysfunction of the adrenal cortex which results in the decreased level of cortisol. Decreasing cortisol removes the feedback inhibition of ACTH; this causes the levels of ACTH to increase

203. D. Phenytoin toxicity

Phenytoin use is not associated with renal dysfunction, increased body weight, diabetes, or infection. On the other hand, phenytoin overdose or supratherapeutic concentration can result in concentration-related toxicity

204. B. Class II

The NYHA functional classes for heart failure are based on patient's symptoms. Class II is for patients with symptoms upon ordinary exertion.

Class I is reserved for patients with no limitation in physical activity despite the heart failure.
Class III is for patients with symptoms upon minimal exertion.
Class IV is for patients with symptoms at rest.
There is no class V

205. A. Metabolic Acidosis

Step 1: Evaluate pH. The pH of 7.6, which is > 7.45 denotes alkalosis. The pH denotes her primary problem of alkalosis.
Step 2: Evaluate ventilation. pCO2 is normal and therefore denotes no respiratory abnormality.
Step 3: Evaluate metabolism. HCO3 of 39 mEq/L, which is > 35 mEq/L denotes metabolic alkalosis.

Therefore, the interpretation of the results is metabolic alkalosis. Mixed acidosis refers to respiratory acidosis and metabolic acidosis occurring at the same time

206. A. Gram-positive organisms

Gram positive are purple (they have a thick cell wall that absorbs crystallized violet). Gram negative are red/pink (they have a thin cell wall that absorbs the safranin counterstain)

207. 127.5 kcal

$$\frac{5 \text{ g dextrose}}{100 \text{ mL}} = \frac{x \text{ g}}{750 \text{ mL}} \quad x = 37.5 \text{ g} \qquad \frac{3.4 \text{ kcal}}{1 \text{ g}} = \frac{x \text{ kcal}}{37.5} \quad x = 127.5 \text{ kcal}$$

208. 15 tablets

$$\frac{30 \text{ mg}}{5 \text{ mL}} = \frac{x \text{ mg}}{150 \text{ mL}}; \quad x = 900 \text{ mg} \qquad \frac{60 \text{ mg}}{1 \text{ tab}} = \frac{900 \text{ mg}}{x \text{ tab}}; \quad x = 15 \text{ tablets}$$

209. 68.5

$$\frac{500 \text{ mg}}{7.3 \text{ mL}} = \frac{x \text{ mg}}{1 \text{ mL}}; \quad x = 68.5 \text{ mg}$$

210. 1.25

0.025 % w/v = 0.025 g/100 mL. Convert this percent w/v to mg/mL = 25 mg/100 mL

$\dfrac{25 \text{ mg}}{100 \text{ mL}} = \dfrac{x \text{ g}}{5 \text{ mL}}$; x = 1.25 mg

211. 322

The molecular weight of K is 39 and the molecular weight of Cl is 35; therefore, the molecular weight of KCL is 74.5
- 74.5 = 1 molecular weight for KCL
- 74.5 g = 1 equivalent weight
- 74.5 mg = 1 milliequivalent weight (0.0745 g)

$\dfrac{10 \text{ g}}{100 \text{ mL}} = \dfrac{x \text{ g}}{240 \text{ mL}}$; x = 24 g KCl $\dfrac{0.0745 \text{ g}}{1 \text{ mEq}} = \dfrac{24 \text{ g}}{x \text{ mEq}}$; x = 322.2 mEq

212. 361

Molecular weight of HCl = 36.5; 1 mole = 36.5 g
1 millimole = 36.5 g/1000 = 0.0365 g = 36.5 mg

$\dfrac{10 \text{ g}}{100 \text{ mL}} = \dfrac{x \text{ g}}{130 \text{ mL}}$; x = 13 g HCl $\dfrac{0.036 \text{ g}}{1 \text{ mmol}} = \dfrac{13 \text{ g HCl}}{x \text{ mmol}}$; x = 361 mmol

213. 1.69

31 lb × 1 kg/2.2 lb × 0.6 mg/kg × 1 g/1000 mg × 50 mL/0.25 g = 1.69 mL

214. 2.75

$\dfrac{1 \text{ g}}{750 \text{ mL}} = \dfrac{x \text{ g}}{350 \text{ mL}}$; x = 0.47 g $\dfrac{17 \text{ g}}{100 \text{ mL}} = \dfrac{0.47 \text{ g}}{x \text{ mL}}$; x = 2.75 mL

215. 2.3

$\dfrac{1 \text{ mEq KCl}}{74.5 \text{ mg KCl}} = \dfrac{2 \text{ mEq KCl}}{x \text{ mg KCl}}$; x = 149 mg KCl $\dfrac{39 \text{ mg K}}{74.5 \text{ mg KCl}} = \dfrac{x \text{ mg K}}{149 \text{ mg KCl}}$; x = 78 mg K

$$\frac{78 \text{ mg K}}{149 \text{ mg KCl}} = \frac{180 \text{ mg K}}{x \text{ mg KCl}}; \quad x = 343.85 \text{ mg KCl}$$

$$\frac{149 \text{ mg KCl}}{1 \text{ mL}} = \frac{343.85 \text{ KCl}}{x \text{ mL}}; \quad x = 2.3 \text{ mL}$$

216. 308

Molecular weight of NaCl = 58.5 1 mole = 58.5 g
1 millimole = 58.5 mg = 2 milliosmoles, since NaCl dissociates into 2 particles

$$\frac{900 \text{ mg}}{100 \text{ mg}} = \frac{x \text{ mg}}{1000 \text{ mL}} \qquad x = 9000 \text{ mg of NaCl in a liter (1000 mL)}$$

$$\frac{58.5 \text{ mg}}{2 \text{ mOsmol}} = \frac{9000 \text{ mg}}{x \text{ mOsmol}}; \quad x = 308 \text{ mOsmol}$$

217. 16

$$\frac{0.4 \text{ g}}{120 \text{ mL}} = \frac{x \text{ g}}{5 \text{ mL}}; \quad x = 0.016 \text{ g} = 16 \text{ mg}$$

218. 65

0.65% w/v = 0.65 g/100 L Converted to milligrams this equals 650 mg/100 mL

$$\frac{650 \text{ mg}}{100 \text{ mL}} = \frac{x \text{ g}}{10 \text{ mL}}; \quad x = 65 \text{ mg}$$

219. 3,250,000 U

$$\frac{5,000,000 \text{ units}}{1 \text{ mL}} = \frac{x \text{ units}}{0.65 \text{ mL}}; \quad x = 3,250,000 \text{ units}$$

220. 2.14%

- Molecular weight of NH_4 = is 53.5
- 1 equivalent weight = 53.5 g
- 1 mEq = 53.5 mg

$$\frac{53.5 \text{ mg}}{1 \text{ mEq}} = \frac{x \text{ mg}}{100 \text{ mEq}}; \quad x = 5350 \text{ mg or } 5.35 \text{ g}$$

$$\frac{5.25 \text{ g}}{250 \text{ mL}} = \frac{x}{100}; \quad x = 2.14\%$$

221. 1 oz

437.5 grains = 1 oz

222. D. Intangible

Intangible costs include the costs of pain, suffering, anxiety, or fatigue that occur because of an illness or the treatment of an illness. It is difficult to measure or assign values to intangible costs

223. C. Cost-minimization

A cost minimization analysis measures cost in dollars and outcomes are assumed to be equivalent

224. C. Cost-effectiveness analysis

Cost-effectiveness analysis (CEA) evaluates the costs that are measured in natural units (eg, cures, years of life, blood pressure)

225. D. Cost-utility analysis

A CUA takes patient preferences into account when measuring health consequences. The most common unit used in conducting CUAs is QALYs (Quality Adjusted Life Year[s])

226. 7

16 lb x 1 kg/2.2 lb = 7.27 kg; 0.08 mg/kg x 7.27 kg = 0.58 mg/hr x 12 hrs = 7 mg in 12 hrs

227. 0.01 ml/min

$\frac{0.05 \text{ mg}}{x \text{ mL}} = \frac{500 \text{ mg}}{100 \text{ mL}}$;   x = 0.01 ml/min

228. 1

Because the time interval between preparation and administration is 6 hours, and the half-life of the radiopharmaceutical is 6 hours, approximately one-half of the original strength has decayed. Therefore, 1 mL of the solution, which now assays at 20 mCi/mL, is needed

229. 90%

The sensitivity of a test is determined by its ability to detect the presence of the disease. The sensitivity expressed as a percentage is determined by dividing the number of subjects with the detected disease (positive) by the total number of subjects that actually has the disease (positive + false negative): 80 divided by (80 + 10) = 0.89 or 90%

230. 0.88

155 lbs x 1 kg/2.2 lb x 5 mg/kg/1 min = 352 µg/min

Because the solution concentration is 400 µg/mL, divide the dosage rate by the concentration:
352 µg/min / 400 µg/mL = 0.88 mL/min

231. 1.5

Q1 x C1 = Q2 x C2;   1 mL x 1/1,000 = x mL x 1/2,500

1/1,000 = x/2,500;   x = 2.5 mL   2.5 mL – 1mL (original volume) = 1.5 mL

232. 0.048

First-order half-lives relate to kinetic constant rate values by the following equation:
$T_{1/2} = 0.693/k$;   14.3 days = 0.693/k
k = 0.048 per day or 4.8% per day

233. 5

The original order requested that the solution be infused over a 20-minute time span. Therefore, 100 mL divided by 20 minutes equals 5 mL/min

234. 7.3

The original dilution would be 100 units/1 mL = 1,000 units/ x mL

x = 10 mL (final volume, of which 1 mL is the volume occupied by the dissolved powder). If a 120 unit/mL concentration is requested, the new volume will be:
120 units/1 mL = 1,000 units/ x mL; x = 8.3 mL
Since 1 mL is dissolved powder, the remaining 7.3 mL is diluent

235. 10%

The prevalence of a disease is determined by dividing the total number of subjects with the disease—(both those testing positive plus those testing negative but with the disease) by the total population tested: (80 + 10) divided by 910= 0.099 or 10%

236. B. 0.2 mL

20 units x 1 mL/100 units – 0.2 mL

237. B. 120 mg

Minimum weighable quantity = sensitivity requirement x 100/ % error; 6 mg x 100/ 5%= 120 mg

238. D. 80

1000 mL/40 mEq x 0.5 mEq/min = 12.5 ml/min;   1000 mL/ 12.5 mL= 80 minutes

239. C. 40 mg

34" = 86.36 cm
BSA = $\sqrt{[(86.36 \times 12)/3600]}$ = 0.54 m2 0.54m2 x150= 81mg/day= 40mg BID

240. E. 70

A SD is calculated mathematically for experimental data. It shows the dispersion of numbers around the mean (average value). One SD will include approximately 67% to 70% of all values, whereas two SDs will include approximately 97% to 98%

241. E. Slightly weaker than desired

There are two factors that may lead to a final concentration slightly lower than the targeted concentration. When aseptically transferring the 20 mL of concentrated dye solution, the technician should inject the dye solution and then draw up 20 mL of the normal saline solution to rinse the syringe of dye solution. Also one must realize that LVPs of 250, 500, and 1,000 mL have volumes greater than the labeled claim. For example, the 250 mL bag of normal saline is likely to have between 260 and 270 mL. Both factors will reduce the final concentration of dye by a small amount

242. D. Drug A

Amphetamines contain amine groups (-NH2)

243. B. Drug C

This structure contains a sulfonamide functional group (-SO2)

244. E. Ketone

This is a ketone structure

245. A. Cyclobenzaprine

This is a typical cyclic three ring structure and represents cyclobenzaprine

246. C. MCV and HPV

LM has not received the MCV or HPV vaccines. College freshman should receive the MCV vaccine if they have not previously been vaccinated. The HPV vaccine is recommended at age 11 to 12 years; however, it can be given in adult females up to the age of 26 who have not previously been vaccinated

247. A. DTaP, IPV, MMR, Varicella, and Hep A

Kaly has received 4 doses in the DTaP series already and therefore needs to receive the fifth and final DTaP dose. She has also received 3 doses of IPV and should receive the fourth dose today. Kaly received her first doses of the MMR and varicella vaccines at 15 months. She needs to receive the second dose of each today. Since Kaly only received one dose of the Hep A vaccine at 15 months, she needs to complete the 2-dose series today. She only needs one dose of the Hep A vaccine

248. E. Sofosbuvir and velpatasvir for 12 weeks

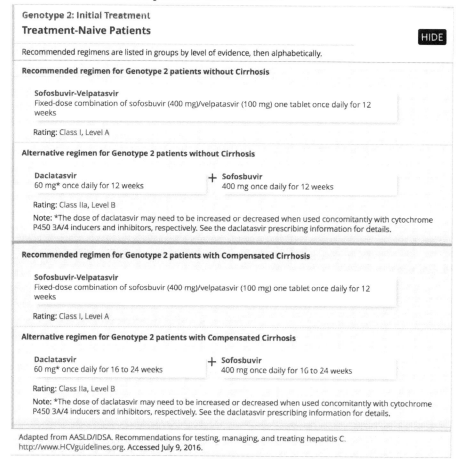

Adapted from AASLD/IDSA. Recommendations for testing, managing, and treating hepatitis C. http://www.HCVguidelines.org. Accessed July 9, 2016.

249. A. Ribavirin

The incidence of hemolytic anemia for ribavirin is 10% to 13%. The FDA requires a black box warning regarding this risk in the package insert

250. D. Reduction in incidence of cyclophosphamide-induced hemorrhagic cystitis
Mesna binds to and inactivates the toxic oxazophorine metabolite (acrolein) in the urine to prevent hemorrhagic cystitis

NAPLEX FORMULA SHEET

Conversions between units
1 grain = 65 mg
1mg aminophylline = (0.8)(mg theophylline)

Waist Circumference Risk
>35 inches for women
>40 inches for men

BMI = [weight (kg)]/[height (m^2)]
BMI = {[weight (lbs)]/[height (in^2)]} X 704.5

IBW (male) = 50kg + (2.3kg)(inches>5ft)
IBW (female) = 45.5kg + (2.3kg)(inches>5ft)

If BUN/SCr ratio > 20, consider dehydration in the patient

Cockcroft-Gault Equation
CrCl = (140-age in yrs)(wt in kg)/(72)(SCr) If female, multiply answer by 0.85

Specific Gravity
SG = weight (g)/volume (mL)

Body Surface Area: BSA = $\sqrt{[(\text{height (cm)} \times \text{weight (kg)})/3600]}$

Half Life: $T_{1/2}$ = 0.693/k

TPN Kcal
Dextrose 3.4kcal/g
Amino Acids 4kcal/g
Lipids 9kcal/g
10% Lipid emulsion 1.1kcal/g
20% lipid emulsion 2kcal/g
Glucose 4kcal/g

Basal Energy Expenditure (BEE) (Harris-Benedict Equation)
Males: $66 + (6.2 \times \text{weight in pounds}) + (12.7 \times \text{height in inches}) - (6.76 \times \text{age in years})$
Female: $MR = 655.1 + (4.35 \times \text{weight in pounds}) + (4.7 \times \text{height in inches}) - (4.7 \times \text{age in years})$

Total Energy Expenditure (activity and stress factors will be given)
$TEE = (BEE)(\text{activity factor})(\text{stress factor})$

Nitrogen Balance
1g nitrogen = 6.25g protein
Nitrogen Intake = (grams protein)/6.25

Corrected Calcium (use when Albumin < 3.5)
Corrected Calcium = (Serum calcium) + [(4-albumin)(0.8)]

Osmolarity
mOsmol/L = [(concentration of substance in g/L)/(MW in g/mol)] (# of species)(1000)

Sodium Chloride Equivalent (E Value)
$E = (58.5)(i)/(\text{MW of drug})(1.8)$ i = dissociation factor

Mol = g/MW   mmol = mg/MW
mEq = (mg)(valence)/MW OR mEq = (mmol)/(valence)

Temperature Conversion
$F = (C)(9/5) + 32$

Absolute Neutrophil Count (ANC) Normal limits 2200-8000
ANC = (WBC)(% neutrophils) (% neutrophils) = segs + bands

Anion Gap (High is >12mEq/L = gap acidosis)
AG = Na – (Cl + HCO3)

Henderson Hasselbach equation
Weak Acid: pH = pka + log (salt/acid)
Weak Base (pkw IS ALWAYS 14): pH = pka + log (base/salt)

Aliquot Measurement

Mean Weighable Quantity (MWQ) = (sensitivity requirement SR)/ (% of error)

Relative Risk (RR)

RR = (exposed or treated group event)/ (nonexposed or placebo group event)
RR <1 reduces risk of event occurrence with treatment
RR = 1 no reduction of risk between treatment vs. nontreatment group
RR > 1 increases risk of event occurrence with treatment

Relative Risk Reduction (RRR)

RRR = [(%event occurrence of control or placebo) (% event occurrence of treatment)]/ (% event occurrence control or placebo)
RRR = 1-RR (relative risk)

Like the book? Help us help you more!

- Please help positively (5/5) rate this book on Amazon.com, search title **"2017 NAPLEX"**, find our book and rate us under customer reviews

- Access our website for more guides at: www.rxpharmacist.com

- Don't have a guide there you need? Send us a recommendation and any comments/suggestions to: help@rxpharmacist.com

Made in the USA
Charleston, SC
10 March 2017